How's That For T

Also by Simon Gray

*Fiction*
COLMAIN
SIMPLE PEOPLE
LITTLE PORTIA
A COMEBACK FOR STARK

*Non-fiction*
AN UNNATURAL PURSUIT
AND OTHER PIECES

*Stage plays*
WISE CHILD
DUTCH UNCLE
THE IDIOT
SPOILED
BUTLEY
OTHERWISE ENGAGED
DOG DAYS
MOLLY
THE REAR COLUMN
CLOSE OF PLAY
STAGE STRUCK
QUARTERMAINE'S TERMS
TARTUFFE
CHAPTER 17
THE COMMON PURSUIT
MELON

*Television plays*
THE CARAMEL CRISIS
DEATH OF A TEDDY BEAR
AWAY WITH THE LADIES
PIG IN A POKE
MAN IN A SIDE-CAR
PLAINTIFFS AND DEFENDANTS
TWO SUNDAYS

*Television films*
AFTER PILKINGTON
QUARTERMAINE'S TERMS

*Films*
BUTLEY
A MONTH IN THE COUNTRY

# How's That For Telling 'Em, Fat Lady?

## *A Short Life in the American Theatre*

SIMON GRAY

*faber and faber*
LONDON · BOSTON

First published in 1988
by Faber and Faber Limited
3 Queen Square London WC1N 3AU

Typeset by Goodfellow & Egan Ltd Cambridge
Printed in Great Britain by
Mackays of Chatham Ltd Kent


*British Library Cataloguing in Publication Data*

Gray, Simon
How's that for telling 'em, fat lady?:
a short life in the American theatre.
1. Theater—United States—Production
and direction
I. Title
792'.0232'0924 PN2291
ISBN 0–571–15139–6

For Judy Daish

1

# 'Hey, Joe, Let's Don't pull the Plug on This one – Yet!'

## Thursday, 12 December 1985

Sitting in my study, my dog Hazel under my desk, talking into this machine as a way, really, of confirming that I'm back home. I arrived in London, disconcertingly, at the same hour as I left Los Angeles. The flight was OK, comfortable in fact, and champagny, though I didn't really enjoy tottering out of the airport with a couple of meals and quite a lot of alcohol inside me, with most of the day still to get through. Actually I feel inert. Irritable and inert. Not perhaps the best state in which to begin a diary. I must remember to record all the dates accurately.*

I was in Los Angeles for the casting of a play of mine, *The Common Pursuit*, which is being done at the Matrix Theatre. The Matrix is a 'waiver' theatre, i.e. its auditorium is so small (it seats 99) that Equity waives all its rules on professional rates of pay, and everybody works for nothing. The actors do it because it gives them a chance to appear in the kind of parts they don't get offered on television – or because they're out of work anyway, and would rather work for no money than not work for no money. I suppose the director and the designers do it for the same sorts of reason. I'm doing it because I'll go anywhere, and do anything, to have an unproduced play produced – although, as a matter of fact, *The Common Pursuit* has been produced twice before. Once in London, at the Lyric Theatre, Hammersmith, directed by Harold Pinter, where it almost but not quite moved to the West End; and once at the Long Wharf Theatre, New Haven, where it almost but not quite moved to Off-Broadway. So the Matrix is my chance to get it on the move again in the States – possibly all the way to New York. I did a

* I didn't, actually heading one report 'April 31st', a day that doesn't even exist. All the dates have therefore to be taken as approximate.

lot of work on the script for the New Haven production, and I've done a lot more since for the Matrix – in fact, I spent a lot of the ten days I've just come back from rewriting sections that I'd substantially rewritten just before going. By the time we finish I hope I'll have got the script absolutely right. Well, as absolutely right as possible.

The casting itself turned out to be the usual exhausting process, only more so. Casting is *always* more exhausting in the States, and casting at the Matrix turned out to be more exhausting than anywhere else in the States, in my experience anyway, partly because a lot of the actors were involved in television series and so their schedules caused problems, and partly because Kristoffer Tabori, the director, and Joe Stern, the producer, were meticulously courteous with the actors. I'm all in favour of that, but sometimes they passed beyond courtesy into what seemed to me very like perversity, if not actual perversion – actors who were seen to be wrong for their parts within two minutes being kept long past their scheduled ten minutes, as if spinning out their ordeal (and ours) made it up to them for their being no-hopers. One chap came in for the part of Nick, who is meant to be a bright young Cambridge-educated middle-class English type on the make, and offered a boisterously anti-Semitic version of an East End Jew, complete with lisp and even a touch of a drool. Tabori and Stern kept him at it, not for the courteous ten minutes, not for an inexplicable twenty minutes, but for forty minutes – lisping, slobbering, whining, wheedling, wringing his hands. Furthermore he *looked* completely wrong, being short and bald, with a beard. (Actually, now I come to think of it, the chap who got the part – Bart Braddleman – is short, balding, with a bit of a beard and is apparently a Sephardic Jew. But he got everything else right. Or seemed to at the time.)

Every casting session ran two or three hours over. We weren't altogether helped by our casting lady, who would sometimes forget to notify us of cancellations, and then of substitutions, so that I would write down my impressions beside the wrong name, which would lead to endless muddles afterwards. 'No good,' I'd say of the actor I took to be – let's call him Sprinkleman. 'For one thing he's far too old. For another he obviously can't do English.' 'Too old!' Kris Tabori or Joe Stern would exclaim. 'He's twenty-six. And what do you mean he can't do English, he *is* English!' 'English! He's from the Bronx, from the sound of him. And at least forty.' And so it went, until the casting lady would suddenly remember that the one I'd got down on my list as Sprinkleman had in fact been replaced by Yorricks, or whatever, hadn't she mentioned it, sorry. Of course Joe Stern and Kristoffer Tabori, being familiar with most of the actors around Los Angeles, could spot on sight the difference between a Yorricks and a Sprinkleman, and knew exactly who they were talking about. The result was that for long stretches of utterly worthless conversation I must have given the impression that I wasn't only highly unobservant, but positively out to lunch.

The casting lady also had a penchant for actors – particularly actresses – with whom English seemed to be a second, if not a third language. There was a Polish girl, for instance, who was kept for a quarter of an hour. But that may not have been their fault because she had trouble first understanding, and then pronouncing her lines, so it may well have taken her fifteen minutes to get through her short scene as a bright, Cambridge-educated, middle-class English girl. In fact the part of Marigold for which she was auditioning – the only female part – went to the director's wife, Judy Geeson. This decision was preceded by some pretty heavy private conversations between Joe Stern and myself. The reason I was against casting Judy Geeson wasn't because I didn't think she was right, or a good actress, but because I'm going to be around from the second week of rehearsals on, and I want to be able to discuss the actors' progress frankly and fearlessly. I mean, I can't imagine myself saying to Tabori, 'Look, what the hell is your wife up to in the first scene?' sort of stuff. And I also want to be his closest confidant and ally. Unlikely if his bed companion and breakfast mate is in the production too. In the end I gave in without ever confronting Tabori directly on the issue, deciding that it was better not to have as my director a chap whose judgement I'd questioned in the worst possible way, by overruling him on the casting of his wife. No doubt she'll be very good. She certainly seemed to be at the read-through we had the night before I left. In fact, she seemed to be the only one of our cast who knew what she was doing.

So what with all the casting hassles, and the intensive bursts of rewriting, I really feel I've been away for months, not a mere ten days. But I've enjoyed telling my family about Los Angeles – not the working part of it, but the place itself, and especially about the little cottage lent to me by Tabori's sister-in-law. I painted pictures at once vivid and lyrical of orange trees, humming-birds and so forth, until I detected from the slightly sickened expressions on the faces of wife, son and daughter that what I was bringing before their eyes wasn't unlike some sugary sequence from the Walt Disneys of my childhood. They probably half expected me to burst into song, or imitate the cute American chatter of the red squirrels.

I shall miss the cottage – Tabori's sister-in-law has rented it out to some Japanese, and Joe Stern seemed uncertain about where precisely I'm going to live when I go back the week after next. He assured me, though, that I wasn't to worry, he knew of a house, a little house, a *nice* little house, just up from the Taboris, and if that falls through and all else fails, I can always stay at the Magic Hotel, gesturing out of his car window (we were on our way to the airport) at a large, institutional-looking building, quite evidently remote from anything in the way of bars, restaurant, and even shops. 'That'll be all right,' he said, 'because it's cheap.' I said, with a heavily warning inflexion, that I hoped it wouldn't come to that, and reminded him that I didn't drive. He said, 'No, no, don't worry, we'll find you something. A nice little house . . .' I must remember to keep Joe on the job when he phones. I've no intention of ending up in the Magic.

Beryl has just come into the study to remind me that we have to be off in an hour to Queen Mary College, for a ceremony in which I'm being made a Fellow.* She said that I looked *louche*, jet-lagged, ill-tempered. I said that that was how I'd looked every day of the twenty years I'd taught there – the effect of an hour on the tube followed by a walk down the Mile End Road – they might be confused if I appeared in a different guise, might not even recognize me. 'Anyway,' I said, in genuine bewilderment, 'why am I doing it?' She explained that I was 'doing it' to prove to sceptics, among whom she numbered herself, that I had a generous, not to say magnanimous spirit. 'But why to them, why there? Can't I prove it to someone else somewhere else later in life?' But Beryl, who always tends to treat my most urgently practical questions as if they were merely rhetorical, advised me to shave, and to shampoo my hair. I'll

* I'd had a rather stationary career at Queen Mary's, starting as a mere lecturer, and ending up, twenty teaching years later, as a mere lecturer. I was disqualified from promotion on the grounds that I never wrote anything – or at least anything useful, like a critical work.

compromise. Shave one cheek and shampoo some of my hair. I'll leave out the bits that are sticking up at the back.

## Sunday, 15 December

Back in my study, Hazel for some reason on the sofa, staring at me with her usual compassionate unintelligence. Joe Stern has just phoned with two pieces of news. The first, infinitely complicated, to do with some airline ticket deal he's made with Stephen Hollis in Dallas – I'm going straight on to Dallas from Los Angeles to co-direct an old play of mine, *Dog Days*, at the New Arts Theatre. Stephen, who is the artistic director and an old friend, is going to co-direct with me. Joe saw an opportunity here to save money by getting the Dallas lot to pay my fare to Los Angeles. In return he'll pay my fare from Los Angeles to New York and back when I have to pop over there for a few days for the *Dog Days* casting. I can see how this benefits Joe, but not quite how it benefits Stephen and the New Arts, although I have some idea that the New Arts has some sponsorship thing going with British Caledonian, which, if I understood it, would probably explain everything. Anyway, there was Joe on the phone going into all the details of flight schedules and doing sums aloud – at one point he seemed to be forbidding me to go to New York on a Sunday because the ticket cost 800 dollars more than on any other day of the week – can this be right? – when I cut through with a question on the subject I really wanted to hear about. The rehearsals of *The Common Pursuit*, how were they going? 'Well,' Joe said, 'the main thing is that Bart Braddleman' (the Sephardic Jewish chap playing Nick) 'has walked out.' On the grounds apparently that he couldn't do it, didn't know what was wanted, couldn't understand what the play was about, and had been offered another job. So Ted Larkins,* an English actor who had looked in auditions as if he ought to be a good Nick, but had given a cute, laidback rendering, has stepped in in his place. 'Oh,' I said, 'I see,' thinking that this might possibly be a change for the better, and deciding not to get too despondent. 'Well, how are things going apart from that?' Joe said he really didn't know, there wasn't much to report on yet because, he said – making the old heart dip, lurch, sway and jump about – they'd only been at it a

* For reasons that will become apparent, I have changed this actor's name.

week, and they'd spent it breaking the play down. 'Breaking it down – what do you mean?' 'Well, you know,' Joe said, 'sitting around the table and analysing it. Scene by scene.' Analysing it. Around a table. For a week. I had thought that that kind of rehearsal had gone out some time in the sixties or so. But there it was again, at the Matrix Theatre, in Los Angeles. I tried not to sound too appalled, but did inevitably say something to the effect that you can really only find out about a play by doing it – straight from the start – moving it, getting the actors to move, say the lines and discover it, the play, in practice. Sitting around tables and analysing is for academics, etc. 'Yeah, well – ' Joe said, 'I dunno. Anyway, that's what they've been doing.' We then exchanged Christmas salutations, looked forward to seeing each other in a few days, hung up. I felt dispirited. And irritated with myself, as I'd forgotten to ask Joe whether he'd found my little house, nice little house yet.

## Monday, 23 December

Had lunch with Judy Daish, my agent, after a bout of Christmas shopping. Remarked that I'd heard nothing further from the Matrix, things must be going badly.

## Tuesday, 24 December, Christmas Eve

One of those link-up telephone calls from Los Angeles, Joe at the theatre connecting with Kris Tabori at his home, connecting with me in Highgate, Hazel at my feet. They were calling to tell me that four days previously – *four days* – John Delancey (Stuart) had come to Joe and said he couldn't play the part, was completely at a loss with it, could he bow out? At the same time Joe and Kris Tabori had come to the conclusion that Clancy Brown – the chap who was playing Humphry – couldn't play the part, and should be asked to bow out. Their solution, therefore, was that Clancy Brown should leave the production; that John Delancey, who insisted that he'd always wanted to play the part anyway, should take over Humphry; that Kris Tabori should bow out as director and take over the part of Stuart; and that a new director, a chap called Sam Weisman, should be brought in. I received this news, one, two, three, rap, rap, rap, on my chin, just like that. Dazed. When I finally managed to speak, I asked why they'd waited four days before they'd let me in on the facts. 'Oh well, you know,' said Joe, 'we didn't want to ruin your Christmas,' 'We wanted to wait', Tabori said, 'until we'd got it all sorted out.' 'It should work out fine,' Joe said, 'except it'll mean a delay in rehearsals.'

I said that I could see that it might work out. Going by the read-through John Delancey would almost certainly make a better Humphry than a Stuart, and Kris Tabori, being the right age, and with the right acting pedigree (as I'd gathered) would probably be a good Stuart, but why, I wondered, bring in a new director, wouldn't it be better to let me direct it, as I knew the play better than anyone else, had been through two previous productions? 'Well no,' Joe said. He had a special thing against writers directing their own work. It never panned out. And the man they'd brought in, Sam Weisman, loved the play, had wanted to direct it himself from the moment he'd finished reading the first (Lyric, Hammersmith) script, had directed Harold Pinter's *Betrayal* with great success the season before, was an old colleague/friend and an associate director of the Matrix. He would do a good job.

Before I could pursue my own claim to direct, Joe shifted the subject – Kris Tabori dropping off the line – to my flight to New York to cast *Dog Days*, explaining that as we were now running late in Los Angeles it would be better if I went to New York later. The juggling with dates confused me – anything to do with dates always does – but I was pretty sure that Stephen Hollis would be fed up at being postponed yet again. I asked him if, under the circumstances, he would break the news to Stephen. He said of course he would, what's his number? I found this rather odd. As he's spoken to Stephen quite a few times, he presumably has the number. Nevertheless, I found Stephen's number, and gave it to him, adding that if Stephen had left for England for Christmas, the theatre in Dallas would be able to give him his number here – I myself didn't have it, as Stephen had just sold his London flat, and would therefore be staying with friends, relatives, whatever. Joe said OK, he'd phone the theatre, try and catch him there, if he didn't, would get his London number, phone him here. We closed down on fond wishes for Christmas, etc., looking forward to seeing each other in the New Year, etc., although I felt my throat constrict as I uttered my share. After all, I'd spent ten days in Los Angeles specifically to help cast the play, and now here we were, with a new director, a new leading man, a new Humphry, a new Nick – what had been the point of my going? And to have waited four days before telling me. And what about the little house – he didn't mention it. I must remember to ask Judy to tell Joe that the Magic Hotel is out of the question.

## Friday, 27 December

Talked to Stephen Hollis, who got in a few days ago from Dallas. Actually getting in touch with him was an irritating and expensive business. As I didn't know where he was staying, I had to do what I told Joe to do, i.e. phone the New Arts in Dallas in order to get his telephone number here in London. After we'd arranged a meeting to go through the text of *Dog Days* I asked him whether he'd heard from Joe Stern about the date changes. He said he hadn't. I phoned up Joe to ask him why he hadn't yet been in touch with Stephen. He replied that he'd phoned Stephen in Dallas, but Stephen wasn't there, he'd gone to London. 'But Joe,' I said, 'I told you that Stephen would probably be coming to London, didn't they give you his number here?' He said they didn't have his number. 'Didn't have his number?' I said. 'But Joe, they've just given it to me.' There was a pause. Then he said, 'Yeah, well I phoned just after he left so I suppose what they meant was that they didn't have his number while he was in transit.' As 'in transit' could only mean while Stephen was in the air, it certainly did seem unlikely that they would have a number for him. I allowed a heavy silence to reign for a moment or two, the implication of which he must have grasped, because he burst into what seemed to me characteristically American bombast. I say American because I've heard its like only from Americans and it always includes phrases like 'I've been busting my ass off', with lots of references to money. What it specifically amounted to was that he'd been 'busting his ass off' to put this show together, in which he had so far invested 35,000 dollars, and yet here I was phoning up to be querulous about his treatment of Stephen Hollis, *so what the hell was going on around here?* Actually it was difficult to follow any clear argument because it wasn't so much speech as a series of angry barks down the telephone which were not quite directed at me. I allowed yet another silence to reign. He then said, 'I've been thinking of pulling the plug on this show.' That was his phrase, 'pulling the plug on this show'. And went on to imply that it was only his grace and generosity that had prevented him from 'pulling the plug' on the show already. As I too began to feel that it would perhaps be advisable to 'pull the plug' on the show, I allowed another silence, a dignified one, I trusted, unlike the previous two which I had intended to be recriminatory. He abruptly reversed tack, apologized for being 'so snappish', and asked me to give him Stephen's telephone number, which I did. He then told me that Sam Weisman was going to be in London in a few days' time and would make contact with me, and that, by the way, he'd fixed up a really nice little house, I'd love it.

We parted, under the circumstances, on fairly amicable terms. Actually it's a recurring feature of my relationship with Joe Stern that almost all our telephone calls contain passages of hostility and, on my side, acute suspicion, none of which is present when we are in each other's company. The telephone seems to bring out the worst in both of us, perhaps because we both depend a great deal on our gestures and expressions to explain our language. Joe in the flesh is one of the most engaging people I've ever met. He's in his mid-forties, and bears an astonishing resemblance to some kind of soft animal, rodent-like but affectionate. He has a pack of straw-coloured hair on his head. In fact, now I come to think of it, he looks like Walter Matthau, always on the move, jerking in and out of rooms, talking a great deal and with great intensity, with a kind of curious Californian-Jewish wit, I suppose it is, although actually he is much more like my idea of a New York Jew – cynical, guileless and funny at the same time.* I don't think I've ever met a man who comments on the different angles of the life in front of him so incessantly – whatever he sees prompts a joke, an observation. He seems not to listen completely when you speak, picking up half-phrases of what you've said and translating them into arias of his own, usually arias of reminiscence, going right back to his childhood.

* He was actually brought up in the neighbourhood of the Matrix, the synagogue which he attended as a child being only a few hundred yards or so down the road. His wife, by the way, runs a synagogue. A peculiar kind of job – at least it had never really occurred to me before that there is a profession, as opposed to a vocation, of running a synagogue, though I admit that I don't quite know what running a synagogue entails, practically.

One of his specialities is a kind of verbal practical joke – springing a series of unrelated questions at you, talking solemnly back to you in your own accent, then switching mid-stream to a Bronx accent, or plunging without preamble into a passage of Pinter, for instance – one of his favourites is Max's speech about horses from *The Homecoming*: 'Horses! Don't talk to me about horses!' – somehow tangling it into the conversation to surreal and heady effect. So much extravagant, free-flowing fun can leave him curiously vulnerable to counter-attack, though. On my last evening in Los Angeles he took me out to dinner – an event he clearly wanted to be very special. As we approached the majestic and expensive restaurant he said, 'Well, I hope you're going to like this place.' I said, very emphatically, 'I *know* I'm going to.' He said, 'How do you know?' I said, 'Because I was here last night.' He looked absolutely appalled. He said, 'What? Oh come on, you were here last night? Oh Jesus, I wanted this to be new – oh Christ, you were here last night?' I had to explain that this was merely a little joke. I was attempting here a little joke. He looked astonished that he'd had played on him the kind of joke he likes to play on other people, and kept referring to it for the rest of the evening. 'So it was a joke, eh? A joke. Well, what about that?'

## Monday, 30 December

Sam Weisman is in London, and phoned to arrange lunch. I suggested Peter Mario's, an Italian restaurant in the Chinese section of Soho – the same restaurant, I now realize, where I first met his predecessor, Kristoffer Tabori.* Perhaps not a wise choice, as it hadn't worked out too well with Tabori, at least to begin with. But then Tabori's appearance in London had been surrounded by mystery. On several occasions he'd phoned from Los Angeles to announce his arrival, naming the day, and then a few days after the day named would phone up to name a further day, on which he also failed to turn up, until at last, after a couple of further postponements, he phoned up on a hitherto unnamed day from

* For years I went there several times a week. I not only had my own table but an understanding with the management that whenever I came through the door the piped music would be turned off. It closed while I was in Los Angeles on my second trip and the premises converted into yet another (surely unwanted and certainly unneeded) Chinese restaurant.

London itself, to announce that he was here. I had a funny feeling about Peter Mario's even as I suggested it, especially when he wouldn't let me give him directions. He said he knew his way around London, and anyway had a terrific street guide, which he loved using. He turned up about an hour late, having got lost. Probably not altogether his fault. I've lived in London most of my life and still get lost, even without the help of a street guide, but being kept waiting always puts me in a rage, which turns into a kind of simmering headache when I have to suppress it.

He's actually got a very personable appearance and manner, large brown eyes, wide, ingenuous smiles, very fluent – rather like a young academic in his first job. Also he talked very well about the play. In the end we parted on the best of terms, though I remember being made uneasy by his habit of addressing me as 'sir', not, I hoped, to draw attention to our age difference, or even (which I wouldn't have minded) to a difference in our professional status – I a battle-hardened campaigner of many productions, he a boy soldier who'd not yet had the sniff of blood (his own) in his nostrils – but rather as if it were some kind of nickname I'd picked up without being aware of it. Not quite 'sir' as when one calls a dog 'sir' in 'Get down, sir!' for instance, but certainly more intimate than hierarchical – which is a kind of contradiction, really. The odd thing is I can't recall whether he's called me 'sir' since. Joe has, once or twice, but with him the intention is simply ironic. 'And how are you today, sir?' sort of stuff. I very much hope Sam Weisman doesn't call me 'sir'. Even ironically. Especially on a first meeting.

As I was recording this I suddenly noticed that I had two cigarettes going. Two. One between my fingers, newly lit. The other in the ashtray, half smoked, damp on the underside, staining yellow near the top, a long trail of ash dangling from it. I've really *got* to give up. On the first day of January I'm going to make a serious attempt. It's probably madness to try with so much tension going on, but then there are always likely to be tensions going on either professionally or on the home front – rows with my children, and worries about Hazel's health. She is now very blind and very deaf, though she is still capable of sniffing the air, twitching her head alertly about, and rushing dramatically to the front door to bark at it with spirited aggression, usually when there is no one there, thus showing that even though her senses may be on the decline, all her instincts are still in some sort of working order. Our walks in the woods are being conducted in a more colourful manner than usual because in this cold weather she has to wear a strange woollen garment that Beryl has manufactured out of an old sweater. For Hazel this amounts to clothing and I think she feels that she has taken a step up the evolutionary ladder. A clothed dog is somewhere on the way towards being a human being, a status which, for some indecipherable reason, she clearly considers worth gaining.

Anyway, to come back to the other subject. I am going to try to give up smoking on the first of January. I remember that Harold gave up during the first production of *The Common Pursuit* at the Lyric, Hammersmith, and was much helped by a nicotine chewing-gum called Nicorettes. So on Saturday I moseyed up to the chemist for some Nicorettes, to be informed that I could only get them on prescription. On prescription. I asked the reason. The chemist wasn't quite sure, but he thought it might be because nicotine chewing-gum could be addictive. I said, 'It can't surely be any more addictive than cigarettes?' No, he said, certainly not more addictive than cigarettes. I asked whether it was harmful in any way and he said, no, not that he knew of, certainly nothing like as harmful as cigarette-smoking. He added that Nicorettes were also very expensive, almost as expensive as cigarettes in fact.

When I got home, I phoned up my doctor at her group practice. As she wasn't there I said to the receptionist, 'Well, perhaps one of the other doctors can help me. I'm giving up smoking in the New Year, and I need a prescription for nicotine chewing-gum.' To which she replied, 'No, there's nobody here who can help you on the telephone. You'll have to make an appointment and come in.' 'Come in?' 'That's right,' she said. 'We can't give out prescriptions on the telephone.' This receptionist was Scots, and sounded as if she were in her mid-seventies, though she was probably only twenty-five – but she had that sort of prissy, Edinburgh accent, every vowel and consonant a salute to morality and education. 'So you'll have to come in.' 'But,' I said, 'I don't want sleeping pills, or heroin. Simply nicotine gum, to help me – ' 'I'm sorry, there's nothing I can do. You have to come in and see a doctor if you want a prescription for your nicotine gum. Because it's a prescription. We can't just let you have one on your say-so over the telephone, you know.' Recognizing that a Scot is a Scot (I'm half one myself) I hung up. Then, remembering that my doctor is, in fact, perfectly normal, pleasant and helpful (Welsh), I wrote her a letter explaining that I was buggered if I was going to sit about for hours in a germ-and-baby-filled waiting room, just to get a prescription for nicotine chewing-gum that I was going to have to pay heavily for, into the bargain. I enclosed a stamped, addressed envelope. At least I hope I did. My preliminary manoeuvres to give up smoking have resulted in the kind of irritation that usually leads to my stepping up my smoking.

## Tuesday, 31 December

Had the lunch with Sam Weisman. He was on time which got us off to a good start. He's in his late thirties, possibly early forties, with rather startling blue eyes – no, not startlingly blue, startling *and* blue, as if magnified unnaturally.* He has an intelligent Jewish face, thinning ginger hair swept back, a goat-like beard, and best of all, a direct uncomplicated manner. We spent the first hour fencing – i.e. not talking about the subject we'd come to talk about. He'd just read *An Unnatural Pursuit*,† and asked questions about casting in London. He could scarcely believe, he said, that Harold Pinter and I had encountered the same sort of problems that he and other stage directors had encountered in Los Angeles. He'd imagined actors over here would queue up, if not actually lie down on their stomachs, for the opportunity of appearing in stuff written by me, directed by Harold. I greedily accepted my share of the compliment while also accepting that this was so much fol-de-rol, and muttering something dark about the independent-spiritedness of our lads and lasses, along with the high quality of our television drama, which offered lots of very good parts for reasonable amounts of money, finally nudged the discussion on to the Matrix, and all its recent turmoil – the director taking over as the leading man, the leading man taking over the part of Humphry, the chap playing Humphry leaving, the chap playing Nick being replaced, and not least, his own emergence as the new director. He allowed me to air all my doubts and worries while calmly assuring me that all could still be saved. We parted on the understanding that we would meet up

* I discovered in Los Angeles that he wears contact lenses. Perhaps they magnify the eyes as well as the vision.

† My diary of the London production of *The Common Pursuit*, published by Faber and Faber (London, 1985) and St Martin's Press (New York, 1986).

again in Los Angeles in a few days' time. Greatly relieved, I phoned my New York agent, Phyllis Wender, to say that I wasn't going to exercise my own option to 'pull the plug out' on the production, though I was entitled to do so, having director approval as well as casting approval. 'Well no, as a matter of fact you haven't, Simon,' she interrupted me. 'As the contract was drawn up after you'd approved Kristoffer Tabori as the director, there seemed no need to put anything in about director approval.' So it was a good thing I'd approved of Sam Weisman, as there was nothing I could have done about it if I hadn't. That's how things stand, then, on Tuesday morning, half-past midnight. I leave for Los Angeles on Saturday, midday, and on Sunday, back in Los Angeles, I'll have to sit through a read-through of the new text, with the new, or rather revised, cast.

## Wednesday, 1 January

Evening. Beryl, her sister Jennifer, Jennifer's two-year-old daughter Alice, and I saw the New Year in with glasses of champagne, after watching a film on television called *The Black Stallion*, about a boy's relationship with a horse, which would, I think, have been a fine film if its last section hadn't been devoted to establishing that boy and horse were American-style winners, i.e. won lots of money in races. Pity, because the first two-thirds had been touchingly about their growing trust and mutual dependence. There was consequently something obscene in seeing the boy turning himself into a successful little jockey, and this fine animal becoming a successful commercial proposition, both looking proud of it. Still, it was a more wholesome experience than we'd have had if we'd ventured out to a party. Nowadays the sights of London, even on the least festive nights, resemble sketches by Hogarth.

Our son, Ben, on the other hand, did go to a party, to which he hadn't been invited. He and his friends had made up a list during the day of five or six parties, to not one of which they'd been invited, but to which they somehow assumed (correctly, as it turned out) they'd be welcome. How news of these parties reached them is quite incomprehensible to me – a kind of town-crier, or town-whisperer, system seemed to be at work. The party they selected, after much consideration, had about forty people at it, apparently, all of them also uninvited. The hosts were two young television producers, both of them small and bearded, who presented each uninvited guest with a bottle of champagne on arrival. This wasn't their night's ration, but a sort of door-prize, as apparently there were bottles of wine and spirits scattered everywhere. Most of the guests were in their late teens; the two hosts were in their mid-thirties, but neither Ben nor his friends could tell me much more about them, not having much inclination to meet them, let alone talk to them. 'But what was it *like*?' I cried, finally, in bewilderment. 'It was all right,' he said. Perhaps he attends such affairs all the time – certainly I only learned about this one because I happened to ask him how he'd spent his New Year's Eve. Lucy also went to a party, a disappointingly mundane one, as it was given by somebody she knew. All they did was dance, drink, smoke, and whatever else people of sixteen do with each other these days.

Stephen came around at about ten, to read *Dog Days* with me. He brought a camera with him. Beryl was slightly surprised to discover him in various of our rooms, taking snapshots of bookshelves, fireplaces, cluttered desks, for the benefit of the Dallas set designer, who wanted views of the inside of a down-market North London residence, of the kind in which you'd expect to find an under-achieving, would-be-philandering literary type, and his adulterous, deceitful and moralizing wife. I said rather frostily that I believed Beryl and I were a cut above the two characters in my play, both socially and morally, turned him around on the stairs as he was making his way up them to our bedroom, camera at the ready, and ushered him into my study where we sat down to our reading of *Dog Days*.

I found myself loathing it. Absolutely loathing it. After the brief opening scene I could scarcely bring myself to speak the lines, they seemed so smart and predictable – as if I'd once written down a number of jokes, and then filled in the feed lines a few years later. Nothing sounded spontaneous, nothing simply happened – everything worked for, then crunchingly arrived at. I therefore disliked the chap who'd written it some fifteen years ago, and by the end of the second act could scarcely believe that in six weeks' time I'd be going to Dallas, to add my name to this little horror as co-director, as well as sole author. I tried to share these doubts with Stephen, who brushed them robustly aside, saying he was delighted with what we'd discovered, looking forward to his part in the production immensely. Perhaps he sees it as his duty to unmask me publicly in western America.

We talked for a short while about casting, bandying names about, until I suddenly remembered Ian McShane, an English actor, who'd worked successfully at the Matrix a few years back, and who more years back had appeared in a couple of Harold's plays. I phoned Harold, who spoke highly of him, and then phoned Joe Stern – McShane now lives in Los Angeles and has become a friend of Joe's – to get his telephone number. What of course Stephen and I had forgotten was the eight-hour time difference between London and Los Angeles. I got Joe at a quarter to five in the afternoon our time, at a quarter to nine in the morning his time, on New Year's Day. I realized this immediately from the confusions of his voice when responding to my New Year's greetings. I went on to give him an enthusiastic account of my lunch with Sam Weisman, and oh, by the way, I interrupted myself, do you by any chance have a telephone number for Ian McShane? Whereupon Joe, who until then had sounded drowsily touched by my concern, became galvanized. 'What,' he asked, 'what do you want Ian's number for?' Oh, merely thinking of him for *Dog Days* in Dallas, I explained. '*Dog Days* in Dallas, well, you know. I just want to assure you that there's no possibility – no *way* – that Ian will be interested in doing *Dog Days* in Dallas. For one thing Ian has lots of commitments, for another he's going over to London where his wife's going to star in a big, big show,* for a third thing he'll want to stay on in England while his new television series is released there, and anyway why should he want to go to Dallas, he's a much-sought-after actor, no *way* will he go to Dallas, why should he want to go to Dallas, who'd want to go to Dallas?'

I tried out one of my pauses, indicating through it that I at least was somebody who, while not perhaps *wanting* to go to Dallas, was nevertheless obliged by circumstances (shortage of funds) to go there. He met the pause with a pause of his own, then said, 'You know. I'm just trying to save you wasting your time.' 'Well,' I said, deciding to shelve examining with Joe the question of his proprietorial, not to say positively possessive concern for Ian McShane, 'he can make up his own mind, I suppose. I mean, he won't object

* Big, big, *big* show called *Chess*, though as I haven't seen it, I have no idea what part his wife played, or perhaps still plays.

to being *asked* if he'd like to go to Dallas, will he? Do you have his number?' Joe abandoned the phone for two or three minutes, then came back with a number that I took to be Ian McShane's, though I got no answer when I tried it.* I thought it wiser not to ask after the little house, whether he was sure it *was* a nice little one, and had he had a video installed yet, etc. (I'd asked both Judy Daish and Phyllis to remind him of my need for a video), feeling that I'd already done enough damage to his first morning of 1986, so again wishing him Happy New Year, see you soon, hung up.

## Friday, 3 January

It is eleven at night. I leave for Los Angeles tomorrow, the plane departing at midday. Nothing much has happened since the attempt to communicate with McShane the day before yesterday, apart from a conversation on the telephone with Harold, on the subject of my giving up smoking. I wanted to know how he'd negotiated the nicotine-chewing-gum – the Nicorettes – stage of his withdrawal, how he'd got from cigarettes to nicotine gum, and from nicotine gum to no nicotine at all. He asked, rather strangely, I thought, 'What do you want to know for?' 'Well.' I said, 'I might one day contemplate giving up smoking and I just wondered about some of the details.' He said, 'But what do you want to give up smoking for? I mean, what are you talking about, I'm sure you don't want to give up smoking.' Well, I said, I did. Everyone wanted to give up smoking, didn't they? I mean everyone who was fool enough to smoke wanted to give up smoking. He said, 'Yes, but I mean you don't want to give up smoking, it's not really – I mean, you've got a few years of smoking left in you.' I said, but what about health and so forth? And he said, 'Oh well, yes, I mean it's not really – I don't think you should worry about giving up smoking.' I asked him how old he'd been when he gave up smoking. He said, 'Fifty-three.' 'And that's – really, I mean the thing is that you should – perhaps you should hang on until you're that sort of age before you give up smoking.'†

* Nor did Stephen when he tried it regularly over the next few weeks. But Joe was dead right. I met Ian McShane in Los Angeles, during *The Common Pursuit* rehearsals, and he made it clear, though with great charm, that no way would he consider going to Dallas.

† I am now fifty-one.

## 2

# Flexing the Life-Muscles

## Saturday, 4 January 1986

Here I am, back in Los Angeles at 7 p.m. their time, having two hours earlier, at one in the morning my time, checked into the Magic Hotel. But it's not at all as I remember it when Joe pointed it out to me from his car. For one thing it isn't cut off, being in easy walking distance of the Grauman's Chinese Theatre end of Hollywood Boulevard, and therefore close to lots of bars, restaurants, shops and cinemas. For another it isn't at all institutional, either architecturally or in atmosphere, consisting of a series of studio flats on three floors. Each of the upper two flats possesses its own balcony, which faces over a kind of courtyard, in the middle of which there is a rather engaging little swimming pool surrounded by a mysterious grass substitute, Astroturf I suppose, which also covers the floor of my balcony. I find the whole effect oddly pleasing, even at three in the morning my time, and am looking forward to sussing out the bar, trying out the restaurant – I haven't located them yet.*

In fact the whole day has turned out to be rather pleasing, in spite of beginning badly by my waking abruptly at seven, summoning a phantom Joe to my bedside and having a row with him on the question of my being booked into the Magic, news of which I'd received through Judy Daish the evening before. These ghastly, schizophrenic outbursts – or inbursts I suppose they are really – must be essential to the workings of my psychic system, but I do wish they'd occasionally take a different tone, loving and tender remonstrances, for instance, with a dash of eroticism thrown in. But if I could manage that, I hope I wouldn't be wasting any of it,

* They weren't there, to be sussed out, tried out, located. The only hotel I've ever been in that couldn't furnish you with a drink or a sandwich at *any* time of the day.

but especially the eroticism, on the phantom of Joe Stern. Things cleared up once I was out of bed, on the move, in the grip of my usual pre-flight panic, but all went smoothly for once,* recrimination-free farewells with my family being followed by a step into a waiting taxi that took me to a punctual train to Gatwick, where I was advised at the check-in counter that I'd been upgraded from 'Super Club', which is neither, to First Class – my natural flying environment, to which I was reintroduced by way of a glass of champagne *before* take-off, when I most need it.

I drank and ate well but not extravagantly, read, dozed, dreamed, read, ignoring the in-flight film (*Pale Rider*, starring and directed by Clint Eastwood – a sacreligious rip-off of *Shane* – I'd seen and hated it in London) and was only disturbed at finding myself, a couple of hours before we were due to land, engaged in another frenzied conversation with the phantom of Joe Stern on the subject of the Magic Hotel. I sucked down a large whisky, to prepare myself for the usual American customs and immigration ordeal. As I always make a point of travelling light, just an overnight bag that I take on the plane with me, I was pretty fast through to immigration – and through immigration pretty fast too, as the pleasantly smiling young official turned out to be sympathetic to my plight – my plight being, apparently, that I was an indigent Englishman trying to pass himself off as a playwright of some consequence. He asked me whether I'd got a return ticket, and when I made a gesture towards my pocket, held up his hand as if he didn't want to be embarrassed by the pantomime of searching I was about to go through before announcing its loss. 'No,' he said, 'just *tell* me whether you have it, let's leave it at that, eh?' I said, 'But I do have it, actually,' though at that second not visibly, as my hand was in the wrong pocket. He said, 'OK.' There was a brief pause, the two of us staring at each other, then he said rather ominously, 'Look after yourself.' The customs officer, a Spanishy-looking middle-aged woman, was disconcerted both by the smallness of my bag and then by the discovery that it was only half full, especially when I told her I'd be staying for six weeks or so, but she decided against a body search.

Kristoffer Tabori and Judy Geeson were waiting for me along with their dog Digby, actually a female, who seemed quite pleased

* It usually does, for once.

to see me, and made no attempt to go for my shoes. On my previous visit she'd taken a positively lascivious interest in my shoes, particularly my left one, which she would seize between her jaws and try to pull off my foot. The Taboris also have two cats, Flora and Asia. On the first night of my first visit to Los Angeles I had entertained Flora, a black and white cat, on my bed – I'd lured her in with a bowl of milk which had been consumed by Digby who'd bowled in ahead of her, then clamped her jaws around Flora's head, and dragged her around the room. Flora clearly resented this but submitted to it passively – wisely too, as it was probably the best tactic to employ to avoid having her head bitten off. That was the only night Flora spent with me. I think she thought I'd lost respect for her, like a Victorian maiden that had been ravished. Yet she continued to haunt my house, frequently spending the night staring reproachfully in through the glass door.

I never saw Asia, her sister, who had vanished a few days before I arrived, but the Taboris assumed that she'd been abducted and consumed by a coyote – if one gets up early enough one can apparently see packs of coyotes swarming steadily up and down the complacent-looking, suburban streets, rather as office workers swarm towards the tube in London, I suppose. If ever a puppy, a cat, or a baby goes missing around here, its absence is generally attributed to the coyotes, which may be a plausible explanation, though I've noticed that even in London babies, cats, dogs vanish, and we don't generally attribute this to packs of squirrels or foxes, nor even to packs of office workers. The Taboris' other pet is a parakeet who had just been released from quarantine when I was here the last time. Her name is Ben, owing to initial confusion over her sex, and she's now seventeen with a life expectancy of ninety. But apart from that – that as she is likely to outlive one by several decades at least, she now and then induced intimations of mortality – I found her a quite enchanting creature, extremely affectionate, and with considerable dignity. Digby, for example, would stand staring into her cage for hours – I mean *really* for hours, just stood staring through the cage bars at her, while she hopped about pecking at grain, or stared back past her, as if Digby were a particularly uninteresting piece of furniture. When she came out of her cage she would flap ponderously around the room before alighting on a Tabori shoulder, where she would sort of purr with her beak, a cluck, cluck, purring sound, of sheer happiness.

When at last she chose to land on me, she gripped my finger with her claw, not a grip for security, but out of affection also, then ran her beak up and down my cheek – although I have to admit that the moment she first came at me was rather terrifying, as she aimed herself straight at my face before sort of collapsing on to my shoulder, though she then set about calming me down with her beak-nuzzling and beak-clucking and claw-gripping. Digby, of course, who had pursued her across to me, stood staring indignantly up at her, then pursued her back to the cage. But I don't believe it would have made any difference if Ben had chosen to make the journey on foot. Her will was evidently much stronger than Digby's, and will is what counts between animals, as between most humans. Anyway, I've never been so entranced by a bird. Never even saw the point of birds as pets before – and actually, because of the methods employed in catching, crating and shipping them, I don't think I could allow myself to have one. But if there are any knocking about, already caught, crated and shipped, then I wouldn't mind doing some sort of deal with it. It could share my study with me as far as I'm concerned. Although I expect Hazel would have some objections.

I asked the Taboris after Flora (fine but still shy), Asia (still missing, presumed dead), and Ben (radiantly happy) as they drove me to a supermarket, then on here to the Magic. They are due back in a few minutes to take me to a nearby restaurant, where we are to have dinner with Joe and Pepe Stern, Sam Weisman and possibly Sam Weisman's wife. Half-past three in the morning my time, and I'm standing with my feet on my turf-clad balcony at half-past seven in the evening Los Angeles time, waiting to go out to dinner. But as we have a read-through of the play tomorrow morning, it's all quite sensible – my plan being to stay awake until around 11 p.m. (Los Angeles time, naturally) in the hope of getting a decent night's sleep.

Before I sign off, I should say something about my other, larger plan – to stop smoking. I've brought with me an enormous load of Nicorettes, enough to see me through at least four weeks. I chewed quite a few pieces during the flight. The trouble was that I also smoked. There was a foul moment when I realized that I had a box of Nicorettes on one knee, and on the other, or just beside it, in the adjoining seat, a packet of cigarettes and my lighter, and that between my lips I had dangling a cigarette, while between my jaws a piece of nicotine gum, as if in some way the latter cancelled out the effect of the former. Altogether during the flight I must have worked my way through half a dozen pieces of gum, without my smoking being in the slightest affected. Which means, of course, that I managed to take far more nicotine into my system than I'd normally have done. Very depressing. I suppose I can claim that the boredom and tension attendant on a comparatively long flight* aren't conducive to a chap's giving up smoking, but then tomorrow I've got to endure the boredom and tension of a read-through, and after that weeks of boring and tense rehearsals, so when in Los Angeles am I likely to give up smoking? I'm desperate to try but when it comes to it suspect I haven't the will, the resilience, the sense of long-term preservation, to give up for twenty minutes, let alone for the rest of my life. All I can say now, with any confidence, is that I don't want to end up with my lungs rotting from cigarettes, while my stomach rots from the gum I'm chewing in order to give up cigarettes. Good night. The Taboris have just phoned to say they're waiting for me in the lobby. Good night.

*Later that night*

Yes, well, it's twenty-past ten in Los Angeles. Or is it? No, it's ten to eleven in Los Angeles. Ten to seven in the morning in London. I've just come back from dinner. Sam Weisman was unable to turn up for some reason (though none was offered) so there were just the five of us. The evening got off to a distinctly ropey start, at least for me. I'd hardly settled into the back seat of the Taboris' car when Judy Geeson informed me that she had some bad news – I was forbidden to smoke in rehearsals. My hackles, what I have of them – and I suspect I've got rather a lot – rose immediately, while Judy Geeson's hackles, what she has of them – and I suppose I can assume the usual human amount – remained infuriatingly dormant. I spoke powerfully from the back, she turned her head slightly sideways to speak gently from the front, while Kristoffer Tabori dropped out of the arena through the simple expedient of concentrating on the steering wheel, the gears, the traffic lights, the signals – behaving, in fact, like a learner driver on his first public outing. According to Judy the chief stirrer up of strife is John Delancey, the

* Given my previous description of the flight as pleasing, there seems to be a contradiction here, but only of a kind that is routine in this sort of self-justification, I think.

actor who started as Stuart and is now playing Humphry. He finds cigarette smoke offensive, Judy explained to me, and when Kristoffer Tabori was the director had organized a 'petition' (she actually used the word) requesting/demanding that nobody – including Tabori, a strictly amateur smoker – should be allowed to puff smoke around the rehearsal room.

I can't remember the details of my counter-attack, but I know I touched on cars (I have a suspicion I called them motor vehicles) as a source of pollution and ill health ('I'll stop smoking in rehearsals if everybody else promises not to drive to rehearsal' – hah!) and then went on to question the propriety of actors (didn't, I hope, use the phrase 'mere actors') daring to dictate to the only author and begetter, without whom none of them, not *one* of them, would be at the Matrix at all (ignoring the possibility that they might be somewhere more glamorous, doing something far more lucrative) and concluded with a threat to the effect that if I couldn't smoke in rehearsals, then I wouldn't be coming to them, would in fact be shortly on a plane to London. She responded to this, as indeed to everything else I said, with deft sweetness, like a nurse explaining away the pain of an operation the patient suspects has been bungled, until I found myself on the verge of demanding that we skip this dinner altogether, let's drive straight on to the airport and the next plane home, at about which point we arrived at the restaurant, where Joe and Pepe were waiting for us.

The restaurant was Joe Allen's, and the dinner turned out to be pleasant. It was good to see Joe Stern in the flesh, rather than as a fantasy antagonist in one of my schizophrenic hand-to-hands. Most of the time we spent discussing old films, very old films, going back to the late forties and early fifties, summoning from the past, probably even from the tomb, such figures as Charles McGraw (superb in the superb *The Narrow Margin*) and a strange German director/producer called Hauss, whose films we'd both seen but the stories of which we only half remembered. All was well, in fact, in spite of Joe's requesting me early on, I think just after the starters had been put in front of us, not to smoke while people were eating – I chose to take this as a knowing little joke on the rehearsal smoking ban and, grinding out my cigarette, lit up another one immediately.

Now here I am back in my sitting room at the Magic, on the balcony, talking into this machine while I square up to the fact that my smoking or not smoking may turn out to be the main story of my time in Los Angeles – which may turn out to be a briefer time than was expected. Revolving also the irony that though I'm desperate to give up smoking, I won't allow myself to be forced into giving it up. Does this mean that I won't, or that I can't? Or that pride, vanity and self-indulgence come before a concern for my own health and the well-being of others? Yes. From where I stand, by the way, I can see across the pool into the studio opposite mine. When I arrived three or so hours ago there was a most elegant black chap lying on the sofa with his feet on a stool, surveying himself in a mirror beside the television set. Now the television is on, he is still in almost exactly the same position, but has at his side a beautiful black girl, whose arms are around him. They are both watching television, but should they shift their eyes a few inches to the mirror, they'll be able to see how they're getting on in terms of ageing. In his case the minutes have already turned into unreclaimable hours, for both of them the day is almost done. Yet they look happy. Happy and comfortable with each other. Behind me in my sitting room as I watch and talk there is Antony Hopkins on the radio playing bits of music from this Mozart, that Bach, his Radio 3 programme incorporated into a Los Angeles musical programme, I assume. So there we have it. Two beautiful black people enfolded, watching television in the studio opposite, here in Los Angeles, while on the radio Antony Hopkins dealing out Bach and Mozart, also in Los Angeles, I standing watching, listening, talking into this machine.

## Sunday, 5 January

Joe picked me up at the Magic at twenty-past nine, and we arrived at the Matrix ten minutes later, the read-through being scheduled for ten o'clock. The Matrix is a very inconspicuous-looking theatre from the outside, almost like a shoe shop it seems to me, but inside it's very charming. You go through a wide lobby, past Joe's office, down a passage that leads to an auditorium, which seats its ninety-nine people very comfortably, much more comfortably than most theatres of this size do. The stage is immensely wide, but in proportion very shallow. When I last saw it it had a set on it for a play with which Joe Stern wasn't involved as producer – he had merely rented his theatre to an independent company, a rather strange company actually as it was formed by a one-time Miss America who had married a chap who wanted to be a playwright, and had written a drag farce–thriller.

I left Joe and Sam Weisman discussing various technical matters, to do with the set, went into Joe's office and sat smoking, waiting for the actors to arrive. They came in in little dribbles, here a pair, there a single, looking like well-dressed convicts. No – not like convicts, like children delivered for their first day of school. The only one who seemed to be at all pleased at finding himself in the theatre was our Humphry, John Delancey, whose intelligent and sympathetic face, not at all the face of the leader of an anti-smoking lobby, by the way, radiated contentment with his lot. Anyway, in the rest came – Wayne Alexander (Martin) smiling furtively, Judy Geeson (Marigold) and Kris Tabori (Stuart) walking close to each other but rather formally, Christopher Neame (Peter) flashing by with an odd saluting gesture, Ted Larkins (Nick) pale and unshaven, as if on the flit, then John Delancey (Humphry) – all of them passing the open door of Joe's office, in which I sat, crying out my 'hellos' and 'good mornings' and 'good to see yous', my mind not so much on them or the play, but on my smoking and the problems raised by it.

Just before ten I went back into the auditorium. The actors were sitting around a table on the stage. I carefully selected a last-row corner seat, from which, as it turned out, I could see only the backs of three of the actors who mainly blocked out the fronts of the three actors sitting opposite them, but at least it was a seat in which I could smoke without fear of a rational complaint. I had my nicotine gum in the adjoining seat.

Absolutely nothing was made of my smoking at all. John Delancey, the one who is meant to have the strong objections, occasionally rolled his eyes towards me, but simply out of curiosity, to see how I was responding, or so I deduced from his looks, which were invariably accompanied by genial and handsome smiles. Sam Weisman, the other chap who, according to Judy Geeson, is worried about smoke, seemed quite oblivious, sitting below me to my left, concentrating on the read-through. It's true that Judy Geeson occasionally looked in my direction. Brief glances. Enigmatic, I thought. Could have been about anything. Or about nothing.

After the read-through Sam Weisman said, 'Thank you, great,

terrific,' Joe said, 'Great, thank you, terrific,' I said, 'Thank you everybody, many, many thanks,' then Sam and I went next door to the Café Melrose, where, over lunch, I put to him various worries I now had about the text, made a few changes in his presence, then when he left to re-address himself to Joe and then the actors, stayed on to make a few further changes. I went back to Joe's office, showed the changes to Sam. He incorporated them into his script and then came with me into the theatre and read them out to the actors, who wrote them down very carefully, sometimes asking for the changes to be read out again. Joe came in, and we began the main business of the day, a run-through.*

A lot of the blocking was both clumsy and fussy, placing actors in static clumps in which they were nevertheless irrelevantly busy, i.e. eating, drinking, shuffling papers, adjusting their positions on chairs, etc., all of which I hated. On the other hand the actors had a reasonable sense of their characters, and the first act had a good thrust to it, better perhaps than had been managed (given the different texts) in either London or at the Long Wharf. But it was clear that still further work needs to be done to the play itself. Every scene needs more economy; and in several scenes the dramatic emphasis is wrong. I hope this is only a matter of a few judicious cuts. I dread the thought of having to do any serious rewriting.

After the run Sam Weisman, Joe and I repeated our 'greats', 'terrifics' and 'thank yous', I still in my corner, puffing away, before Sam Weisman went back to the top of the play, and began to work slowly through the first act. After about an hour or so he stopped, and talked generally to the actors about their problems, concentrating specifically on the word 'pain', noting the presence of 'pain' in the text, the lack of it in the actors' account of the text. 'We gotta find the pain. *You* gotta find the pain.' he said, several times. I didn't really know what he meant by 'pain', unless, of course, he assumes that as all life contains pain it becomes axiomatic (if tautological) to assert that any character in a play has in some way to communicate it. I don't know. What depresses me is that the actors seemed to think that there was some profound value in the word, in fact behaved as if they were expecting it and would have been disappointed not to have it fired at them – they nodded,

* In a run-through the actors try to perform their parts, on their feet and on the move; as opposed to a read-through, with which we'd started proceedings, when the actors, seated, simply read through their parts.

blinked, swayed their heads, painfully confessing their failure to come through with the pain. Sam concluded on a wave of resonant statements and interrogatives, actually the same statement and interrogative, frequently repeated – 'Ya know. I'm talking about the pain. Know what I mean? Ya know. The pain. Know what I mean? Hear what I'm saying?' – and then all the actors eventually departed (including Judy Geeson) except for Kristoffer Tabori, who wanted to pursue with Sam Weisman the idea of the pain in his part as Stuart.

It was missing somewhere, he couldn't find it, especially in the first act, after he discovers Marigold is pregnant, and then again when he discovers that she's had an abortion – where in the gaps between these discoveries should he locate the 'pain', how express the 'pain', where is the 'pain' that runs through this man's life, *is* this man's life? By this time I'd come to hate the word, thinking that it's best applied to specifics, like a throbbing tooth, a headache, an extra-strong spasm of guilt over this or that betrayal, unpaid bill, unreturned phone call, etc., but not wishing to push into the discussion in a too bluntly Anglo-Saxon style – especially as Sam Weisman was responding to Tabori's re-employment of the word with sage paragraphs, energetically delivered – I inserted myself shyly between them and begged them both to remember that yes indeed, I said suavely, there is 'pain' knocking about in life, and of course we must be aware of its presence in the play, but we mustn't forget, must we, that in the first act the characters are young people, who feel sure that when they make a decision, the decision sorts life out. But of course what we discover, don't we, as we go on is that the definitive decisions tend not to be definitive. Life, 'old life itself',* won't allow them to be. I went on for some time in this vein, sounding, I suspect, rather like an elderly vicar ruminating aloud to the local literary society on the moral themes in *Middlemarch*, but my intention was to get as much mist as possible around the idea that Tabori and the other actors should go looking for the 'pain' in their parts – I knew what kind of production *that* could lead to.

Sam Weisman, who's clearly attended a few postgraduate seminars

* A phrase that Stuart used at the end of Act One in the London version of *The Common Pursuit*. I cut the phrase when rewriting the play for the Matrix, and it never found its way back into the text.

somewhere or other,* came surging straight out of the mist with another dangerous monologue to do not only with 'pain' but with 'life-muscles', a term with which I'm already familiar through conversations with Joe Stern.† I must try to find out which of them induces this vocabulary in the other. Anyway what he actually said to Tabori, who with his friendly youthful manner and large bespectacled brown eyes, resembled an exceptionally eager student, was that we all have this 'muscle', this 'life-muscle', that some of us allow to go undeveloped, so that when a crisis comes, and we need the power of our 'life-muscle', we find not only that it's become useless, but that it's a hindrance, even. I must say that while I quite enjoy the idea of a life-muscle, I find it disconcerting when offered to an actor making inquiries about his part. All I care about is the kind of discussion that leads to a result on the stage, and I don't really see how talk of finding the 'pain' through the discovery of the life-muscle can lead to anything on the stage – except posturing and meaningful pauses. But I may be wrong. Perhaps this is the way you have to talk to actors in Los Angeles, perhaps they're conditioned to it, and would feel deprived without it.

Anyway, I did my best to get some mist swirling again, with further prattle about encouraging the audience to understand and *enjoy*, a word I kept hitting, *enjoy* the ironies of my piece by encouraging the actors to understand and *enjoy* the ironies of their dramatic circumstances, through the language in which they speak about them. I mean, I said, one of the *pleasures* of the play, surely, is that it slightly offends our moral expectations: we want people, ourselves included, to be punished for our vices, rewarded for our virtues, whereas there were times in *The Common Pursuit* when it seemed to be working the other way round – on and on I went, smilingly aiming their attention towards cheerfulness, jolliness, upness, hinting that the darker strands of the play would express themselves more fully in a bright atmosphere – until Tabori took himself off, his head I hoped full of mist rather than muscles. Sam Weisman then talked briefly, and I'm glad to report practically, of what he'd noticed in specific performances, and I got Joe to drive me back here.

It's a quarter to seven, I have a malt whisky in my hand, another

* Yale, I subsequently discovered.

† Joe Stern also liked to talk about the need for actors 'to go to that place they don't want to go to' – I could never make out where that was, but then I'm not an actor.

already sluicing warmly through my system, and I feel, in spite of my dismay at Sam's monologues (I'm clutching the back of a chair in my kitchen, in the hope that it's made of wood – it looks and feels like wood) that in the end this production is going to turn out OK. I have an intuition that it will, in fact, just as I had an intuition from the beginning that the London production would in some way go wrong. In a minute I shall saunter down to Hollywood Boulevard, choose a restaurant for my dinner, then have an early night. I quite enjoy the pleasures, or are they vices? – yes, they're vices – of solitude. I shall pick out a restaurant, and have a leisurely meal with a book. With a bad book. Sidney Sheldon. I've got a Sidney Sheldon in my bag for just this sort of situation.

Oh, by the way – I'd forgotten. I phoned Joe before recording this to give him a heavily edited version of my views on the production so far. He said at one point, 'I don't mind being rejected as long as I'm not dismissed' – which had what I take to be a Hollywood ring to it. I was about to reply that I wasn't sure I had a preference, but decided not to pursue it. And now here I am, out on my balcony, my tape recorder still in my hand, on an evening that's nippy and humid simultaneously, with a sort of pervasive muckiness in the air, which is, I suppose, the famous Los Angeles smog. From the room next to mine there comes a confused blaring of tempestuous music and gunfire, as if the radio and television were both on together. Every room in the hotel is somehow public. In the ones opposite me, on the other side of the pool, I can see flashes of this and that through the thin curtains – a man sitting at a table, eating rapidly as he writes onto a legal pad; a coloured woman of about twenty-five with a child; a laid table. I don't know whether this highly visible privacy is characteristic of Los Angeles, or simply a charming accident in the design of the Magic Hotel. Anyway off I shamble with Sidney Sheldon to find a restaurant. Good night.

I still haven't left. I'm back on the balcony holding in my hand a curious kind of muzzle it looks like, anyway a plastic construction with a strap and a patch of white cloth – actually it looks like a cricket box,* though I would think that it's meant to cover the mouth and nose. I found it hanging on the back of the bathroom door when I went in a few minutes ago (after I'd last spoken) to have a pee. It could of course be some kind of disguise given out

* A cricket box is a white plastic construction that looks like a muzzle, though its function is to protect the testicles of batsmen in the game of cricket.

free to guests who want to do a spot of mugging, but it's more likely to be something to do with the smog, a filter, I assume. But it's been quite smoggy all day, and I didn't see anyone wearing any kind of muzzle on the streets around the Matrix. I must find out more about it. I must find out what this is for. If it *is* a filter, I can take it into rehearsals, and clamp it over the mouth and nostrils of anyone who complains about my smoking.*

## Monday, 6 January

It's eight twenty on a nippy, fog-bound Los Angeles evening. I'm reporting this in a state of some exhaustion, as I have been at the theatre since half-past ten this morning. The day got off to a bizarre start. While I was waiting in the Magic lobby for Chris Neame to pick me up and take me to rehearsals, I suddenly realized that I couldn't go on expecting people at the Matrix to give me lifts. I went to the man at the desk, a sort of remotely sunny, always smiling guy with a beard, about thirty, I suppose, perhaps younger. I said, 'Look, can you give me a number for when I need a cab?' The smile remained on his face but it was an uneasy smile. He said, 'What? What do you want?' I said, 'A number for a cab.' He said, 'Well, I dunno, I dunno. You want a number?' I said, 'Yes, that's right. I want a number for a cab. So I can phone up for one.' He said, 'You mean you wanna phone up and *talk*?' I said, 'Yes, well, to get one around actually.' 'Get one around?' he said. 'Get one around?' I said, 'Yes, you know, get a cab around when I need one.' 'Well,' he said, 'there's only one and it sort of – you've seen it, it lives on the premises.' I said, 'What?' He kept on smiling through all this, smiling, but he also looked extremely worried, if not slightly frightened.

He obviously found me menacing in some way – not surprisingly as it turned out that he thought I wanted a number for a cat. Cat. In fact he thought the telephone number I was actually after was of the cat that hangs about in the hotel, a very charming cat that sits at the edge of the pool in the morning, and whom I met on my first evening – in fact, he was in my room, as if waiting to receive me. Unfortunately the Taboris, who came up with me, brought Digby along. Digby, of course, growled at the cat, who responded with a

* It was, in fact, a muzzle for protection against the smog, or so John Delancey informed me. I never, in my weeks in Los Angeles, saw anyone wearing one, though.

cuff to Digby's eyebrows, making them bleed and sending her yelping about the room, actually dancing back at one stage, her front paws in the air, while the cat, maintaining its dignity, walked slowly and thoughtfully out of my room, out of my life, to all intents and purposes. I'd dearly love to get him or her back, especially at night, when I feel the need for some living company, but even I hadn't thought of making contact by telephone. But how am I going to manage in a society in which people are mad enough to assume that you're mad enough to believe that all you have to do, when you want a cat, is phone one up and ask it around? Call-cats, like call-girls, I suppose.

Even the elementary and necessary things here are complicated by this sunny, almost radiant, incomprehension. Actually not *always* sunny, almost radiant, now I come to think of it. There was that odd experience I had the last time I was here when Joe and Pepe Stern took us out to dinner at a very expensive ranch-like restaurant. The waiter asked me if I wanted a salad. I said, yes, just a lettuce salad, please. Something odd happened to his face. He said, 'What do yer mean?' I said, 'Just a lettuce.' He said, 'What's that?' I said, 'A lettuce, you know, a lettuce. I only want a lettuce. Nothing else but a lettuce.' He said, 'Well, I dunno what yer mean. What yer talking about?' His voice got tougher and tougher, as if at any moment he was going to take me out to a nearby alley at gun point. Fortunately Judy Geeson explained what I meant by a lettuce, putting the proper name to it. Apparently in California they have all varieties of lettuce, which means you can't have just a lettuce. It's got to be a something lettuce. And furthermore I don't think they actually use the word 'lettuce' at all. They call it a something salad. But I don't believe this semantic confusion really explains the increasingly infuriating effect my use of the word 'lettuce' had on the waiter, who was, I remember, tall and rather distinguished in a Latin way, exactly like a *consigliere* in *The Godfather*. But I should keep him in mind whenever I fall too easily into the habit of assuming that incomprehension here is at least benevolent.

I went to the theatre resolving not to smoke, resolving not to interfere too much in rehearsals. I wasn't successful on either count, though I did manage to chew gum for an hour without smoking which I suppose has to rank – how pathetic – as an achievement. But I didn't go for more than ten minutes without interfering. It would have been quite a good morning, all in all, if I hadn't been rather disconcerted by something Ted Larkins told me over lunch. I'd invited him to discuss his accent with him. He's been assuming a chirpy Cockney one, which I think quite inappropriate for Nick. But before I could get on to the subject he blurted out that he was finding things very difficult because after he'd only been working for four days – called in without warning to replace Bart Braddleman – Joe Stern had driven out to his house after rehearsals and suggested that he should leave the production because, he said, he didn't think that Ted could do it. He couldn't see the 'pain', he said, in the man. The 'pain', the 'reality' and the 'pain' in the guy. And he also apparently wondered aloud to Ted Larkins whether Ted Larkins could act. He had the feeling that perhaps Ted Larkins couldn't act. 'Couldn't *even* act' apparently was the phrase he used. So there was that to be dealt with.*

We spent the first part of the afternoon going through Act One, Scene One which seemed occasionally to take off, but more often to sink into a kind of dull posturing. Proceedings weren't helped by John Delancey, who may well be (I suspect is) talented, interesting and intelligent, but nevertheless seems to feel a need to articulate every passing thought and stray doubt about every line and intention and motive in the scene, thus constantly holding us up. I was further irritated by the way that the previous director (Kristoffer Tabori) had filled it with a lot of unnecessary activity: for instance, constant recourse to the coffee pot. I always hate the coffee/tea syndrome in plays – that is, when one feels that a director has stuck a beverage on stage for the characters to help themselves to, in order to create a bustle and urgency quite unrelated to the text. Thus the chap playing Peter (Chris Neame) entered the room carrying not only his gown and some books and papers (as specified in the text) but also a sandwich, and made straight for the coffee pot, so that within seconds of his arrival we had him munching a sandwich, gulping down coffee, getting out of his gown, messing about with his books, all this while talking to various other characters on stage. American actors have a fixation about food, it seems to me, as if they can't act unless they're eating.† Anyway,

* There is no record of how I dealt with it.

† Though I'd forgotten that Chris Neame is English, I still hold to my position about American actors and eating. Note any American play, television series or serial, whatever. Perhaps they feel it adds a dash of realism, or perhaps the actors simply happen to be hungry when the scenes are being shot.

there he was, munching on this *enormous* American sandwich – all sandwiches in America are enormous; in Los Angeles they seem to be twice as enormous as the sandwiches in New York – saying his lines and getting out of his gown and putting books and papers down.

Joe was standing at the back of the theatre watching, but went off just before I had the coffee pot taken away, then the mugs taken away, and finally the sandwich taken away. When he came back, he was appalled to see that all the business had been surgically removed, saying, 'But we needed all that to energize the scene.' I said, in what I concede was a rather pompous manner, that if the scene didn't 'energize' itself through the characters and the events, then no amount of coffee-making, coffee-pouring and sandwich-munching would compensate. 'Yeah, yeah,' he said, he understood my point, but at the same time we didn't want this to be a play about people just sitting down and talking to each other, then standing up and talking to each other, then sitting down and talking to each other. I said, 'Joe, if the scenes don't carry because the conversation isn't interesting, then we should perhaps forget it.'* Because, I said, the drama of the play comes through people talking to each other. That's all they do. Talk. There's no getting away from it. He looked baffled, made one of his short, metaphysical speeches about the purpose of movement, the 'muscle' of energy, withdrew.

After rehearsals Kris Tabori, Joe Stern and I went to a bar. A chap with a moustache, in a peculiar white chamois top and chamois trousers, kept turning up to ask if we were being served with a drink, and when informed that we weren't, bustled off to arrange it, then returned to ask if we'd been served, bustled off to arrange it – it took about half an hour for the drinks to arrive, delivered by a very elegant young faggot with a plump moustache, a thick mane of hair and extravagantly good manners, who kept enjoining us to have a good evening,† enjoy our drinks now, you're very welcome, kind of stuff, that constituted a serious interruption to a story Tabori was trying to tell about an elderly West Coast

* i.e. 'Pull the plug out.'

† On my previous visit a young and attractive actress and I had been instructed by a waiter to 'have a good night'. Various retorts had sprung into my mind, but luckily not to my lips, as the response to them might well have been a fork through the throat delivered by the young lady or the waiter, or possibly both.

actor with whom we were all three acquainted, whose main assets on stage were a deep, trembling voice, a strangely trembling body – offstage he spoke and moved quite normally – and a racking cough, which he probably couldn't help, as he chain-smoked, but which he didn't try to suppress either.

According to Tabori this actor once appeared in a Shakespeare production – I forget of which play – directed by a young man, also from the West Coast, who refused to give him, or indeed any of the other actors, any notes whatsoever. Furthermore, the young director remained very guarded about what the set was going to look like, where the furniture (if any) was going to be placed, even where the exits and entrances were to be. At last, impatient with so much secrecy, the elderly actor demanded to be given a note, any note, on his work so far. The director led him off to a quiet corner of the rehearsal room, whispered to him briefly. The elderly actor looked at him, then repaired to the green room, where he was found stumping up and down in a fury, bellowing in his onstage trembling voice, '*Be more real*! He won't even let me know where the fucking doors are, but he tells me to *be more real*!' Now this story, interrupted as I say by the faggoty waiter who'd taken half an hour to get us our drinks and then kept molesting us with his sunny but imbecile courtesies, seems to me to bring into focus sinister elements both professional and social in Los Angeles life. But would it do any good if I went around shouting, '*Be more real*!' Would it, in the end, even get a cat up to my room?

## Tuesday, 7 January

Yes, well, I'm extremely cold actually. It's one in the morning and there is a curious icy mist around Los Angeles which makes me feel as cold as I would feel in London in January – having spent a very hot day indeed. Every time I went out of the theatre I felt heavy, almost inert with the heat. And then suddenly it goes from that to this.

Anyway, to report on my day. I didn't have to be in the theatre until eleven so I loitered about in my flat for a time, and then sat on the balcony, staring down at other geriatrics who were in short trousers or swimming suits, sitting around the pool, reading magazines. I thought of going down to join them but decided against it – I think mainly because I suddenly remembered the last time I'd sat by a swimming pool, just before Christmas when staying at the Tabori cottage. I'd have felt pretty good in my deckchair, a glass of champagne and my cigarettes to hand, if I hadn't been so aware of my stomach, pale, bloated and even slightly wrinkled. I'd thought: so here I am, undeniably middle-aged, sitting effetely by a swimming pool in Los Angeles like a gangster boss in a movie – all I need is a terminal visit from Clint Eastwood. So within minutes I was back in the cottage – dressed, still smoking and sipping at the champagne, but at least out of sight. But nobody this morning, around the Magic pool, seemed to be expecting a visit from Clint Eastwood. Most of them seemed quite pleased to be where they were, whatever the condition of their stomachs. One very old chap, wearing sort of Hawaiian shorts, and a blue peaked cap, was reading a book with Victorian – no, Edwardian, more like – binding. It had a kind of Rider Haggard look to it. Every so often he'd put the book down and smile. And why not, down there in the sun with his Rider Haggard, or whatever?

The thing I remember most vividly about the day's work is what happened to Ted Larkins. He made some real progress in the morning, suddenly seeming to flower into a richly comic, whirling motor of a Nick; but in the afternoon, at the run-through, went to pieces almost at once – as soon, in fact, as he saw the producer, Joe Stern, sitting in a seat in the middle of the stalls, staring intently at him. The theatre is so small and there was the director, Sam Weisman, sitting at the front; there I was, sitting at the back because I was smoking; and there, with his peculiar straw-coloured hair and Walter Matthau muzzly face, was the producer, Joe Stern, staring at him. So he completely disintegrated. It was most extraordinary. Everything that had been done during the morning, everything that had been both precise and emphatic, vanished and he became your chirpy little Cockney sparrow all over again. I yearned for the director to call an end to the proceedings and say: let's all go and have a drink and talk about something quite different.

Afterwards Sam Weisman made various observations, some to the point and some of them in his psychologizing American fashion about the nature of the characters, the nature of acting, where you have to be as an actor, reaching into yourself and finding yourself and then finding that the self you've found isn't the self you need because you've got to go on and make that self into the character self. So forth. Odd, because he also slipped in quite a lot of useful information about what the actors should understand this or that line to mean, how they should work towards this or that moment in a scene. But really, whether being useful or useless, he couldn't touch publicly on the main point, the dominating point, which was Ted Larkins's performance. (I wish to God Ted Larkins would shave before rehearsals, by the way. He always contrives to appear with a heavy shadow, which makes him look as if he's on the skids.) What he did say to Ted Larkins, not touching at all on his acting, either in general terms or in detail, was that perhaps he should wear some heavy boots to rehearsal, to root him in the part. Ted Larkins said he didn't have any heavy boots, only ordinary shoes or trainers. Well, Sam Weisman said, he was sure heavy boots would be a help. They stared at each other in intense vacancy for a moment, then Sam Weisman turned back to, or forward to, life-muscles, I suppose, while I continued to wonder why Sam Weisman thought a heavy-booted Ted Larkins would help Ted Larkins to create a fleet-footed (physically, as well as mentally) Nick. A heavy-booted *and* five-o'clock-shadowed Ted Larkins would place Nick among the down-and-outs on a Camden Town Tube platform, bumming pennies and cigarettes – anyway certainly not (as Nick ends up) in a television studio, running an intellectual chat show.

After rehearsals Ted Larkins drew me aside to say what I already knew – that the moment he'd seen the producer who'd wondered to his face whether he could *even* act sitting staring at him from the stalls, he'd lost every shred of the confidence he'd picked up during the morning. I tried to find some sympathetic words, while (I have to admit) feeling that if he went to pieces before the producer, how would he cope before an audience, then watched him go off, depressed, some way behind the other actors. I was about to leave myself when Joe stopped me, there, in the auditorium, saying he'd like a word, got a minute, Simon? I said yes, I supposed I had a minute, and down we sat, with Sam Weisman sitting to the side, like a referee, while Joe quizzed me on the text – the meaning of a line here, the value of a scene there. It went on, this interrogation, for two hours – *two hours* – in spite of my attempts to explain that I was still thinking about the text, didn't want to discuss it until I'd had the chance to consider each part in relation to the whole, some few run-throughs on from now. But Joe, who relishes discussion and debate, the offstage drama of the theatre, went on remorselessly, saying, 'Simon, one question. *One* question. Just one *question*,' actually raising a finger to indicate the figure 'one' for his one question. He must have raised about a hundred 'one' questions in the course of the two hours, his finger raised in front of his Walter Matthau face with its bushy straw hair on top. Up would go the finger, up would come the question until finally, exhausted and fairly angry, I said I'd had enough, see him tomorrow. During all this Sam Weisman was mostly mute, though I discovered that Kristoffer Tabori had somehow found his way back into the auditorium, and was listening in from a seat further along, to the side, in the shadows.

I got Tabori to drive me to a restaurant called Musso and Frank's, on Hollywood Boulevard and fairly close to the Magic. I sat at the counter and had a lobster salad, trying not to stare too hard at the guy next to me – he was about seventy, corpulent, with newspapers piled in front of him and meals seeming to come in at him from all quarters, beginning with a number of hors-d'oeuvres and followed by a large platter of swordfish, and then some other main dishes. There was something about his devotion to his food and his newspapers that I found, after the tumult and rigours of the Matrix, rather comforting. After dinner I slouched into the first available cinema and found myself watching a film called *The Jewel of the Nile*. I fell asleep a quarter of the way through, woke up just before about halfway through, to discover that nothing had improved on the screen, and left. Came home. Am about to go to bed. And that's really all I've got to say – oh, except that I don't think I'm going to make it to Dallas for the New Arts production of *Dog Days*. For one thing, I've become too involved in what's going on at the Matrix. For another, I'm already so tired that I don't believe I can even make it to New York for the casting. For a third, I don't really want to direct *Dog Days* anyway. It's such a boring and repellent little play that I'd rather not be associated with it.

## Thursday, 9 January

It's nine thirty in the morning, and I'm pacing about my living room in the Magic, trying to recall the events of the last two days. It's hard to concentrate, though, as it's very hot – the sun striking blindingly through the windows, and out on the balcony there's no breeze at all. One of my preoccupations – my many preoccupations – is with my clothes. For some peculiar reason I packed for New York, where I'm going to spend only four days (if I go there at all) and forgot to pack for Los Angeles, where I'm going to be for at least another month, or for Dallas which is also hot, where I'm going to be for at least two weeks. So here I am in the heat, with three pairs of unusable heavy trousers, and the pair of medium-weight cords that I arrived in and am still wearing. I'll have to go out and buy some light trousers later this morning. If I've got the energy.

But let me try and remember the events of the last two days. The reason I've missed out on the reports is that I've been too depressed by what has been going on, and failing to go on, in the rehearsal room that I couldn't bear the prospect of hearing myself recapitulate it. I have a suspicion, though, that the source of the problem has been myself, my impatience. I have twice been where this production has to get to, while the actors and the director are still groping to discover the proper direction, which – it's axiomatic – they must do to some extent on their own, otherwise it'll be a false journey to a false destination. Yes, I know all that. But sometimes the routes they're taking are so obviously wrong, so obviously leading nowhere, that I sit in a kind of seething frustration that leaks around the rehearsal room, making the actors jittery, and unsettling Sam Weisman, who therefore – anxious to maintain his own dominance – finds it difficult to refer to me. I still haven't made up my mind whether Sam Weisman is any good as a director, but I frequently wish he weren't, so that I could elbow him out of the way* and get on with the job myself – in which case I would, of course, uncover all the patience I lack now.

Anyway, there we are, or were, rather, the day before yesterday – my sitting in the back corner of the stalls, resenting every wrong move and stress of the actors, the actors aware of it. And resenting every wrong direction, and even sometimes half-right direction of the director, the director aware of it. And resenting myself for neither interfering vigorously, to a positive purpose, nor keeping still and affable, biding my time. As a consequence I left the Matrix at the end of a long day feeling foul, had myself dropped off at

* I seem, at this stage, not to have noticed that Sam Weisman had a couple of elbows in good working order of his own.

Musso and Frank's again for what I intended to be a consoling dinner. I can't remember whether I've described this restaurant properly yet, but it's large, two large rooms with upholstered leather seats in booths for four and six. The atmosphere is rather like that of an English club or a certain style of Republican (or so I imagine) New York restaurant. I'd got hold of a *Guardian* and a London *Times* from the news-stand opposite the restaurant, and was looking forward to settling into one of the booths to read them over half a bottle of wine and scallops – looking forward to absenting myself from the angers of the rehearsal, in fact. But I wasn't allowed to a booth – though most of them were empty – this grey-faced and rather sinister maître d' conducting me instead to one of the swivel stools at the counter, where the light is too dim to read comfortably by. It's very American, or so it seems to me, to refuse to allow you to sit where you want to sit because there's some code that has to be enforced, even when it's irrelevant. Anyway, the irritation of being compelled to swivel away at the counter lingered in spite of the perfectly decent mussels and wine, and was intensified on my leaving when I discovered that they'd locked the front door, which meant that I had to go out through the back, through the parking lot, and around to the street. I remember walking back, composing grave letters to Musso and Frank, both of whom I visualized as thickset, middle-aged Italians smoking cigars and wearing rings, with a pride in their jointly owned establishment and therefore worthy and sympathetic recipients of my communications. I reported my admiration for their food, for the ambience they'd created, etc., and then went on to say, regretfully but with subdued passion, that it was a pity therefore that in the end I'd found my evening not only uncomfortable, but positively uncivilized. And *furthermore* – ! It is extraordinary, this aspect of myself that is bad enough at home but becomes far worse when I'm abroad and on my own – presumably because I haven't a wife or friends to help turn it into comedy. So I seethed away, behaving within myself as if I'd been debagged by Musso and Frank, rather than merely inconvenienced by their minions in a very minor way.

Anyway, back to the Magic, where the foul state induced by my day at the Matrix and the foul state induced by my evening at Musso and Frank's blurred into a further, undefined foul state, the figures jumbled together, Musso, Frank, the actors, Sam Weisman, Joe Stern all seeming to be part of a lunatic world, vicious caricatures – I mean not only viciously caricatured but also caricatures in themselves vicious. I paced about smoking and drinking Scotch, thinking I ought to be recording the day's events, unable to do so.

The next day (yesterday) I woke feeling as if I'd been poisoned. Rehearsals didn't begin until four thirty, a lousy hour for me as I can never think energetically in the late afternoon. Also it meant we wouldn't finish, given the normal eight-hour stretch, until midnight. I spent the first part of the morning on the telephone to Beryl. I keep trying to cut down on these appallingly expensive calls, but on the other hand I think they're emotionally necessary – for her, I hope, as well as for me. Afterwards I went for a walk, steaming along Hollywood Boulevard in my medium cords and a heavy shirt, with the intention of buying some appropriate togs. I went into a likely looking shop where two moustachioed gays, bandido-moustachioed gays, one of them wearing a sombrero, refused to take their eyes off me for a second. I became extremely self-conscious, going about fingering material but really feeling as if I were, or anyway appeared to be, touching up the garments sexually. I turned and left abruptly, trouserless,* but did manage to find a shop that sold Silk Cut. I bought a carton, and was steaming my way irritably back towards the Magic – the street up to it was for once quite crowded – when a chap I've seen hanging about in the Matrix office, a kind of assistant to Joe Stern I think he is, passed me in a car, shouting out of the window as he did so that he'd be back in forty-five minutes. I thought, why should he be back in forty-five minutes? Back *where* in forty-five minutes? Did he mean back in my hotel in forty-five minutes? If so, why? I couldn't remember any arrangements to meet Chip Estees† anywhere, at any time – and then recalled that one of my campaigns here has been to get a video installed, so that I can watch films late at night, when I'm too tired to do anything, including watch films on a video. I further recalled that there'd been some talk of the video arriving after lunch (yesterday). So perhaps Chip was on his way to collect it, passing me on the street by coincidence at about two o'clock. This all turned out to be correct, except that Chip didn't come back

* Apart from the pair I had on, that is.

† Actually his name may have been Chuck Johnson, or Chip Johnson, or Chuck Estees. As I no longer have a copy of the Matrix programme I can't be sure which permutation is the correct one. I have settled for calling him Chip Estees.

in forty-five minutes, at a quarter to three, he came back at five to four, five minutes before I was due at rehearsals. I had to stand about smiling pleasantly, fulminating within, while he figured out how to install the video. He read the instructions aloud slowly and carefully, put plugs into sockets, extracted them, reversed them, so forth, until he finally declared that he'd done it, it should work now. I hadn't got a tape to test it with, so I have no idea, really, whether it will work or not. All I know is that it's sitting there bathed in sunlight, winking at me as its flashing clock tells off the minutes of my life.

Chip drove me to the theatre, which therefore meant that I had to make conversation with him. He's a nice man, very handsome, very polite, but a trifle literal in that American way, tending to unravel your little jokes and asides before your very eyes, so to speak, and to give you information that you've asked for only out of courtesy, without expectation of response. In other words, talking to him made my ill temper worse. And arriving late at the theatre, with the actors and the director hanging about waiting for me, made it worse still. I sat down where I'd been sitting the day before, a few seats away from Sam Weisman, who said, 'Oh, one thing. Could you do me a favour? Could you sit at the back so I don't get your cigarette smoke? My voice was really very bad last night.' I twitched immediately, then said that I would indeed sit at the back. I would INDEED sit at the back, I would INDEED. Actually I sat at the back of the back, nostrils flaring, eyes narrowed, psyche smouldering, and watched the scene.

Every word the director and the actors said struck me as being wrong. Quite simply wrong. I tried to remind myself of everything I'd said to myself yesterday and everything I'd said on the phone to Beryl about being patient and letting them explore the characters and find their own way, but finally found myself up on my feet and emphatically, not to say melodramatically, stubbing out my cigarette and slipping out. Not slipping out really, because I had to plod right past the director's table, and then go up the aisle and past the office. Joe was on the phone – he's always on the phone – looking extremely serious, so probably he was talking to his bookie.* I gestured that I'd like to speak to him when he was free. He followed

* Joe is an almost professional gambler. For years he supported his family – and presumably the Matrix – from what he won from bets on football and baseball matches, and in regular poker games.

me next door to the Café Melrose – which, by the way, is run by Japanesy looking people, who don't look thoroughly Japanese – where I put my problems to him.

I said that I thought my main difficulty was that I was not having what I was used to having with my directors, a discussion after the day's work over a drink. Sam Weisman has got a very young child, possibly even a baby, and a wife with a flourishing acting career, and therefore dashes off immediately after rehearsals, presumably to take domestic charge. Perhaps he even wants to see his baby. Or his wife. Or both. While I understand his situation, or think I do, I said to Joe, it does mean that he and I never meet in the valuable – because relaxed – period after rehearsals, to exchange notes (I meant, of course, for Sam to get *my* notes), which is why, I explained, I find myself intervening so often during the rehearsals themselves. As I think I've said before, every time I talk to Joe on the phone, especially long distance, I suspect him of bluffing and even of lying, but the moment I'm with him in the flesh I'm convinced that he's a decent and honourable man whose company, furthermore, I find myself enjoying. So we talked very amicably, he saying that he'd got wind of the fact that I was manifesting my impatience because one of the actors, Chris Neame – it would be Chris Neame, somehow, English and late of the Royal Shakespeare Company – had said that when I sat in the front row, next to the director, he found my face too present, my personality too overpowering, my feet too large, my cigarette smoke too effusive – in short, I put him off his stroke and stride. I had to concede to Joe that there was a certain wheedling and pathetic justice in what Neame had said – otherwise I myself wouldn't have felt so strongly that I'd been having a negative effect. We talked it out, Joe agreeing that the solution was for him to ask Sam Weisman to organize either the rehearsals or his domestic life in such a way that we always spent time by ourselves at the end of the day.*

I went back with Joe to the theatre. He side-stepped into his office and the telephone, I went on into the auditorium – it was now about six in the evening, I suppose – and I suddenly found it quite easy to intervene. The rehearsal took off, Sam Weisman and I developing for the first time a true spirit of collaboration, talking

* We never did – at least not until we were in previews. But I don't know, as I never asked, whether this was because Joe didn't pass on the message, or did and Sam Weisman refused.

across the stalls but quite openly and effortlessly about each problem as we saw it arise. How this happened I don't really know, although I assume a good part of it had to do with Joe – he'd found some way of releasing me from my tensions, perhaps, and had sent me back less fraught, and therefore less destructive. Anyway, the rehearsal positively flowed along, I becoming for the first time spontaneous instead of deliberate and measured, Sam Weisman receptive, quick to pick up my points and anxious to share the development of his own. I came back to the Magic feeling quite cheerful, indeed rather self-approving at the way in which I'd managed to deal with my irascibility and impatience, though inwardly acknowledging that it was really the conversation with Joe that had turned me around. I slept well, had a good breakfast, and here I am now, on my balcony in the sun, finishing off this account before setting forth to buy myself a corkscrew and a bottle of champagne – I wouldn't mind a glass or two of champagne before I go into rehearsals, which begin at midday. This evening Mr and Mrs Sam Weisman are taking me out to a show, I don't remember which one. Tomorrow I'm going to dinner with Roddy McDowall, an English actor long domiciled in Hollywood, who began his career as a child star, and is more recently famous for his remarkable impersonation, when incarcerated in an ape's body and head, of an educated ape.* I met him some years back, just after he'd played the lead in *Otherwise Engaged* in Florida. I've very much liked him on the few occasions we've met, so for once I feel OK. Perhaps Hollywood will come to suit me, even if I don't come to suit Hollywood.

## Friday, 10 January

This morning I decided to try out my video machine. I have been feeling uneasy about it as Chip Estees seemed to me to sink the plugs into the sockets in a rather arbitrary fashion. I went down to a shop called 'The Wherehouse' – a very hot walk in this hot weather – to hire some tapes. The Wherehouse, which had been recommended to me after a lot of thought by the sunny at the desk, turned out to be an amazing building, dwarfing a shopping arcade that looked as if it had been built as an afterthought to the car-park

* In *Planet of the Apes* and various sequels.

opposite. The ground floor was devoted to 'hardware' and tapes for sale, the upstairs floor to an enormous video library. This library was without air-conditioning and therefore very hot. I sweated copiously in my thickish trousers as I went about trying to make my selection – I was after decent thrillers. Even indecent thrillers. The heat, and a large, centrally placed television screen, from which came loud and random excerpts from pop videos or violent films, induced a headache that made my progress both lethargic and unpleasant, but I finally got together three films that looked promising from their covers – men with guns, girls screaming, that sort of thing – and took them to the counter where I had to go through a wearisome American business – numerous dockets and receipts produced and signed, my American Express card checked out.

When she appeared to have finished ('she' being a medium-sized black girl with acne – I noticed the acne as our relationship quickly developed into one of implacable hostility – she also had a rather shapeless body) she said, 'Now could I have some identification please, sir?' I said, 'What sort of identification?' She said, 'Yer driver's licence, please, sir,' I explained that as I didn't drive I didn't have a licence. You could have cut her incredulity with a – I don't know what you could have cut it with, but it hung there thickly between us, her incredulity, and not just her incredulity, her suspicion. Suspicious incredulity, presumably from encountering for the first time in her life a middle-aged man whose toes weren't actually sticking out of his shoes who claimed he couldn't drive. I suppose she worked out that I'd been banned for drunken driving or whatever, and was trying to save face. Anyway she said, well, she was very sorry – 'Very sorry, sir, but you may not have the tapes without identification.' I said but surely my credit cards were identification enough. So it went. I got hotter and hotter – suppurating with heat – and angrier and angrier, but still managed to *explain* to her in what I thought was a reasonably poised manner why her request was preposterous, as I could apparently *buy* the tapes on a credit card without showing identification, just as I could buy meals in restaurants without showing identification, etc. She kept saying, 'It's to protect you, sir, it's to protect you.' I kept insisting that I was prepared to be unprotected in this matter.

Eventually she called over some young jerk with a sort of seventeen-year-old moustache wisping across his upper lip, who said that it was a house rule and then called over somebody else who then, unbelievably, went and got somebody else. So I actually ended up with five, I think it was, people from the Wherehouse, all of them explaining to me that (a) it was against company policy to accept credit cards for television rentals without identification, and (b) that they themselves didn't actually understand why this policy existed. Occasionally the girl, the acned black girl with whom I'd begun the negotiation, would interject that I didn't drive. 'You see, he doesn't *drive*.' I could see *their* suspicion growing. In the end I felt rather as if I were surrounded by policemen, who at any moment were going to handcuff me and drag me down to the station for attempting the use of a credit card without being able to drive. I began in fact to find something very suspicious myself in my not being able to drive. In the end I went out shouting what I hoped was dignified English abuse, without fully raising my voice, and at least avoided having my shoulder bag searched by the heavily armed guard at the door.

On the pavement I spotted a grimy-looking liquor store further up the arcade, slogged my way towards it, bought some bottles of white wine and champagne – enough of each to fill four carrier bags and strain my arms – then slogged up the hill in the heat, averting my face from the heavy traffic fumes. As I neared the Magic – a mere hundred or so yards from it, in fact – I had the consolation of trudging damply past a liquor store which advertised a delivery service, thus rendering every aspect of my little shopping expedition gratifyingly pointless.

I'm glad to report that from there everything got worse. It was a truly dreadful day in the theatre. No doubt some good work was done here and there, but everything was coloured, and in a sense nullified, by Ted Larkins's rapid decline as Nick. He went from merely going to pieces – which he'd managed when trying to perform in front of Joe – to a self-sacrificial passivity. His voice had also developed a rhythm, a feeble rhythm but a rhythm nevertheless, in time to which I could have nodded my head. I suppose he'd surrendered, demoralized by his previous débâcle, and was now dutifully offering himself up to the axe – I don't know. All I know is that he can't possibly have believed that what he was doing bore any relation to the dynamically mischievous Nick that the scenes needed and that he'd once or twice come close to giving us. Sam Weisman seemed incapable of effecting any change, speaking an occasional jerky sentence that for once, mercifully I suppose, didn't carry him on into a muscle-monologue. He just ran through the scenes again and again, almost as if hypnotized by his own helplessness, or by the limping rhythms of Ted Larkins's delivery, perhaps.

In the end, in despair, I left the auditorium, went out on to the pavement, where I saw Joe standing a few yards away, almost on the corner.* He asked me how it was going. I said, 'Dreadful.' He said, 'What's the problem, Larkins?' And I said, 'Yes, problem.' He sort of raised his eyebrows. I raised my eyebrows back, then heard myself saying, 'Any chance we can replace him?' I don't believe I've ever said those words before in all my time in the theatre, though of course I've heard others say them, once or twice. 'Yes, but who with?' Joe replied, 'That's the problem.' I found myself – speaking and thinking at the same moment – saying, 'Nathan Lane, the guy who played Nick at the Long Wharf. He was brilliant. Wonderful actor.' I went on to explain that I knew Nathan was free because Caroline Lagerfelt,† just back from New York, had phoned yesterday to say hello, pass on greetings from mutual friends, among them Nathan Lane, whose Broadway show, a musical version of *The Wind in the Willows* (Nathan playing Mr Toad) had closed after three days. Why don't you think of Nathan for *Dog Days* in Dallas, Caroline had said *en passant* – a suggestion I'd found intriguing, because although Nathan is not exactly right for *Dog Days*, his talent makes him right for almost any part, including the ones he's not exactly right for. I'd decided to pass his name on to Stephen Hollis, and see him when and if I went to New York – all this to explain why his name was already in my mind, and sprang so quickly from my lips, there out on the pavement with Joe. Joe said, 'Well, would he come out?' I said I thought so – Caroline

* It didn't occur to me at the time to wonder what he was doing there, but I do remember that he was neither coming nor going, just standing. I now find something odd in the image of Joe, who doesn't smoke and is always so active, just standing on the corner of the street.

† I first met Caroline Lagerfelt when she was cast as the wife in *Otherwise Engaged*, on Broadway. Since then we've done five plays together. Though her first language is Swedish, she speaks both American and English (she went to school in England) with outrageous ease and naturalness. In fact she's a kind of linguistic schizophrenic, able to switch from soft southern counties English to savage New York in the course of a sentence. She lives in New York, but pops over to Los Angeles from time to time to work in television.

had mentioned that if nothing interesting were offered to him soon, he was going to come to Los Angeles and check out television possibilities. Anyway, I said, 'We can always ask him. I know he loves the part.' Then I also remembered that Nathan and Ted Larkins were friends. Almost the first thing Ted Larkins had said when I'd met him on my return to the Matrix was that Nathan sent his love. I found this rather disconcerting – after all it's likely to make for less awful feelings all round if the chap one is replacing is unknown to the chap one is replacing him with. Nevertheless, I said I'd ask Nathan in confidence whether he would be interested in coming to the Matrix, where we could offer him the chance of working hard in an uncongenial atmosphere for no reward. Unless you count doing a disservice to a friend as a reward.

The conversation with Joe depressed me, not only because of and on behalf of Larkins, but also because of the hardness that had surfaced in me so unexpectedly, in such a matter-of-fact fashion. I wished – still wish – that the idea of replacing Ted Larkins hadn't come from me. I wished – still wish – that the idea of replacing him with Nathan Lane hadn't come from me. I suppose I'm glad that both ideas came from somewhere, but behind the obvious moral embarrassment lurks a sense that we haven't done as well by Ted Larkins as we ought to have done, that we've given up on him too easily, or have allowed him to give up on himself too easily. Not, of course, that it's too late. Nathan hasn't yet been signed, Ted Larkins hasn't yet been, in the great American theatre euphemism, 'let go'.* Perhaps the situation can still be redeemed. No, it can't.

It was in this state of mind that I went off after rehearsals with Mr and Mrs Weisman to a show whose name I've already forgotten, which turned out to be playing at a theatre miles away from the Matrix. The journey was interminable, and the destination, when we at last got there, massively unprepossessing, the theatre being in a complex that contained the kind of car-park that people in films drive at each other in, guns blazing. We sat at a counter in one of the restaurants, had some fish snacks and guessed, in a desultory way, at the ages of various long-serving film stars,

* I've heard of an English actress, a jolly and uncomplicated girl, who was cast in a Broadway production. When told by the director and producer, in the middle of a rehearsal, that they were going to 'let her go' she assumed they meant allow her to slip off for a cup of tea. She thanked them both accordingly, thus notching up another one for the myth of the stiff upper lip.

then went into the show, which was really a kind of *Oklahoma* without the music. People stood about in *Oklahoma*-like togs on a set that consisted of an *Oklahoma*-like log cabin in an *Oklahoma*-like field. The play was co-authored by an elderly and distinguished actor who'd obviously taken on the job with the sole purpose of providing acting work for himself and his equally distinguished actress wife. His own character is meant to be a kind of ghost visible only to his wife (onstage *and* offstage), a conceit taken from *Harvey*, itself a pretty elderly, not to say decrepit play featuring an alcoholic who conjures up a rabbit as his boon companion, a part played by James Stewart in the film. The part, that is, of the alcoholic, not of the rabbit. Anyway, in the *Oklahoma*-without-music play this old ghost is still pottering about the old homestead, even more infuriating than he'd been in life because after all he was meant to be dead, which in a decent society should have meant the end of him. There was one particularly revolting scene in which he and his wife re-enacted the birth of their son, thus giving us the spectacle of the elderly leading lady groaning away on a table, in heavy labour, being tended to by her elderly but dead double-husband who was shouting the baby out as if he were a coach on a football field. Throughout the play the old ghost stood in strange, insignificant* postures or ran nimbly about, with special little skips for ascending to or descending from the porch. Of course what he was really pantomiming was, 'Aren't I in good shape for a guy of seventy-five? Especially for a *dead* guy of seventy-five?' The audience – the theatre is enormous, seating about 3000, if I heard correctly, *and* it was sold out – loved it. There were ripples of warm laughter and sighs of affection at every single cuteness. Fortunately I managed to train such visible malevolence on to the stage that at the interval Sam Weisman suggested we leave. I got myself dropped off in Hollywood Boulevard, saying I'd walk from there, not to worry, thank you for a wonderful evening – no, I couldn't have said that, could I, as we'd left at the interval – then hurried myself to Musso and Frank's, sat on a swivel seat at the counter and ordered myself up a batch of Chivas Regals,† then escorted myself home, in a rather dozy state, watched a bit of television, hit the sack.

* I think this must be a mistranscription for 'and significant'. Pity. For interesting echo, see *The Common Pursuit*, Act One, Scene One, Nick reading from a letter 'delicate, insensitive poetry – oh, delicate *and* sensitive poetry. Pity.'

† A very expensive Scotch whisky that I had to make do with at Musso and Frank's, as they don't stock malt whisky there.

## Saturday, 11 January

In the morning I dragged myself out of bed with something like a headache. Not a drink headache, but the kind of headache you get at the prospect of the day ahead. I had an ill-judged breakfast and then phoned Nathan Lane. To my horror I got him straight away. I told him, in the solemn tones one assumes for this sort of occasion, that our conversation had to be both confidential and inconclusive. We *were* having trouble, I went on, with the part of Nick. In fact, we were beginning to think we might have to find an alternative, what did he feel about this? He said, 'Great, I'd love to do it.' Just like that. Almost before I'd finished. 'Great, I'd love to do it. What seems to be the trouble with Ted?' I gave a judiciously edited account, then asked him whether their friendship would be a complication. He said, 'Oh well, that'll just have to be something, I don't know, to sort out. That's the way things go. A bit of a problem.' But he made it quite clear that it wasn't a problem that would in any way affect his coming out and playing the part. We left it that all future negotiations would be between himself and Joe Stern. I hung up feeling immensely relieved and slightly sullied. Immensely sullied. But there we were. I then cabbed into the Matrix and reported the conversation to Joe, who managed to look astonished, delighted and distressed all at once. We went in together to watch the rehearsal, standing at the back, in the shadows, like a couple of assassins, all our concentration on Ted Larkins. He was worse than the last time I'd seen him, as if he'd given up even on the ghost of Nick – all he could do was say the words, make the moves.

During a break Joe and I passed the news about Nathan Lane on to Sam Weisman. He received it with the same astonishment, though with more delight and less distress than Joe, but a few minutes later we were into one of those conversations common (I imagine) to most inexperienced conspirators – you know, worrying about how Chris Neame (our Peter), who is a great friend of Ted Larkins, will take it; and how John Delancey, a man of evident decency and clear moral views, will take it; and of course how Ted Larkins himself will take it – so forth, on and on, until we backed into a compromise, deciding that we must make one further attempt with Larkins in case he'd simply fixed on some misconception about the part, that a few key words might clear up. This will cost us a few more days, but will make us all feel we're behaving properly.

We resumed the rehearsal, but before it was properly under way the caretaker of the Matrix, who is about twenty-three years old and has a funny little fuzz on his chin, burst in to announce that Sam Weisman's car had been broken into by a large black guy, he guessed, he'd seen running down the alley at the back of the theatre. We went out and surveyed the car.

The front window had been smashed in and the radio three-quarters pulled out, wires trailing everywhere, a real mess. According to the fuzzy-bearded young caretaker, the black guy hadn't been carrying any tools, and as there weren't any rocks around, he must have done all the damage with his bare hands – an extraordinary feat, really. We stood looking at the wreckage for a few minutes, then Kris Tabori set off in his car and Sam Weisman went running off, both looking for the black guy, and I have to note now – something to do with the inhuman, increasingly inhuman, side of my nature – that I was frightened that they'd find him. Frankly I didn't think they'd have much chance with someone as big and powerful as this guy must be – in fact they might get badly hurt or killed even – and where would that leave my play? I didn't want them killed anyway, but I have to admit that the future of the play was really my first thought. Furthermore, I realize now that I showed not even a courteous interest in the condition of Weisman's car. Being a non-driver, I have no interest in cars, people's relationship to them, even when I'm being driven about in them. I must remember to express sorrow and concern tomorrow.

Both Tabori and Weisman returned intact. Weisman – having to go down to the police station to file a report – called off rehearsals for the day. John Delancey drove me back to the Magic, offering to come up and have a go at fixing my video. It took him a long time – about twenty-five minutes – as most of the plugs were in the wrong socket, while one of the pins in one of the plugs was bent. He had to cut the pin off and insert the naked wires into the set. It's probaby been made quite lethal, but I admired the calm dexterity and logic with which he first detected the problem and then solved it. If it is solved. I haven't had a chance to test it. By the time he'd finished I was late for the Roddy McDowall dinner, to which Delancey offered to drive me. I had virtually no clothes, even though I'd got Delancey to stop off at the laundry where I'd left some (so, come to think of it, Delancey functioned first as my valet, and then as my electrician, and then as my chauffeur). But the point is that even with my laundry back, I still hadn't anything reasonable to change into. In fact all I'd got were the threadbare black cords I was in – still am in – a pair of soft brown run-down shoes, and only one light shirt, which I was also in (though I've changed it today). Suspecting that Roddy McDowall's was going to be a smartish affair, I had to phone up in front of Delancey and tell Roddy McDowall I was coming straight from the theatre, wouldn't have time to change out of working gear, hoped this was OK, etc. Delancey listened to these lies and apologies with a sympathetic smile.

Naturally, Roddy McDowall lives miles away. Everybody in Los Angeles lives miles away, not from anywhere, because there isn't actually an anywhere to live miles away from, but from each other. It was therefore a long drive through increasingly lush suburbia – like Surrey on the rampage, both in foliage and in architecture – through gates,* down a short wide drive to a flunkey or two waiting to park cars, and then into the house to be served a (thank God!) enormous drink by another flunkey, with Roddy McDowall and a group of prosperous-looking guests gathered around a fire. Recognizably present were Coral Browne, Vincent Price, and above all the actress Lee Remick, one of my all-time favourite ladies – on the screen, that is, I'd never met her in the flesh before. She's got these adorable teeth. The thing about them is that they just slightly protrude over her underlip when she smiles, and the effect, on me anyway, is simply annihilating. I go straight to pieces. Whenever I see that smile on the screen I go to pieces, and there she was in the flesh, looking pretty good and smiling that smile on the other side of the room.

I hustled myself shyly over to her and said what a great fan of hers I was, especially in that film – I couldn't remember a single film she'd been in. Not a single film. I stared at her blankly, then managed to dredge one up. 'You know,' I said, 'you know, with Gregory Peck. And Robert Mitchum violated you.' She said that she'd never been in a film in which Robert Mitchum violated her.

* Now I think about it, I'm not sure that there were gates. I might have been confusing my arrival with an arrival once made by Dana Andrews in a movie that I saw when I was ten or eleven years old, the title of which I have forgotten. I've also forgotten the story, and the names of the other actors.

She wished she had. And smiled her smile.* I blundered on to the effect that the film was made so long ago I couldn't remember it properly, thus indicating that not only could I not remember her through the years, but that there had been so many, many years, how could I hope to? – also giving the impression, I think, that I'd been in short trousers while she'd been playing grown-up parts. A pity, as I really would like to have expressed my – my – anyway, she was rescued by Roddy McDowall, a perfect host in every respect, who bore me away to meet a lady whose name rang a bell. An extremely engaging lady, with a Welsh accent and a very Welsh kind of charm. So I talked a bit about my own Welshness, fishing for her identity, and finally proposed indirectly that she might be an actress. She said no, she wasn't but her daughter, Kate Burton, was.

Dinner itself was fine. I made amends with Lee Remick, who sat next to me, not by suddenly remembering her films, but by recalling that I'd read somewhere that she'd lived for a long time in London, which gave us a subject to talk about. Then I had a gossip with Coral Browne, that I would have enjoyed even more if I hadn't been conscious of myself chain-smoking away in frayed togs, down-at-heel shoes, rather like the Boudu tramp in the Renoir film, only without his insouciance. At least I didn't belch.

After dinner we sat by the fire, drinking. I talked mainly to Vincent Price, avoiding a number of other people I sort of sensed were famous but didn't recognize. It was a really nice conversation – Vincent Price telling me about his early days as an actor/art historian – and I was just beginning to relax, looking forward to my next drink, when people around me began to go. This, as I think I've already noted, is the Los Angeles style. People go early, from anywhere. Perhaps they wake up early. Perhaps they're about their day before dawn. Or perhaps there's simply something in the air that makes them semi-comatose after twilight, I don't know. There was a protracted discussion among the other remnants as to who was to drive me home. I was chagrined to note that there wasn't too much competition for this job, though I was pleased when Vincent Price and Coral Browne finally elected themselves. Off I went in a capacious car, Price driving with gentlemanly dexterity, Coral Browne beside him, I lolling in the back at ease, and feeling rather lively. When I got back here, to the Magic, I watched a bit of *The*

* I've since remembered that it was Anne Francis that was violated by Robert Mitchum. The film was called *Cape Fear* – a humdinger.

*Godfather* (on a tape lent to me by Joe Stern) on the video, which means that John Delancey's labour wasn't in vain, opened a bottle of champagne – I'd shared the last drop of my whisky with John Delancey – and after getting up to the scene where Sterling Hayden is shot through the forehead by Robert de Niro* in the Italian restaurant, turned off the video, and dictated this. Am now going to bed.

## Sunday, 12 January

Woke up feeling like absolute hell, made myself a rather disturbing breakfast of bacon, peppery sausages, toast and instant coffee, and decided over it that if only I could get the right pair of trousers, all my main problems would be resolved. But how in Los Angeles without a car *and* on a Sunday did one come by the right pair of trousers? I put this question to Caroline Lagerfelt when she phoned to inquire after my health, the state of rehearsals, etc. She said there was a famous mall – 'mull' they pronounce it here – which is open every minute of every day of the year, where I'd be able to find trousers galore. I accepted her offer to drive me to it. Just before she arrived Lucy phoned to announce her return from Switzerland – we'd given her a week's holiday there as a Christmas present. She'd had a wonderful time, she said, why didn't I take up ski-ing? I explained about the dangerous complications that could arise from broken limbs at my sort of age. She said that I wasn't *that* old. I said that one was as old as one felt, and I felt old, at least when it came to ski-ing. It was very sort of loving to hear her voice, especially as I'd been worrying about her a bit – Beryl had phoned yesterday (Saturday) to point out that she'd been expected back on Friday, and still hadn't returned. Then Caroline, and off in her car, in the heat, to the 'mull'. (I'm dictating this on my porch, looking across to one of the other porches where I can see an extremely delightful-looking dog, staring through the plate-glass window at his departing owners, who are obviously off for the evening. The dog, with a look of dignified desolation, is now getting up and is walking out of sight. Perhaps to pee in their bed. Reproach or piss – what dogs like to do when you leave them alone when they don't want to be left alone, which is most of the time.)

* Or was it Al Pacino?

It was hopeless, of course. Quite hopeless. I either stood about in trousers that came down over my feet at one end, and almost up to my armpits at the other, or in trousers so short and tight that I felt the slightest move would result in popping buttons, a gaping fly. I also suspected that word was getting around the 'mull', and that people were coming from its distant parts to look at me. I gave up, thoroughly demoralized – how can it be that for all my credit cards, and with an absolutely routinely proportioned body (given my age) I couldn't find one, not even one, pair of suitable trousers. I took Caroline through this again and again (though in no way blaming her, let it be said) as she drove me to the Matrix, where I was blocked in the lobby by Sam Weisman. He wanted a little time alone, he said, with Kris Tabori and Judy Geeson. Did I know what he meant? I didn't, but said, 'You're very welcome,' and felt it, really felt it, because what I wanted to do was to have a quiet sandwich and a glass of wine and not think about anything for a bit.

I went next door to the Café Melrose with a two-day-old copy of the London *Times* which I'd picked up on the way in, and devoured the wonderful drama of Heseltine's resignation. Then I sat back and encouraged myself to grow resentful at Sam Weisman's wanting to work alone with the two actors. What was it he didn't want me to see? Or was it Judy Geeson who didn't want me to be there? It had seemed to me that both she and her husband had been slightly alarmed when they saw me arrive. They'd obviously assumed, I thought in retrospect as I sat over my white wine and some peculiar confection of crab and poached eggs (which turned out to be mainly poached eggs), that I wasn't going to turn up this morning – had they already arranged with Sam to keep me away? I went through my usual procedure, smoking numerous cigarettes, drinking numerous glasses of wine and cups of coffee, finally and seethingly deciding that the culprit was Judy Geeson – no doubt because she wanted to be free to 'explore' and 'examine' and all that sort of stuff without the pressure of the author's presence, etc., and so forth. I rose abruptly, hurried next door, and bumped straight into Judy Geeson in the lobby, who said, 'It's a pity you weren't in rehearsal because Kris and I have the feeling that actually Sam is working a bit against the text.'

The rehearsal for the rest of the day was unspeakable. A clear case of an actor drowning before one's eyes. Poor Ted Larkins.

Every time he began to do a scene he would stop, almost at once, and involve Weisman in some irrelevant question – as, for example, when do I see this letter, when shall I move to this chair, what do I do when I get to the chair, what do I do when I sit down, which letter do I pick up – anything that would delay having to give us a performance. And Weisman, instead of being solicitous and helpful, manifested impatience – irascible impatience – almost constantly. Larkins would speak two lines and ask a question which would result in an interminable but ill-natured discussion. Then another two lines, another question, another interminable, ill-natured discussion. The atmosphere was absolutely ghastly.

At long last Weisman gave up on Larkins and ran the whole of the first scene, which gave me a chance to see what he'd been up to with Judy Geeson and Kris Tabori. It was really quite interesting – if one's interested in such technicalities – because the scene, as I wrote it, is constructed so that things happen in stages. First we have a look between Stuart and Marigold; then we have a bit of charged conversation; then we have proximity; and then a kiss, the kind of kiss that leads to bed. Now Sam Weisman has always been keen to *start* the scene with a kiss. So what he'd imposed on it while they'd been working without me is a kiss at the beginning, then another kiss, then some businesss with coffee, then a further kiss, then the conversation, then a further kiss, followed by bed. In other words, a muddle, because the scene begins where in a sense it should end and simply goes on repeating itself with interruptions for coffee and talk. I shall have to do something about it.

The rest of the run had some good things in it: a very nicely developing Martin (Wayne Alexander) and nicely developing Humphry (John Delancey). But of course the scenes with Nick – Ted Larkins – were dire. It was sad, and rather horrifying really, to have to sit through them. In fact I didn't, slipping instead up to the Mexican bar, where I had a few drinks, then got a cab to Musso and Frank's. I was just settling down to nothing in particular – a kind of self-absence – when I suddenly remembered that I didn't know what the call was for tomorrow. I phoned Sam Weisman who told me that it was for seven o'clock in the evening,* then went on to say that he and Joe Stern had had a dreadful conversation with

* The arbitrary-seeming times at which rehearsals began – anything between ten in the morning and seven or eight in the evening – is explained by the fact that the director and some of the actors were also pursuing successful careers in television.

Larkins. Larkins had kept on probing about his part, what it was he still needed to find, and they'd been unable to help him, Sam said, because they knew he was beyond help, though he had the feeling that Larkins's next move would be to phone me. Well, here I am, just back from dinner to discover a message from Larkins asking me to phone him back – he'll be up until half-past midnight. I can phone him any time until then to have a chat. It's only ten thirty but I can't face phoning him.

## Monday, 13 January

When I woke up this morning, I brushed my teeth, had a shower, breakfasted on coffee and bacon, hung about for a bit, then finally forced myself into phoning Ted Larkins. I said enthusiastically that I'd got his message, did he want to talk to me? And he said, yes, that was why he'd phoned, because he wanted to talk to me. Why else would he phone? And could he come round? I said, 'The thing is, Ted, I'm not really quite up yet, the day hasn't taken full possession of me, can I phone you back after I've had a bit of coffee and brushed my teeth, etc.?' He said that was fine by him – he was very nice, very calm. I hung up and did in fact brush my teeth again and made some more coffee. Then I phoned Beryl, discharging all my panic and resentment at the prospect of having to do to Larkins what, clearly, the producer and the director were unable to face doing. As soon as I'd hung up I phoned Larkins and said, 'Come on, why don't you come on round at ten thirty?' I sat on the sofa, wondering what I should say to him, then suddenly realized that I'd forgotten to shave. It was while I was shaving that the line I ought to take became clear to me. I waited for him until just after ten thirty, then went down to the lobby and there he was, coming up the steps. We walked past the pool, talking about the Astroturf which was causing sparks to fly up from our shoes, and about how dangerous life is in Los Angeles even when passing alongside a pool in the sunshine, and on up into my room. I offered him some champagne which he refused, saying – it made my heart sink – that he had to do some work 'on a certain play'. I poured myself a glass of champagne and said, rather abruptly, 'Shall I speak?' He said, yes, he would like me to speak. So I spoke.

What I said was that it seemed to me that I could talk for ever about how he should play Nick, but it was all irrelevant because 'what we have here is a basic situation and another situation arising out of a situation'. In other words there were two situations. From then on I managed to become slightly more lucid. He was miscast, I said, seriously miscast, because Nick was an expansive, bizarre, outgoing figure and he, Ted, was by nature rather inhibited, shy – introverted in a word. In trying to think of what it was in Nathan Lane's performance that was so different from Ted Larkins's I'd come to the conclusion that Nathan had only to move an inch forward to be Nick, whereas Ted had to make a jump of miles, forward and to the side, to be Nick. I made a point of stressing that it wasn't Ted Larkins as an *actor* that was the problem, but Ted Larkins in a part in which he had been inappropriately cast. Furthermore, I said, it was clear that he was not getting on with the director. There was so much tension between him and Weisman that every time he tried to perform he went into a state of shock, which led him in rehearsals, as for example, yesterday's, to keep stalling by asking utterly irrelevant questions. I'd like to think that I was both gentle and brutal. *Simultaneously* brutal and gentle.

After a pause he said he would like a glass of champagne after all, he rather needed one. I poured him a glass and handed it to him. There was another pause before he said, yes, this was exactly what he'd wanted to hear, he agreed with all of it. He was miscast as Nick as he was really a shy, diffident, out-of-the-corner-of-his-mouth actor, that was his nature, he couldn't help it, how therefore could he be an ebullient, forward-thrusting Nick, especially with a director who kept shouting at him that he needed basic acting lessons? I agreed that he couldn't, and then virtually repeated what I'd said – one tends to go on saying the same things in these situations because (a) one can't think of anything else to say, and (b) there isn't anything else to say. He downed another glass or two of champagne, we parted on the best of terms, it being understood between us that he was going to withdraw from the production.

I phoned Joe Stern and told him that he was now free to contact Nathan, then went on to Musso and Frank's for some lunch. Came back and hung about on the porch of my apartment with the sun beating down, gazing at the people lying around the small pool below, among them a man I took to be English, handsome and middle-aged, who was pulling on a very fat cigar and reading a book – I above him in my thick clothes, sweating and guilty.

I went in for the seven o'clock run-through. A pointless exercise as without one of the characters it was inevitably lop-sided and uninformative. There was of course a rather odd atmosphere, over-relaxed, and at times almost hysterical – survivors celebrating, I suppose. They might also have been celebrating the fact that Sam Weisman is going to be away for the next four days, directing a television show to which he committed himself months ago, and they therefore thought that they were getting that time off. Not so, as I've arranged with Joe and Sam to work with the actors on the text, long stretches of which are still bothering me. I'll also take the opportunity to rearrange the blocking, and have a proper look at Judy Geeson and Kristoffer Ṭabori in the first scene. Though I believe I forgot, so to speak, to mention that to Sam Weisman.

## Tuesday, 14 January

When we began work on Act One, Scene Two, Joe plonked himself down right beside me in the front row of the auditorium. I said, 'You're not going to sit there, are you?' He said, 'Yes.' I said, 'Well, I'd rather you didn't, if you don't mind.' He got up and went out – without a flounce. He's not the flouncing kind – but nevertheless making it dramatically clear that he'd taken offence. When I got back to the Magic I phoned him to apologize. Instead of acknowledging what I said, he went off at tangents of rage, not confronting the issue directly until the very end, when he suddenly said, 'OK, you're being aggressive now, I'll accept that. But when we get into previews *I'll* be aggressive. I get very aggressive in previews. And you'll have to accept *that*.' I said I would, but hung up feeling offended in my turn. Went to bed, still imaginatively on the line to Joe. Probably better that he didn't hear what I had to say.

I walked up to Musso and Frank's thinking about the flabby writing in the scene between Martin and Stuart in the first act. After the meal – I remember absolutely nothing about it – I went for a walk in the vicinity of the restaurant, a sleazy section of Hollywood Boulevard, where I suddenly encountered a chap I've become familiar with since my arrival, carrot-haired and wheeling about on skates. From the back he looks about twelve or thirteen, at a distance from the front you realize he must be older, at least sixteen, but when you see his face close to, you discover that in spite of his carroty hair and boyish body, he's actually about fifty.

Tonight he came zooming towards me, then skidded around on his skates and zipped away, whipping around other pedestrians who paid him no attention. I paid him very little attention myself, having become used to androgynous or over-muscled creatures on roller-skates zooming, zipping and wheeling up and down the pavements just as I've become used to people lying about in the gutters of this part of Hollywood, lifting their hands for compensation for the blight I haven't personally inflicted on them. I went on walking, turning eventually back towards the Magic Hotel, keeping my mind fixed on the screne between Stuart and Martin in Act One, Scene Two.

## Wednesday, 15 January

While Wayne Alexander and Kristoffer Tabori were collating the new script, Joe Stern, Chip Estees – who was fussing about with the theatre computer writing a play or a film script, I couldn't make out which – and I traded Irish, Polish and Jewish jokes. We kept each other amused (for about three hours, in fact) until Tabori and Alexander came into the office, looking rather tired, to say good night. They've done a remarkable job, performing not only actors' parts, but also critics' and secretaries' parts, while I've merely performed a playwright's part, and that in an antique style, sauntering about with a cigarette in my hand, altering lines on my feet, getting Tabori and Alexander to perform the cuts and changes so I could hear what they sounded like, but not of course condescending to anything practical as, for example, scribbling changes into my text, getting the text sorted out, typed up and collated. No wonder they looked tired, poor boys, especially when entering an office relaxed and jocular, echoing with laughter.

Joe drove me to Musso and Frank's for a quick supper, after which I came back here to confront the video situation, which is as follows: John Delancey's ingenious wire implant of a few days ago hasn't really worked, because the wires keep slipping out. Chip arranged for an engineer from the video shop to come out and fix it properly. I warned the sunnies at the desk that the engineer would be arriving, and left my key in my box in reception, so that he could be let in. When he arrived the sunnies turned him away, on the grounds that, as there was no key available, he couldn't be let in. On hearing this from the sunnies, I walked ponderously to my box, took out my key, and held it up for their inspection. They smiled at it sunnily, making little exclamations – 'Oh, gee ...' and 'Well, wow ...', not so much apologies as cheerful little appreciations of my rather smart conjuring trick. But then the Magic Hotel is named after the Magic Castle, an extraordinary Gothic building a little way up the road, where professional magicians exhibit themselves, so perhaps the sunnies thought I was a Magic member, practising. I don't know. All I know is that the saga of the video goes on. I've had it now for nearly two weeks, and it still doesn't work. In London you could have it installed and working in two hours. In New York I expect (though I've never tried) you could have it installed and working in two hours. In Rome, Paris, Vienna – but here in Los Angeles you cannot get it installed and working in under two weeks, no matter what sort of fuss you make, to whom you appeal. It's now ten past one in the morning. We're hitting Thursday, the day when Nathan Lane gets in from New York.

## Thursday, 16 January

At the Matrix Theatre in Los Angeles the actors scarcely ever arrive punctually for rehearsal, turning up fifteen or twenty minutes late, having come from television shows or auditions or love affairs, whatever, and furthermore are likely to leave rehearsals abruptly, for the same sort of reasons. This morning John Delancey mentioned, quite nonchalantly, that he was up for a television series called *McGovern*, or *McGiven* or something, and if he got the part would be out of rehearsals for ten days. I think my face, which, being Welsh, can be alarmingly expressive, expressed quite a few, if not all, of my feelings on this, but I'm not sure he noticed. A part of the niceness of nice people is that they assume you're nice too.

At lunchtime I discovered that Nathan Lane had arrived and was next door at the Café Melrose. I scurried the fifteen yards or so down the pavement and into the Melrose, and there he was, Nathan to the life, sitting at a table with various foods spread in front of him. He'd had to get up at 4.30 a.m. to catch a plane at 6. He was full of fun and had his usual corporeal energy, though there wasn't much energy in his eyes, which were half dead from fatigue. Kristoffer Tabori and Joe Stern joined us, and there was a lot of talk about this show and that show, who'd seen what and what they thought of it – one of the things about the theatre, there's always a subject to hand to cover the preliminary social manoeuvres.

We went back to the theatre for a read-through, to give Nathan a chance to slot into the company, and for the company to see how he slotted in. We couldn't start immediately, of course, this being the Matrix. The read-through was to be in the Green Room, i.e. an upstairs attic, very hot, with the sun pouring through the skylight. Christopher Neame and Joe Stern made an elaborate business out of opening the skylight, both of them fussing with cords and sticks and mutual advice until they'd so worked it that a little dash of air came through, accompanied by extra lashings of light and heat. At last, hot and uncomfortable, we began. It went on and on. The only good thing was Nathan, who, given the circumstances of his arrival and the fact that he hadn't done the part for a year or so, was marvellously energetic and ripe. Kristoffer Tabori was still finding his way – not surprising, I suppose, as he has a long rewrite to deal with in Act One, Scene Two. My feeling about the play itself was that its shape was right in that it had a curve and it led to climaxes, but that it was too safe. There was a certain deadness or at least dullness about it, and almost an over-shapeliness to the rewritten Act One, Scene Two. But we plodded on, working our way through to the end of Act Two and there ending the day's work, though I addressed a few rather sharpish words to the actors about the importance of observing the punctuation and the language of the play. Christopher Neame was particularly bad, or good (depending on your point of view), at paraphrasing, getting not only whole passages, but simple sentences, even quite short ones, wrong. In fact was all over the book, as was John Delancey, who seemed so mechanical as Humphry that he gave the impression of being over-rehearsed in lines that he nevertheless hadn't learnt properly – a dispiriting combination.

I went back and had my usual meal at Musso and Frank's, where they've consented to give me a booth, at last, and then shambled up to the hotel, where there was a message at reception to the effect that the video engineer, who this time had been allowed into my flat, had been unable to fix the machine, and therefore proposed replacing it with another, far newer one, though needless to say, hasn't yet done so – there's the old set in its usual place, non-functioning as usual. No, that's not fair, partially functioning. It can throw pictures on to the screen, scarred and jagged, as if they've been in an accident. I phoned home and talked extensively to Beryl about what had been going on in Los Angeles. I was about to go to bed when I was suddenly struck by the idea that perhaps I had failed rather in boldness, let's say heroism, in Act One, Scene Two, and began to restructure it in my mind.

## Friday, 17 January

I woke at seven thirty and tried to recapture everything I'd thought about Act One, Scene Two during the night, writing it down on a legal pad, juggling with lines until it was time to go into rehearsal. I began by addressing myself to the problem of Delancey's slipshod robot of a Humphry, but wasn't helped by Joe Stern coming in and settling down beside me, saying, 'Do you mind if I sit in?' I began to make a gesture of denial, then remembering the consequences the last time I'd done this, said, 'Of course, Joe,' though what I wanted to do, actually, was to take him by the scruff of his neck and the seat of his trousers and hurl him down the stairs to his office below. I proceeded rather haltingly, acutely conscious of Joe's presence – he's got a kind of continuous smile when he attends rehearsals, I've noticed, a cynical and despairing one, and every so often he shakes his straw-coloured head, to signify unspoken but emphatic dissent. His performance, of which I was more conscious than of Delancey's, was interrupted by frequent calls to the telephone. We could hear his voice coming up from the floor below, then the patter of his feet, or rather the stamping patter of his feet as he came back to join us, sitting down beside me in this humid attic of a Green Room and then going off again.

We had to break in mid-afternoon when a lady from the *Los Angeles Times* came to interview me. She was small, about sixty, very intense but perfectly agreeable. We went to the Café Melrose, where I seem to spend most of my life when I'm not actually spending it in the theatre or at Musso and Frank's or festering away here in my hotel room. She'd brought with her a copy of the American edition of *An Unnatural Pursuit*. She seemed, rather oddly, to have a great familiarity with the essays at the back of the book, but none at all with the actual diary, though she kept referring to it confidently and inaccurately. When we'd finished, I had a long session with a *Times* photographer – a young man of very exotic extraction, from the looks of him, and very charming, but with a perverse idea of the kind of picture that would convey the spirit of rehearsals. He insisted on my sitting awkwardly on the knife-edged rim of a seat in the middle row of the auditorium, so I wasn't merely facing away from the actors, I actually had my back to them. He also asked me, even when I was smiling, to smile, so I ended up grimacing – pretty viciously, I suspect.

After he'd left I turned my attention to Judy Geeson and Kristoffer Tabori in their scenes together, reblocking them in an attempt to discover normality, playfulness and sexual tension. One of the things that continues to depress me about Joe Stern and Sam Weisman is their tendency to think that every scene has to be moved about rapidly, rapidly – people scurrying here and scurrying there, no conversation ever unfolding without scurrying. I took out all the moves in which Judy Geeson was called upon to race about the stage, delivering her lines while, metaphorically, anyway, pummelling her fists against the chest of her lover – onstage lover, offstage husband. I went through it again and again, getting it at least calmer, and I hoped slightly more concentrated, until about seven thirty, by which time I was pretty exhausted.

Back at my hotel I found a message to say that the video engineer had installed an entirely new video that he was sure worked perfectly, and therefore he couldn't understand why it didn't actually transmit pictures on to my screen. He had spoken to his boss, who was prepared to return my money. For some reason this message was left not to me, but to Chip Estees. I tried the machine out. Sure enough, there was no connection between the tape whirring away on the video and the active but blank television screen. Depressed and angry, I set out for a meal at, of course, Musso and Frank's, and was disconcerted to discover the restaurant absolutely packed, I think for the first time in my experience. The only seat available was at the counter, right opposite the grill, where I had to sit with lamb chops and steaks and swordfish steaks grilling away almost under my nose. There was a gap at the counter which I thought at first was to allow me space to swivel about in, but in fact turned out to be for the waiters who swivelled me about as they pushed past me to collect the food. I was also swivelled about by customers, as they elbowed their way past on either side. A miserable evening. On my way back there was the ravaged-faced roller-skater with long red hair jumping, nimbling about on his roller-skates and suddenly coming towards me as if intent on rape.

## Sunday, 19 January

I woke at about eight, having had the most appalling nightmares, *appalling* nightmares, to do with my family and their safety. I lay in bed, smoking and pondering – fretting. Eventually phoned Beryl to make sure that everybody was all right, then got up and had breakfast. Went down to the Chinese laundry on Hollywood, collected the clothes that I'd dumped there the other day, came back, dumped them, phoned the video people. I was put on to a very Los Angeles chappie called Dave, who kept on saying, 'I empathize with you, I deeply empathize with you, I empathize with you, Mr Gray, over your problem – it's been two weeks now,' and all that stuff. He went on to say that he'd consulted with the manager who had decided that they no longer wanted to have anything to do with me because (a) whatever was wrong was not their fault, and (b) even if it was their fault they didn't want to have anything to do with me. They would rather give the Matrix Theatre their money back. I shouted some abuse and hung up.

Sam Weisman phoned. We arranged to meet at the Café Melrose at eleven thirty, half an hour before rehearsals, so I could tell him about the various changes I've made while he's been away. At eleven o'clock I phoned for a taxi, collected Nathan (who is staying at the Magic, by the way, in a small, dark room, without a balcony, close to the lobby – he hates it) and down we hurtled to the Café Melrose where, as seemed almost inevitable, Sam Weisman was not waiting for me. In fact, surging into the café exactly on time, and finding it full of people who had taken it over for a convention, I had to surge straight out again, to hang around in the theatre until Sam Weisman turned up at five to twelve – he'd forgotten his scripts and had had to drive back home to collect them. We stood on the pavement in the boiling sunshine while I told him roughly what I'd done over the last four days. Then we went in – there was the usual further waiting about, because some of the actors hadn't arrived. But at least the floor is being laid, a marvellous floor, it looks, and soon the set will be going up. The trouble is, I haven't got much confidence in the set. I went over the model when I was here for the casting, and pointed out to the designer – a tiny, intense chap, with a rather fey manner – that the couple of small revolves with which he proposed to make the shift from present to future at the beginning of the play, from present to past at the end of it, won't work as the play needs them to work. David Jenkins managed it (I admit he had a bigger stage, and better facilities) in the Long Wharf production, to absolutely heart-stopping effect, time as well as space seeming to shift about in architectural blocks.

My fear with this design is that the two revolves will carry off some of the furniture, but not all of it; and then we'll go down to black while the rest of the furniture is struck or replaced – in fact, a conventional set change requiring a lengthy pause. Exactly what I don't want, and that I've written into the text mustn't happen. When I'd aired my objections he'd emitted little cawing sounds of recognition and agreement, but I suspected he hadn't listened to a word I'd said – he probably believes that playwrights should stick to writing plays, and not bother their ugly little heads with such technical matters as sets and scene changes. At the end of the session he'd greeted one of my suggestions – it was to do with the placing of a window – with an appalled pause, and then said: 'I dunno, I dunno but there's something about that that just makes my flesh crawl. It makes my flesh crawl. To think of half a window on stage makes my flesh – it just craaawls!' And he did a shake with his whole body to illustrate what he looked like when his flesh crawled. I'd known then that he and I were never really going to be in sympathy – on any matter in life, probably, but certainly when it comes to discussing sets for my plays. But I may have been wrong about him. He may have registered everything I said about what the play needs, and is now coming up with wizard solutions. I hope so. But I don't believe so.

Sam Weisman worked through the play from the top with great effect, accepting with equanimity the changes I'd made in the first act, including the elimination of all the kisses and tousling in the first scene. Best of all Act One, Scene Two seemed to me, almost for the first time, to be fully alive and vigorous. This was partly because of Nathan, who has had a galvanizing effect on the rest of the cast. Several actors – Chris Neame, for example – went quite white when he came on. There they'd been, working on the play for weeks and weeks and weeks, and suddenly enter Nathan, shooting about with energy and wit, thus informing the other actors of what the scene should really be like; and they, who had been plodding along happily, tranquilly, finding a bit here and finding a bit there, now had to deal with a chap who was actually finding it all. Terrific.

Oh, I mustn't forget the one serious interruption – to do with the video naturally. I reported the morning's conversation to Joe, who then set about the phone like a madman, calling up all kinds of people, some of whom seemed to be merely friends, until John Delancey came into the office and did the obvious thing, i.e. phoned up the firm itself. He had a polite but, from my point of view, entirely incomprehensible conversation, and then Joe, Delancey and I sped to the Magic to look at the video. It took Delancey about thirty seconds to see that the video was plugged into itself instead of to the television set, and also that there was something wrong with the plug. So down we went – through the heat, really torrid heat, of Los Angeles, in Joe's car with the top pulled back, to the video shop, where we had a series of extremely comfortable exchanges with the manager. People in Los Angeles seem always to be extremely comfortable, even when they're hideously in the wrong as was this man, who has spent two weeks not putting in my video. Clearly in the wrong but very affable with it, gracious even as he handed over a new plug. After rehearsals I put in the plug in the manner prescribed by Delancey, sat down and at last, at last, was able to watch a film. So, as I say, a really good day all round. I've got nothing more to report except cheerfulness so let's leave it at that for once. Right? Good night.

## Tuesday, 21 January

It's ten past one in the morning and I'm in the Algonquin Hotel, in New York. The knuckles of my left hand are bleeding, so I must have grazed them. I don't know when or how, as I've only just noticed, but I can't recall any incident on the way from the airport, or altercation down in the lobby that could account for it. I must have done something just now, alone here in my room. I'm lying on the bed – in the bed, as a matter of fact – attempting to staunch the flow of blood while speaking into this machine. I've got two days to cover. Two momentous days I'd no doubt say, if I were reporting on a change of government, or a nation at war.

Yesterday I went into the theatre at twelve o'clock. The day before had been – as I think I reported – cheerful and productive, the atmosphere positively jolly. Sam's first day back. Second day back a slightly different kettle of fish. In fact, all in all, I'd rate it as the worst day I've ever spent in a rehearsal. It began when Sam arrived a trifle late and, without warning or even warming up, launched a fierce moral assault on the actors. I don't know if he was merely in a bad mood and was therefore working on a kick-the-dog principle, or whether there was a strategic intent – that a nice day should be followed by a nasty one, to keep complacency or the gods at bay. Anyway he stood in the middle of the auditorium and went at them, crudely, abrasively, robustly, while they stood about on the stage, too bewildered at first to take offence even. I was pretty bewildered too, but at least, unlike the actors, I could escape – which I did, into the Café Melrose next door, where incidentally I was given a cuddle by the semi-Japanese owner, to whom I've become known as Salmon. Whether he can't pronounce my name properly, or is pronouncing his understanding of it properly, I have no idea; but at least his intentions were reassuringly affectionate. So there in the Café Melrose, over a bottle of white wine and a dish of snails, sat Salmon. During the course of the afternoon, Salmon got through two dishes of snails – no mean feat, as they came in a heavy and tasteless white sauce – and two bottles of white wine. Every time I popped back into the Matrix I caught Sam in the middle of another row – or possibly at a later stage of the row he was in the middle of when I'd first left. It was impossible to tell, as there was no context for me to put the rowing in. So white wine and snails in white sauce at the Melrose for Salmon, rows at the Matrix for Simon, were the order of the afternoon and the evening, until Salmon finally cleared out of the Melrose, and Simon looked in on the Matrix for what he intended to be the last time.

Most of the actors had left, but Sam Weisman was still there, conducting an assault on Nathan Lane. Sam was sitting in his usual seat, his director's seat, with his head half turned over his shoulder, talking rapidly and abrasively. Nathan was sitting in the row behind him, so he could only hear what Sam was saying by leaning forward. It was very odd as well as unattractive – Sam seemed almost to be making a point of not listening clearly to what he himself was saying, let alone to what Nathan was saying in reply. It was over-the-shoulder stuff and not quite over-the-shoulder stuff – looking half back at Nathan, then glaring at the stage, then looking half back at Nathan, then looking somewhere else, then half back at Nathan – his voice rasping on and through Nathan's increasingly desperate interjections. The burden of his message appeared to be this: 'Try and calm down your performance, get it down to something less complete and strong for the moment, because the other actors are having trouble keeping up with you – in other words, you're putting them off, you see.' That was the message, and not one I would have found myself agreeing with, even if expressed with delicacy, but delivered by Sam with his head turning over his shoulder and his head not turning over his shoulder, it came out something like this: 'Hey, you guy – you guy there that's playing Nick, don't you go giving us your big performance yet, we're not ready for it yet, hold back on your big, big performance, you guy playing Nick.' I don't mean that that was his actual vocabulary or sentence structure, but that was the effect, so off-handedly violent that Nathan could scarcely make sense of it. All that he understood was that he was being ordered not to be the actor that he is, playing the character that he's playing – his very soul as an actor was being 'fucked over' in fact was how he put it, though not to Sam, of course, to me afterwards, when we went to Antonio's for a drink.

Being full of white wine and snails, I wasn't up to a drink – just the one made me feel I was going to fall over the counter – but I dimly grasped that it was crucial to calm Nathan down. So we got on to the subject of the Long Wharf production, Nathan reminiscing about Michael Countryman, who had played the part of Martin, a sublime performance, delicate and funny and *simple*, anyway *seeming* so simple; and Peter Friedman as Humphry, with his brilliantly fussy Scottishness, deeply moving towards the end; and of course himself, although he didn't say it, as Nick.* And now here he was, at the Matrix, being fucked over, his very soul as an

* I still remember Michael Countryman's, Peter Friedman's and Nathan Lane's auditions. Ken Frankel and I had seen lots of actors for each of the three parts, responding on the whole quite positively to quite a few of them, until Michael came in for Martin, Peter came in for Humphry, Nathan came in for Nick. In each case I had that unmistakable stirring at the back of my neck – recognition, identification – that here was my Martin, my Humphry, my Nick. And not because they were 'right' for the part, but because they were evidently fine actors that I wanted to involve in the production, who were *also* right for their parts. Such moments come very rarely in casting. To have experienced three within a few days justified all the boredom and irritation that invariably attends long sessions of casting, and also justifies in retrospect the morning treks from New York to New Haven, the late-night treks back, on the most sordidly uncomfortable train I've ever had to travel regularly on. It even justifies having to live in New Haven for a week or so, the only town in the States I positively hate (in spite of Yale) – its atmosphere, for me anyway, being a combination of the dreary and the dangerous. I always expected to get mugged there. Of course I frequently expect to get mugged in New York, but quickly, viciously, expertly. In New Haven I expected to be mugged dully. Slowly and dully. So I can scarcely speak more highly of an actor, can I, than by saying that meeting him justified spending a week in New Haven?

actor being fucked over – he didn't understand it, what was going on, I mean Jesus – ! So forth. I said that probably all Sam wanted to do was to protect the other actors, encourage them to come through at their own pace, not make them feel that they had to force themselves along to where Nathan was already, that therefore he was indirectly, and in a somewhat unusual style actually paying Nathan a *compliment*. So forth. But it wasn't any good really. Nathan had been fucked over in his actor's soul, even if by compliments.

When I got back to the Magic I sat in a heap on the sofa, depressed by the day's white wine, snails, and lethal one drink at Antonio's, and most of all depressed by the way I'd simply withdrawn from the horrors of the Matrix. I wasn't sure what I could actually have done, short of interposing myself between Sam and the actors, and then I wasn't *altogether* sure that such interposing would have been welcome – perhaps in Los Angeles, or at the Matrix anyway, they go in for occasional blood-letting, need it even, would become leaden and despondent without it. In which case Sam was merely fulfilling a part of his duties, his tribal duties – like a kind of witchdoctor. Or a group therapist. I phoned up one or two of the actors, to check this theory out, initiating the conversations with a thickly cheerful salutation and an inquiry into health, well-being, etc., to be informed that well-being, health, were all at a low ebb, though tempers had never been so high. In fact, the general consensus was that never before had they been treated! Were thinking of leaving the production! Last time ever at the Matrix! So forth.

I phoned up Joe, described what I'd seen and what had been reported to me, and put it to him that he was in danger of having on his hands six disaffected actors, one disaffected playwright, and as far as I could make out, one completely unaffected director. Joe was upset, above all humiliated, saying, 'Oh shit, fuck. Fuck, shit. What am I gonna do? Oh shit. Oh fuck.' It was an inordinately long conversation, and furthermore it was long-distance – is Los Angeles the only town in the world where some of the inhabitants have to call each other long-distance? – so it was also very expensive, which did nothing to raise my morale, especially as I had in front of me a telephone bill amounting, because of my calls to England, to something like —— .* I suppose I then stumbled down to Musso

* I can't bring myself to specify the sum.

and Frank's for dinner, then stumbled back to the Magic, to bed. I don't remember. Or rather, can't be bothered to.

Anyway, that was my yesterday. When I woke this morning, with the prospect of the flight to New York in the early afternoon, I decided I couldn't face a morning at the Matrix. I phoned Joe and dished out some flimflammery about having to go to the laundry to pick up my clothes, then what with packing, this and that – . He drove straight through all this by reminding me of my responsibility to the Matrix, the actors, the production, myself, himself, our life-muscles, etc., along with a direct and colloquial appeal: 'Oh, c'mon Si – Big Si – you gotta go in. You gotta. To see how it goes. Hey Si?' So of course in I went – having first extracted from him a promise to drive me to the airport – to see how it was going. What was going was Sam, full tilt, to an audience that consisted only of the stage management, as the actors hadn't yet arrived. He was storming up and down the aisles, up and down the stage, bellowing away about his scripts, which he'd left in the theatre the night before and now couldn't find. He was also bellowing about the revolve, which he'd come in specially early to check. It refused to work. So there he was, at it when I arrived. I sat down in the stalls and watched him. He was still at it when the actors arrived.

It was really quite eerie – this short, red-bearded man running fumingly up and down the aisles, then across the stage in front of us, demanding his scripts back, demanding that the set be made to work, demanding all kinds of other things as well, including, it seemed, the right to exist from a recalcitrant God. Then he homed in on the stage manager, whom he accused of having stolen his scripts or she'd thrown them out with the other rubbish; or she'd buried them up in the California hills – it was hard to make out precisely what he thought she'd done with his scripts, and more particularly why she'd done it. All that was clear was that he'd suddenly located her at the centre of the conspiracy to keep him apart from his scripts. Now the stage manager is an extraordinary girl – well, not girl, woman really, as she must be into her mid-thirties – very thin, hollow-cheeked, chain-smoking, with a kind of desolated look, but extremely efficient. She clearly loves the Matrix and the kind of theatre Joe is trying to produce in it. Sam, seeing her sitting there hunched, gaunt, smoking, aimed himself directly at her, warning her that his scripts should never again be allowed to vanish, that the revolve should never again be allowed not to revolve. At one point he turned, and shook his fist around the auditorium. And there we all were, sitting watching him shaking his fist and bellowing his abuse. Suddenly he stopped. He didn't wind down or deflect himself on to another subject. He simply stopped, mid-bellow, on the subject of the scripts and the revolve, and started up immediately, in mid-bellow, on the subject of Act One, Scene Two. The rehearsal had begun.

Not for long. Act One, Scene Two, the curse of *The Common Pursuit*, had been rewritten so completely during Sam's absence that the two actors involved – Kristoffer Tabori and Wayne Alexander (who'd put the new text on to the computer, and then collated it) – still hadn't had a chance to learn it properly. Nor had Sam had a chance to digest it properly. He turned to me and snarled out an intelligent question about the meaning of some new or changed lines, but in such a way as to suggest that he was snarling at Kristoffer Tabori for having failed to learn the new lines properly. Whereupon Tabori threw his script to the ground, stamped on it, screaming that the speech he was accused of failing to learn had never been in the script before, how had he possibly had time to learn it? Whereupon Sam snarled back – forgetting that he'd originally addressed his snarl to me, and not to Tabori – that the speech had always been in the script. Whereupon Tabori screamed back,'This speech has never been in the script before.' Whereupon Sam snarled back, and Tabori screamed back, until they were snarling and screaming simultaneously. Both of them, of course, were in a sense right. Though the speech had never been in the script before (Tabori), a version of it had been (Weisman). Where Tabori was in the wrong was in thinking that *he* was being criticized for not knowing the speech, when in fact *I* was being interrogated about the purpose of the changes I'd made in it. Where Weisman was in the wrong was in giving such general offence so offensively that somebody in earshot was bound, sooner or later, to take it personally.

I don't know how genuine Tabori's tantrum was. His gesticulations and counter-screamings were so extravagant that they were more like an impersonated dementia than the genuine article. Weisman met whatever it was with a contemptuous disdain, finally walking out of the auditorium, saying, 'I don't know what's going on here but I'll wait. I'll go out and we'll have a break while you get yourself together, and when you're ready I'll come back in, yer know what I mean? Yer know what I mean?' Kristoffer Tabori and Wayne Alexander, who are old friends, went slouching off, laughing angrily. I waited a few minutes, then shambled after Weisman, a cigarette between my lips. I found him by himself, goating about with his beard in a corner of the lobby. Having reintroduced myself to him, so to speak, I said, 'Those lines you were asking about, we'd better discuss them.' He said, 'Yeah. Right.' We got into the text for a time, cleared up the point he'd raised, then I said, 'Let's go back and tell the actors what we've decided,' and he said, 'Yeah, right, let's go talk to the actors.'

I went back in to the rehearsal and discovered, after I'd begun to address the actors about the text, that Sam Weisman hadn't come with me. Suddenly Joe Stern came scooting down the corridor, lifted an index finger and said, 'Come with me.' I looked at him fairly steadily* and said, 'What?' And he said, 'Come with me.' I said, 'Why?' And he said, 'We've got to sort this out.' As we shot towards his office he said, 'You've gotta tell him exactly what you think and feel.' So in I went. Sam Weisman was sitting at Joe's desk. After I'd left him in the lobby, he'd come in to Joe to complain about the actors. In return Joe had reported to him what I'd said to Joe the night before about the state of the actors, etc. He sat there, looking utterly defeated, a goat demoralized. We then had a reasonably civilized conversation, though it was prefaced by an illogical, formless but passionate speech from Joe about what it was he wanted from the Matrix, from the theatre generally, from life itself. Then he nodded to me. I said to Sam Weisman that the problem seemed to me that sometimes he forgot to talk to people simply and directly, in themselves – you know, me as Simon Gray, Kristoffer Tabori as Kristoffer Tabori, Wayne Alexander as Wayne Alexander. He talked to me as if I was the 'awther' and he talked to Wayne Alexander as the guy who was playing Martin, and to Kristoffer Tabori as the guy, as the actor guy, who was playing Stuart. I said that what we wanted from him was a degree of patience along with a recognition of our personal identities. He began by flannelling angrily along and then suddenly looked bewildered and then equally suddenly became extremely sweet and talked about himself, and his sense of what was going on in the company and his failure to talk to them – he didn't know what it

* I don't know what this means, but I like the image – Alan Ladd in *Shane*.

came from – and at the same time defended himself by claiming that 'they' were all against him. Of course Joe, keeping his own psychodrama going, kept interrupting with diversions to do with his and Sam's relationship and further statements about what it was he wanted from the theatre, life, etc.

Throughout all this I was aware that I really ought to be on my way to the airport, to catch my plane to New York. At the same time I was really desperate to bring the conversation to a proper conclusion. So I said that I thought Weisman should go back into the theatre, not to offer explanations and apologies, but simply to talk to the actors in the same tone as he had talked to Joe and myself, i.e. as if they were there in the room with him. In the end, hesitantly, he agreed to do that. Joe and I left him in the office still brooding, and scampered off to Joe's car. When we got to the airport – a hectic drive – I discovered he'd got me a round ticket that seemed to have cost only $30, and involved my changing at St Louis, travelling steerage. Furthermore he'd failed to get me the aisle seat he'd promised. I found myself sitting in the middle of a row of five seats, deeply uncomfortable and hating every minute of it, unable to read properly because the lighting was so bad, unable to drink properly because the stewardess was always too deeply involved in coo-ing negotiations with the other customers, mostly florid and travel-practised businessmen, to get to me. Once down at St Louis I checked that the interconnecting flight left in an hour's time, which at least gave me opportunity for a drink. I shambled into the first visible cocktail bar – a very peculiar bar actually. It was crowded, with only one girl serving. She was rather sexy, in a skirt cut almost up to the hip, with a bulging blouse. She was also very sharp with the dialogue. Whenever anyone called for a drink, she would say, 'I hear you, I hear you, I'll be with you in a minute but listen, I go through this 350,000 times a day, wait your turn, if you don't like it, go on to your plane' sort of stuff. She was in her late twenties, I suppose, but she had the command of dialogue of a woman who had been playing this part for forty years. Fortunately she was struck by my English accent and got me my drink – a large Scotch – fairly quickly, which I nursed until ten minutes before my plane was due to leave.

So what was St Louis to me? To me St Louis was an airport with piped music, a cocktail bar and a waitress, which might be a better St Louis than most people encounter, except that the cocktail bar and the waitress were located around Gate 42 and I had to get to Gate 16 in under ten minutes which meant my running along conveyor belts* and then across lobbies and then further lobbies and then on to conveyor belts again, arriving at Gate 16 just as the plane was about to take off. I'd been told at Los Angeles that from St Louis I would certainly have – no question, they'd already booked it for me – an aisle-seat smoker. But there I was again, squeezed as before in a row of people, smoking angrily – another uncomfortable flight, at least physically. But psychologically the further I got from Los Angeles and Sam Weisman and the traumas of the Matrix the more comfortable I felt. I'd had the foresight to arrange with Phyllis Wender, my New York agent, to have a limo waiting for me at La Guardia which, inevitably, wasn't there. After a long wait for a taxi, a fairly short ride to the Algonquin, I was back in the hotel and in the suite – 310 – in which I've spent so many nights of my life. The card on which I signed in displayed my signature from previous visits over the years. They looked identical to each other and my fresh signature looked identical to them, as if I had forged it rather than just scribbled it down. I had had three large Scotches on the plane, I have to own up to that. I was also therefore not only very tired and exhausted but pretty drunk. Nevertheless, the first thing I did here at the Algonquin was to settle into the familiar and comforting lobby, and order myself another large Scotch. I sat there for hours, brooding, then came up here to my room. It is now, I might say, five to – can this be RIGHT? – it's five to fucking three in the morning, my knuckle is bleeding again because I've just ripped off the kleenex or whatever . . .

## Thursday, 23 January

Flew back this afternoon with the two male parts in *Dog Days* cast – Stephen will have to cast the two female parts from Dallas-based actresses as the theatre can't afford living expenses for four out-of-town actors. I had my ticket changed so that I travelled direct, business class, aisle-seat smoker. A very agreeable journey except that I couldn't, alas, resist a glass of champagne when we took off, then another glass of champagne, then wine with the meal and then, I'm afraid, a whisky or two after the meal. By the time I

* For passengers, not for luggage.

got to Los Angeles at seven in the evening I was pretty drunk. Joe met me and took me to the Magic. On the way he told me that the ghastly row and subsequent conversation that had taken place just before I left had cleared the air, everyone was working very hard, everything was going well, Sam Weisman was working with Kris Tabori and Wayne Alexander at that very moment. At the Magic the sunnies at the desk passed on angry messages left by somebody called Donna at the video shop, demanding to know the serial number of the video, and saying that it was some kind of contravention of the contract (what contract?) to have the machine in the hotel – as it had been booked by the theatre it had to be in the theatre. I don't know if I've mentioned it but I discovered before I left for New York that for some reason I cannot wind the tapes back automatically, I have to sit pointing the remote control at it with my thumb pressed on the backwards scan button for about twenty-five minutes before the tape gets back to the beginning.*

I managed to stay up for a bit but not very long. Reeled into bed.

## Friday, 24 January

A lot of stopping and starting as we went through the new text. Chip had managed to lock into it lumps from about five previous texts – apparently he'd got the discs mixed when feeding them into the computer. I had to break to give an extremely exhausting interview to a chap from a local theatre magazine. As he himself is a playwright, the conversation had to be at a high level between two serious artists of the theatre. I could have put up with gossip or anecdotes, but not with having to go through a solemn pretence of being seriously interested in such subjects as construction – especially when in the middle of reconstructing a computer-garbled text of my own.

Back in the theatre there was a prickly passage with Wayne Alexander. I overheard him saying to Kristoffer Tabori: 'I miss it, I really miss it.' Assuming he was talking about a cut line, or even a cut speech, I said what I always say when actors are protesting about cuts, viz: 'I'm sure you're going to miss all kinds of stuff for a day or two. Then you won't even remember it was there.' He

* John Delancey – who else? – eventually solved this problem for me by finding the appropriate button on the machine itself. The tapes couldn't be wound back by remote control. So much for American technology.

turned on me, twitching. 'You don't even know what I'm talking about,' he said tightly. 'You don't know what I'm talking about.' Of course he was perfectly right. He may well have been talking about missing a person, a place or a pet, and not a line or a passage from the play. I should remind myself from time to time that the actors have lives outside the rehearsal room. 'Right,' I said, 'Sorry. But look, for Christ's sake, does everyone have to be so touchy around here?' He muttered something and turned away, and I left the auditorium in a huff for a glass of wine at the Café Melrose. Came back, saw Wayne Alexander spotting me, then saw him bustling around the side of the stage to trap me in the corridor, where we apologized to each other, embraced, cuddled, slapped each other's shoulders affectionately and that was that. It really has to be that actually because, you know, if one were to take seriously everything that everyone – I include myself – gets up to at the Matrix Theatre, one would spend one's life planning either homicide or suicide.

Later, I had a long talk with John Delancey, taking him upstairs to the Green Room to be private. I said that what he had to do was to stop imitating or impersonating Humphry and just *be* Humphry. Unprepared, alive to all the possibilities of experience. When he first goes to Stuart's room he should expect to find Stuart there, as had been arranged, and therefore be *surprised* to find Martin instead – at the moment he enters as if he already knows he'll find Martin, thus getting the scene off to what looks like a rehearsed start. In other words, John, live the play minute by minute, don't report on the dialogue and the character – that sort of thing. He went in for being tremendously enlightened, exclaiming, 'Of course what you're talking about here is acting.' 'No, no,' I said. 'I'm a writer, I *never* talk about acting,' although what I was actually doing was talking about acting. My principle (for as long as I can sustain it) is that when I'm hovering about as the playwright I always pretend to be talking about the text and the character, and never about acting – *especially* when I'm talking about acting.

During the afternoon we ran Act One, Scene Two and I do believe that now – but Jesus Christ, I've said this so often about Act One, Scene Two – but I do believe that now it works. There was a run-through followed by a break before a technical run, which gave rise to one of those great Matrix moments. Joe, assuming that the break would be brief, dashed out to a fast-food store and came back loaded down with pizzas and Coke and beer for the actors just as the actors, having been informed by Sam Weisman that the break would be quite long, were taking themselves off to restaurants for a proper meal. There was therefore a scene between Joe and Sam about the redundant pizzas, Joe expostulating about the waste of money and time, Sam insisting he didn't know that Joe was going out for pizzas, Joe arguing that nobody had told him there was going to be a longer break – it really is like being adopted into a close-knit family of lunatics. All of them lunatic in a quite different way.

## Saturday, 25 January

Great improvement from John Delancey. For the first time he came into the room walking and speaking naturally, *actively* listening to people, rather than simply waiting for them to finish so that he could deliver his own lines. Joe watched this, looking extremely pleased with himself. Later I discovered that Joe had also taken John Delancey off for a private talk. One of the things the run revealed to me is that the Epilogue requires rewriting. I shall try to do that on my way to the theatre – I'm off in a few minutes, having arranged to meet Sam to discuss it at quarter to twelve, rehearsals beginning at twelve. It is now twenty-five past eleven so I'd better get a move on. But I shall probably get there and Sam won't be there. He's generally late. Off I go.

*Later*

I rewrote the opening of the Epilogue in the taxi. It really required not so much rewriting as shifting lines – the best I can do because I'm not up to writing fresh dialogue. It took exactly the length of the taxi drive to do it in. Sam was indeed not there. When he did arrive he went scudding past me straight into the theatre, completely ignoring my greeting of 'Good morning, Sam.' This is one of the minor, but grit-like irritants of the Matrix. People are quite likely not to return a 'good morning' or a 'good evening', unlike almost everyone else in California. Almost everyone else in California says, 'How are you today?' and 'Have a good day' and even on occasions, more dangerously, 'Have a good night.' But this is not true of Joe and Sam, and especially of Sam. I followed him into the theatre and said, 'Good morning, Sam' again, rather forcefully, and this time got a response. We then sat down and discussed the Epilogue. The day passed with fretful lumps of rehearsal here and fretful lumps of rehearsal there. Then we did a run. It went surprisingly well, in that the play seemed to work at last. A great weight off my shoulders. I now have the play that I should have written in the first place (London), or at least in the second place (Long Wharf). So on that score I feel pretty good.

After rehearsals I popped into the shop next to the Café Melrose, to buy some razor-blades. It's a curious little shop, which seems to offer for sale almost nothing but a few tins of beer, disposable razors, newspapers, chocolate bars – in fact rather like a shop run by Pakistanis or Indians in London, except that it's run less efficiently and contains fewer saleable goods. There in front of me was a strappingly built transvestite or transsexual, I couldn't make out which, and his consort, who in any other company would have been thought astonishingly effeminate. They were fondling chocolate bars, passing them backwards and forwards to each other, trying to test the texture and even get a whiff of the flavour through the wrapping, all the time talking in what I suppose is a normal transsexual/transvestite manner about which sort of chocolate bar they most preferred. When they went out the woman behind the counter, who is Chinese or Korean, burst into laughter and then sealed her face into a courteous grimace when two oldy-worldy queers came padding in. Now the point about this is that it took place not on Sunset Boulevard or in some other exotic part of Los Angeles, but in an around-the-corner shop where they sold – or didn't sell, as it turned out – G2 razor-blades, but did sell disposable razors and cans of beer and a few bottles of appalling wine, warm and sweet, one of which I was fool enough to buy.

## Monday, 27 January

Today coming back from lunch at Musso and Frank's, I made a study of the stars on the pavement. These stars are of metal – bronze, I think – set into the pavement with the name of the star on it. I'm told that the stars have to pay for this honour. So one finds oneself trampling across, say, Yvonne de Carlo, then Elvis Presley, then Broderick Crawford, and then one's foot hovers over the name Frank Primrose, for instance. Frank Primrose! I mean who could that be? A producer? A director? A cameraman? Probably a scriptwriter. So what happens is that one recognizes three or so names in succession and then there is a name that means nothing and something falls away inside you. You feel that either you ought to know this name or this name is attempting to claim your attention, having no credentials to claim it with – a pathetic call from beyond the grave, though embedded here among the stars.

## Tuesday, 28 January

Look, let's come down to the bare knuckles on this one. Today is Tuesday, and from Saturday, Sunday, Monday through to Tuesday nothing has happened in my life at all except that I have gone, when it's open – it's not open on Sundays – to Musso and Frank's for lunch or dinner, depending on what time rehearsals have been called. I've gone into the theatre, observed run-throughs, made my notes and given comments, most of them exasperated because all the technical stuff is days, if not possibly a week, behind. The sound hasn't been properly organized yet, the lighting cues are disastrously unworked out, and as for the set changes – that guy who a month or so, it seems to me a lifetime, ago, when I proposed that the windows should be *there* rather than *there*, said the thought of it chilled his blood, and did a kind of wince and squirmish and smirk, and when I tried to explain to him the dramatic importance of time in the play I could see that he wasn't listening, I could see that he was NOT listening, because all he was thinking of was his monumental sets – has now stuck us with his monumental sets. Not only has he not managed a proper working revolve, managing instead two little revolves that don't work properly, he also hasn't managed *any* system that gets people shunted in and out quickly enough for us to go from one period to another visibly and dramatically on stage. There he is now, fluttering around, looking mildly embarrassed at the fact that his sets not only don't work but actually dwarf the actors with great slabs of phoney masonry. So we have this problem to deal with. Even though I don't believe there is any way of dealing with it. Nevertheless I've gone on whining at Joe and Sam Weisman, nagging and whining and occasionally shouting and pounding my fist against my upper thigh until something is at last being done to try to achieve the shifts in time succinctly, if not dramatically.

On top of which I've been yet again and yet again and yet again rewriting Act One, Scene Two. I'm beginning to wonder if this scene can ever be got right, if there isn't something radically flawed in the construction of the play. I don't know. I do know that it works better than it did in London and at the Long Wharf but I'm not sure that it works better *enough*. We also had costumes on display tonight. Most of them looked OK. The day was full of hiatuses. We'd get through a scene and then have to stop for something like an hour while scene changes and music and lighting cues were worked out. In these intermissions I would gambol up the road and have a drink or two at Antonio's and gambol back extremely ill-tempered to discover that they *still* hadn't sorted out the cues and the changes. There was a terrific moment when Sam Weisman was trying simultaneously both to rehearse scenes and to get the lighting and the set change and the sound cues right, while the actors, one after the other, were protesting at being forced to continue to rehearse the text when they still hadn't got their actual costume changes and their other physical changes, like moustaches added on here and moustaches taken off there, worked out. One couldn't help but sympathize with them, one couldn't help but sympathize with Sam Weisman. His ginger-bearded and balding head sank on to the palm of his hand and he just stared at the ground while Joe took over. It's the kind of situation I think Joe enjoys, dealing with the actors' problems with sympathy and concern and dealing with the director's problem, the director sitting dejected – he looked like a monument to dejection actually – to one side, and the playwright, one has to say, slightly drunk from his trips up to Antonio's, lurching around somewhere at the back. On the subject of Antonio's, by the way – they come before you've even sat down and strum guitars at you and sing into your face. And they continue after you've sat down, with your drink in your hand, singing and strumming at you. It would be quite a nice place to go to if they would only leave you alone.

But to come back to the technicals, all I can say is that it is like almost any technical experience I've ever had in the theatre, only far worse. Everything takes vastly longer. Nothing functions with precision. They can't even let me know accurately when I should arrive for rehearsals – the schedule changes from moment to moment. For most of the time we can't even depend on a full cast, as the actors are also out and about doing their bread-and-butter TV soaps and series. At the moment our leading lady, Judy Geeson, who is trying to get American citizenship, keeps having to go up for immigration clearance with her husband, our leading man, who has to sit beside her and present her case. I don't know what sort of case he has to present. Surely there should be no problem as she's married to an American. Perhaps Tabori has to persuade them that she's innately American enough to be married to him.

## Wednesday, 29 January

Spent seven hours in the theatre, two of them in the disgusting early-afternoon heat, hanging about, waiting for Sam Weisman, who had asked me to meet him. Two hours late is something of a record even for Sam Weisman. He had been at the sound studios, too absorbed to telephone, or something.

I suppose rehearsals went all right, and I kept my demeanour, I hope, civilized as I insinuated my notes and got some of the blocking in Act Two changed. But my nerves are on fire with irritation, exhaustion, frustration – I don't know what it is – just the day-in day-out experience of the Matrix, I expect. One of the things that inflames them further – my nerves, that is – is the amount of eating that goes on. What makes it particularly repulsive is that they don't bring in genuine meals, but always something that poses as a piece of natural food, a 'nutritional' salad or a 'slimming' sandwich. Some of this food, or non-food or whatever it is, invariably falls out of their mouths and dribbles down their chins, what they retain in their mouths they eat with almost smacking noises. I have to say this. I mean this won't be in the published diary,* but I do have actually to observe that I have never seen so much eating going on in my life before. All the time. Today, during notes before the technical run, one of the actors sat on the floor in a kind of circle of packages of nuts and raisins and biscuits, little non-nutritional or anyway non-toxic biscuits, and his hands were going into one or the other, his lips smacking away, while lumps of biscuits and nuts and raisins were tumbling out of his mouth on to the floor and were then flicked away by his hands which then went back among the biscuits or the nuts or the raisins. I've developed a kind of counter-attack. Whenever they eat I puff smoke into their faces from whatever angle I happen to be at from them. I also have

* This is demonstrably untrue.

a goblet - a plastic goblet – of wine in my hand, or late in the evening, like this evening, a plastic goblet of malt whisky in my hand. There I stand amongst them, puffing and sipping at them, and there they stand, gobbling and slurping back at me.

I left at 10 p.m. in the middle of the technical, Joe having offered to drive me to Musso and Frank's. We were just crossing the parking lot to his car – there's always a parking lot in Los Angeles, you can't get anywhere without crossing a parking lot – when my watch, which I deeply cherish because it has so many associations, just fell off my wrist. Fell off my wrist and dashed itself in what seemed to me an act of wanton self-destruction on the parking-lot cement. The glass splintered, some of it falling through to the face of the watch, preventing the second hand and the minute hand from moving, and this watch, which maintains so many connections to my life back in London – whenever I look at my watch, I remember who I am and where I am, or it seems to me that I do – had suddenly become an utterly useless object. It *fell* from my wrist, *fell* and became an utterly useless object. I took it in to be repaired, of course, and am in the meantime wearing a replacement lent to me by Joe Stern. It's very heavy with a steel strap, and it's the kind of watch that I most object to. I like simple numbers, Arabic numbers, but this one hasn't even got Roman numbers, it's got dashes except for the twelve and the six and the nine and the three. It originally belonged to Joe's father, now dead, and has come down to Joe's son who no longer wears it, but wants it back for sentimental reasons. So I'm under a serious obligation not to lose this watch. I don't know how I could lose it actually, short of having my wrist chopped off, because it's never going to fall off of its own accord. Its metal is going to stick tightly to my wrist, like half a handcuff.

Joe got me to Musso and Frank's just in time for a meal. I sat in the cubicle with the intention of reading but couldn't because there was an extraordinarily loud and garrulous television star, I assume she was from the nature of her conversation, talking to, presumably, her agent, about why she was shy and found things difficult and how she couldn't stand some other actor in her television series who seemed to her to be cheap in the way that he got laughs. Her agent, if he was her agent, was being soothing and sympathetic. He looked exactly like Woody Allen, only a few feet taller. I became so involved in their conversation that I stayed on and on until we were the only people left in the restaurant.

When I got back to the Magic I was informed by the smiling Californian youth at the desk, who also looks a bit like Woody Allen, that all the telephones in the hotel were out of order. It was impossible to make an outgoing call or to receive an incoming call because the week before or so they had put the telephones on to a computer and the computer, as computers invariably do, had failed them. 'So,' he said cheerfully, 'there are no messages for you, Mr Gray, but then there couldn't be any messages, Mr Gray, because the telephones aren't working,' and he gave me this Woody Allen smile. And I must say I wanted to smash this Woody Allen smile into all kinds of lumps and welts because for one thing it meant I couldn't get a morning call, for another thing Joe was going to phone to let me know the rehearsal time. I therefore dealt with this Woody Allen chap in my least charming and sympathetic manner. In fact I launched an attack on what he must have felt was his private life, his sexuality, his purpose in the world, his right to a place in the universe, I called everything about him into question. At one point – at no stage in this conversation did I raise my voice, by the way, which I think must have made me more disgusting – I kept it at a kind of angry, low, growling malcontented level – at one point he said, 'It's no good shouting at me, it's not my fault,' and I said, in my angry, low, growling voice, 'But I'm not shouting at you, am I? Am I shouting at you?' And of course he had to admit that I wasn't shouting. It was most unfair. But I think it was his Woody Allen smile – which he wore even when asking me not to shout at him – that did it. My consolation for having behaved so badly is that I have at last come full circle in Los Angeles. From a functioning video and a telephone that never worked on my last trip,* through functioning telephones and a non-functioning video, back to a working video and non-functioning telephones. And so from my balcony at past one in the morning, recording this, my voice no doubt still growling with malcontent, I offer a mild gesture with my fingers to the soft, muggy star-dappled sky before taking myself off to bed.

* There was an infuriating dummy that sat prominently on the sitting-room table of the Taboris' cottage. The Taboris kept asking the relevant company to reconnect it. One afternoon a gang of men in plastic helmets appeared. They scaled trees, foraged in the undergrowth, then left with merry salutes of 'see ya then' and 'you're very welcome'. The telephone, when I tried it, merely whistled into my ear before falling dead again. What I missed most, of course, was the making and receiving of impulse calls – as well as the making and receiving of anonymous calls. A diminished life.

## Thursday, 30 January

I spent the morning on the porch reading some Chekhov short stories, hating the sun whose presence seemed to me an impertinence, given that it's late January. On one neighbouring porch there was an elderly French couple, he in his bathing trunks, with a kind of masking cup over his nose and various creams on his face, and she in and out of the sitting room with various drinks for him to sip at, with the smells of an elaborate French meal in preparation drifting from their porch to mine. I don't think that anyone in this hotel is a native Californian. They're either New Yorkers or even more foreign. Currently in residence are some black Gospel singers, six of them blind. They trundle carefully around the pool with their sticks but apparently are quite sensational on stage in a spiritual musical about Oedipus. The apartment next to me, on the other side from the elderly French couple, appears to be inhabited entirely by a child of about three. She comes out on to the porch, she goes back in, I hear her squalling, I hear her chortling, but I have never seen or heard an adult in attendance. I suppose there is one. Unless, of course, she's a midget. If so she's an inarticulate midget, that chortles and squalls as a means of communication. But I don't believe that, she must be a child. I'm sure she's a child. She looks a perfectly healthy normal three-year-old child – four year old? three year old? She can't speak, what age does that make her – two year old, I suppose, if she can't speak. The telephones still don't work, by the way.

But what do I know of Los Angeles? I know the little stroll down Hollywood Boulevard to Musso and Frank's – I go down Orange Street and turn left into Hollywood Boulevard and there are these freaks – cocaine addicts, drunks, black guys with bangles and leather straps around their wrists, guys sitting on motorbikes revving up, with police cars bunched powerfully beside them – turn into Musso and Frank's, have my meal, come out again and back up to the hotel. Or get delivered from the theatre to Musso and Frank's and walk back up past these creatures. It seems to me the most cut-off and isolated life. I'm DESPERATE to be at home. DESPERATE to be at home, running about my usual life, seeing all the people I want to see, trying to do some writing in my study with Hazel at my feet, away from this almost unendurably boring existence. That's the key word in all this. Boring. All the dramas at the Matrix, all the life lived or not lived in the Magic Hotel, all the tramps down Hollywood Boulevard to Musso and Frank's, or up Hollywood Boulevard away from Musso and Frank's, I've managed to convert into a routine that is dreadfully boring. Though sometimes I quite like it all.

## Friday, 31 January

I bumped into Nathan in the manager's office where we were both trying to make phone calls – all the other phones are still out. While he was making his call I signalled that I was going to my room to get my bag. When I came back he'd vanished. I went to his room, he wasn't there. I went back to the manager's office, he wasn't there. I checked back in my room, then back in his room, then back in the manager's office, gave up and set out for Musso and Frank's. Halfway there, along Hollywood Boulevard, I spotted Nathan in one of the public telephone booths. He explained that as his call was of an intensely personal nature, he'd decided that a public booth would guarantee him more privacy than the manager's office, especially as the manager and his assistants sit around listening in on your end of the conversation. What is odd is not that they listen in – who wouldn't? – but that they make no attempt to disguise it. There they sit, not even turning their heads away. They simply smile and listen, and I'm sure one would see them nodding at the points one was making if one didn't find oneself irritably turning one's back on them. Not that turning one's back offends them. When I did it yesterday, in the course of a conversation in which I was arranging to meet Joe at Musso and Frank's, then glared pointedly around at them when I'd hung up, one of them asked me, in his usual sunny style, whether, if anyone wanted me, he should say I'd be at Musso and Frank's with Joe. Of course this may turn out to be a more effective way of getting them to pass on messages than just asking them to – for one thing they seem actually to take in what they're not intended to hear.

Over lunch Nathan told me that after I'd left the theatre last night Sam gathered the cast together and held a conference that lasted well over an hour, in which they were invited to say what scenes they wanted to rehearse today. When it was Nathan's turn to speak, he opted for his two scenes in Act One. Sam's reply was he wasn't interested in hearing Nathan's views, this rehearsal time was for the other actors. This upset Nathan quite a lot. He couldn't see the point, he said, of having to hang about for an hour in order to be asked what he wanted to rehearse, if he was then going to be told that nobody wanted to know what he wanted to rehearse.

We got to the Matrix at one thirty – the time settled on at Sam's conference – and then sat around for forty-five minutes waiting for the other actors and the director to show up. It was then discovered that we couldn't have a rehearsal anyway, because the set designer, who has made such a hash of the set, with his enormous, tomb-like rooms, and his revolves that don't work to any purpose other than to shift the furniture interminably about, was busy on the set. What he'd been busy at was quite incomprehensible to me when I saw the set later. It looked exactly as it had done before and worked in the evening run-through just as badly as it had done before. He'd probably been putting some books in the shelves and arranging some papers on the desks. That's about his speed. Anyway, the main rehearsal was abandoned. Instead, Tabori, Wayne Alexander, Sam Weisman and I went up to the attic Green Room, where we set about examining in detail the new text of the dreaded Act One, Scene Two.

We were making pretty good progress, Sam talking about what resources he thought Alexander and Tabori needed to draw on in a particular passage, I explaining what I took to be the intentions behind the lines, when there was a sudden altercation between Sam Weisman and Wayne Alexander, who, as I think I've already noted, is a rather sensitive sort of chap, and now took exception to Weisman's manner, exclaiming that whenever he tried to say something about a line, a scene, a passage, about anything at all in fact, Weisman would interrupt him. Now it's perfectly true that Sam is one of the world's great interrupters – he finds it barely possible to allow you more than two sentences before cutting across and summing up your sentences for you and then – usually – dismissing them. Wayne, in his sudden breakdown, or outburst, went on to say that he'd had enough of this, he wasn't a complete fool, you know, Sam, he wished he'd be allowed to finish when he spoke. Sam let him go on for a bit, staring at him in a slightly peculiar, hunched, unfocused way, and then cut across him, 'Yeah, but what I was trying to say about the scene,' and so Wayne, expostulating away about never being allowed to finish a sentence, he had contributions to make which ought to be listened to, found himself interrupted in full flow, and everything he'd said disregarded. He rallied, started again on an even higher note, and again Sam just sat hunched, staring at him, and then again cut across him, saying, 'Yeah, but what I'm saying to you about this scene is – ', whereupon Wayne threw up his arms in despair, disbelief, and capitulated.

This altercation between Weisman and Alexander was fairly swiftly followed by an altercation between Weisman and myself. I'd just explained the meaning of a line over which Tabori and Alexander had been confused, and they were articulating their new realization, in the way that people do, with such phrases as 'Oh, I *see* . . .' and 'So that's why my next line never made sense . . .' and so forth, just a casual little interlude, really, a kind of verbal tea-break, into which Sam Weisman surged with a long, rasping windy sentence that went something like this: 'Ya know! Ya know, it's very difficult, this is very difficult to sit here like this, doing this, and, ya know! it's very important the author should be here, but it's very difficult for me, ya know! and what I don't want is to have the two actors talking between themselves about something *you've* said to them. Ya know!' And on from there, windily, but raspingly, his point being that if the actors understood each other's intentions, as identified by the author, they would cease to be spontaneous. I became pretty windy and rather rasping myself, asking him whether he meant that I shouldn't be too precise about the purpose of a line or a speech because the actor not directly involved might find out too much about the processes of the actor directly involved. Yeah, he said, that's what he meant, going straight on into one of his statements about acting and the acting process, and what he was trying to do here which was to teach the actors something about acting, instead of paying all this attention to the literals. 'The literals' being, I suppose, the text and its meaning. But they needed to know what it was they were acting, I said, and as for not informing one actor in the presence of another actor about the meaning of a line, did he propose that we approach the actors *separately*?

I wish I could give an accurate rendering of our respective tones, Sam Weisman's angry, but somehow abstract snarlings, my own fury, intensified by the consciousness of the plastic mug of white wine in my hand, which I felt put me at a moral disadvantage to such an extent that I over-enunciated every syllable, to make it clear, in the characteristic drunk's fashion, that I wasn't drunk – though, in fact, I wasn't drunk. We went on and on at each other, disputatiously, discourteously, with Wayne Alexander occasionally offering to explain Sam Weisman to me, me to Sam Weisman, and Kris Tabori putting in some good, solid work as the embarrassed onlooker, until I finally found myself telling Sam Weisman that his behaviour was unprofessional and improper – I was sick to death, I said, sick to death of these horrendous conversations one always seemed to find oneself in at the Matrix, especially with him. There was a long, brooding silence, interrupted only by little scuffling noises from Joe's office below, which alerted me to the fact that he'd been listening in, and then we carried on, inhibitedly polite to each other, and so made far less progress than we'd been making up to the rows. Over the last few days, in fact, when we'd been in accord almost continuously.

Joe drove me back to the hotel, admitting that he'd heard most of what had gone on, encouraging me to report my anger, and even develop it – full of sympathy and concern, but nevertheless looking rather pleased, as he always does when there's a tempest about.

But, my God, what an ordeal it's been at the Matrix! I suppose the main problem is that nobody is getting paid. When actors are being paid they can accept an ill-mannered director as simply another professional hazard. When they're not being paid they resent any slight – anyway, certainly feel that they should be treated as courteously as they usually are when they're being paid. And Sam Weisman, himself not only unpaid but sacrificing the huge sums of money he could be earning as a television director, doubtless feels the actors owe him respect and total obedience, if not adoration, on that account alone. So what we have here is a ghastly kind of amateur set-up, except that everyone concerned is professional. The worst of both worlds. Or at least so it seems to me, as I sit here on my balcony at six in the evening, the tumbler of malt in my hand not sufficiently softening the prospect of having to be back at the Matrix in an hour and a half's time. We're having a fully dressed run before a small, invited audience. One thing I can be sure of. We won't start on time. The cat that I can't get up to my room is sitting at the edge of the pool, by the way, dipping its paw into the water. It looks worried, as if it's lost something.

*Later*

I got to the theatre on time, to find that they hadn't yet finished a technical run-through. Joe caught me in the auditorium, raised a finger to his lips, then beckoned me down the corridor into his office, where he gravely informed me – apropos our conversation in the car – that Sam had been deeply offended by the things I'd said to him this afternoon. This both surprised me and cheered me up. I'd begun to think that Weisman, who is so prone, whether consciously or not, to giving offence, was unable to receive it. I thanked Joe for the information, checked up on the technical again, popped into the Café Melrose for a hamburger, checked back on the technical, to find it at exactly the same place as when I'd left – even down to the actors' positions, while the stage-hands, running about in the darkness, seemed to be shouting out exactly what they'd been shouting out the last time I'd heard them. The small audience – very small indeed, about ten people – had been invited for eight thirty. We began at half-past nine. Apart from that it went well, I thought. The play certainly works, and the actors seemed to know what they were doing. John Delancey, although stiff and unyielding, has enormous natural authority – he's almost hypnotic – so that one doesn't too much mind the inflexibility of his delivery. I shall never warm to Wayne Alexander's Martin, it's a highly skilled and well-judged performance, but morally wrong, a snakey friend rather than a good friend who does – has to do – something sneaky. Kris Tabori had a fine first act, dropping all his Lee J. Cobb mannerisms (gesturing and strutting about), being instead calm and natural. In the second act the mannerisms returned – instead of a literary editor, we got an actor doing some 'acting'. But then the second act was generally less good. Not surprisingly, as all the effort recently has gone into Act One, and particularly Act One, Scene Two. I think the exchange between Martin and Stuart near the top of Act Two, Scene One is too long in the writing. I'll have to cut it by a beat or two.

All in all, though, everyone was rather pleased. The sparse audience seemed to enjoy it, at least. Nathan and I decided to go off and have a sandwich alone together, Joe having offered to drive us to a restaurant or café. But then began one of those interminable Matrix discussions about things like moustaches, overcoats, etc. It was now past midnight, everyone hungry and anxious to be off, and yet – it could only happen at the Matrix, I've never known anything like it – no one could escape from this conversation, once it had begun. It was like a net that they'd entwined themselves in. Finally I had to remove Joe virtually by force. Before getting into Joe's car, I had a brief conversation with Sam Weisman on the pavement, saying, 'Look, Sam, about our little dispute. We could have an interminable post-mortem on what you meant, what I meant, so forth, but I'd much rather we both just forget it, do you agree?' He looked vastly relieved, said yes, he did agree, we said fond good nights, so I was rather surprised when he turned up at Joe Allen's just a few minutes after we did. He worked so hard at being genial that all you saw was the work, which meant that the geniality grated on the nerves – mine anyway. And I suspect I worked so hard at responding to his geniality that all *he* saw was the work, rather than the response, so no doubt I grated on *his* nerves, in turn.

Joe and Nathan, on the other hand, were relaxed. They began to tell theatre jokes, Joe getting into one, rather long one, about a guy who had writer's block, had no money, didn't know where his next meal was coming from. One morning, after a night of tossing and turning, he went downstairs to find the script he'd been blocked on not only finished, but brilliantly finished. He took it to a producer who loved it instantly and paid him half a million dollars for it. A few months later he was tossing and turning with writer's block, although he'd bought himself a house and a new car, and was living in fairly comfortable style. He went downstairs and there, neatly on the desk, was the script he'd been working on, brilliantly finished. He took it to the producer who loved it and this time paid him a million dollars. The next time he was blocked and lay tossing and turning, he heard the typewriter going. He hurried downstairs and discovered an elf sitting at the typewriter, typing furiously away. It turned out that this elf had written all his other scripts for him, so he said to the elf, 'Well, listen, I must give you something.' The elf said, 'No, no, I don't want anything, I just enjoy the work.' He went on typing until he'd finished the script. The writer took it off to the producer, who loved it, paid him one and a half million. This went on for some time, the elf writing script after script, the writer selling them for 2, 3 million, until the writer got rather desperate at the elf's refusal to accept anything in return. He offered him women, and the elf said, 'What would I want with a woman? I'm an elf.' He offered him a house, a car, trips abroad, but the elf would accept nothing, always saying, 'I don't need it. I'm an elf.' Until the writer said, 'Look, this is terrible, there must be something I can give you, let me give you something. Please. *Anything*. For *my* sake. Name it!' After a pause the elf said shyly, 'Well, look. There is – well, a little thing – look, do you think I could have a share of the writing credit?' The writer stared at him. 'Share my writing credit! What do you think I am – fucking crazy?'

I got back here at two o'clock. Just now, in fact. To discover that the phones are still out of order. The sunny at the desk talked of their being fixed in the morning but made, smilingly, no promises. Now that I've got the video working, I'm too tired to watch anything on it.

## Saturday, 1 February

Left the hotel with the phones still on the blink, having been told that they'd be fixed by ten o'clock, then twelve o'clock, then three o'clock. Joe had arranged to pick me up at twelve thirty for lunch. He arrived at one fifteen, by which time I was feeling almost ill with hunger, having had nothing for breakfast but a glass or two of champagne. He drove me to Musso and Frank's in the rain. While he parked the car I walked back to the jeweller's to collect my watch. There was a Pole there, a laughing Pole – I hadn't *left* the watch with a laughing Pole – who told me I must have come to the wrong shop because they had no watch there along the lines of my description, try further down the street. To my own triumphant astonishment, and to his evident bewilderment – at least it stopped him laughing – I produced, probably for the first time in my life, a receipt, and further told him the make of the watch, so there was no getting out of it, he had my watch somewhere. He made some phone calls in Polish, then announced that it would be ready in an hour. As his English wasn't too hot I had to pantomime my anger before slogging back through the rain to have lunch with Joe, and a friend of his who'd joined him, an American actor who 'did' English* – a perfectly pleasant fellow, no doubt, but not somebody I wanted to meet at this precise moment in my life, what with non-functioning telephones, my unreturned watch, the first preview

* i.e. specialized in playing English parts.

coming up in the evening. The lunch seemed to go on and on, the conversation centring mainly on McEnroe and Borg, though shifting now and then to Harold, with whom this actor who 'did' English had once worked. I found it hard to concentrate, Borg, Harold, McEnroe sort of mixing themselves up in my mind into one composite figure on the other side of life's net, so to speak – especially as the food had a very dominating personality. I'd ordered kidneys, but what had arrived were not kidneys as we know them, too enormous to have come from any farmyard animals of my experience. They lay there on my plate, seeming to stir occasionally, as if *challenging* me to eat them.

Eventually I got Joe to agree that it was time to go, especially as I had to pick up my watch before heading on to the theatre. Out the three of us went, into the Musso and Frank car-park, where we bumped into a television producer Joe knew, to whom he insisted on introducing me. I stood in the rain in my shirt-sleeves – everyone else, I noticed, had on some kind of rain-defying apparel – while Joe and the actor and the producer, a big black-bearded, shambling figure, reminisced their way back to their early youths. When I was sufficiently soaked I reminded Joe about my watch, plodded off to collect it. I was met by the Pole, his eyes dancing with merriment, who informed me that it would be ready in a half an hour or so. I threw a tantrum, heaving about his tiny shop, knocking against things. Because of his limited understanding of English I chose words that everyone in Los Angeles uses all the time, even foreigners. I don't think I actually went as far as 'mother-fucker' but I deployed 'shit' frequently and noisily, then wrote down the telephone number of the Matrix, and told him to phone the second my watch arrived. Then back through the rain to Joe in the car-park, and on to the theatre, to discover Sam, for the first time ever, not only there before me, but already in the throes of rehearsal. I was half an hour late. He's generally a minimum of forty-five minutes late. But just yesterday I'd made such a point about the endemic unpunctuality at the Matrix, and given Joe, within Sam Weisman's hearing, a lecture about it, that it was particularly mortifying to be late myself the very next day, thus giving Sam Weisman the right to treat me like an interloper, a right he tried to exercise. I wasn't having any of it, stopping him constantly, checking his comments, discussing various points to the full. I have to admit that he dealt with me with remarkable forbearance, and managed to give the actors clear and good notes. When I watch him at his best I believe the play is in safe hands. I just wish that our temperaments and our vanities didn't collide so readily – eagerly, even – and that he didn't so often move from the illuminating to the obscure in half a sentence. What was evident and reassuring was that the two actors, Wayne Alexander and Kris Tabori, have reached some accommodation with him, settling for picking up what they can. Of course, they are now about to go before the public, and *need* the feeling that they are in the hands of a director.

At about 5 p.m. the jeweller's phoned to say that my watch was ready. I had Chip Estees drive me to the shop, where the Pole triumphantly – rather as if he'd manufactured it himself, he was so proud of having it in his possession – handed it over to me for the sum of $12, a trifling amount given the comfort it has restored to my wrist, to the whole of me, as a matter of fact. I went on to the Magic, but decided not to go into the office to find out whether the telephones were working because I thought that if they weren't the complications arising from the subsequent row would probably lead to violence, the police, handcuffs, gaol. Every day on the way to the theatre I pass a shop that offers bail bonds. I would hate to think that Beryl might have to fly over to Los Angeles and take out a bail bond as the result of altercations I'd had from not being able to reach her on the telephone. When I entered my room the telephone was ringing. Yes, actually ringing. Rick Quinones, someone I hadn't seen for nearly thirty years, when I was twenty and he a few years older, he a student from Midwestern University in Chicago, taking a course in French literature at the University of Clermont-Ferrand and I, *en route* to Cambridge from Halifax, Nova Scotia, teaching English to French students at the Collège-Technique in Clermont-Ferrand. He was married to a beautiful American girl called Laurel, who became pregnant halfway through our year there. The only contact I've had with him since came through the post a couple of years ago in the form of a pamphlet of poems by Laurel, along with the announcement from Rick that she'd died of cancer. He is now lecturing at Claremont College, not far from Los Angeles. We arranged to have lunch on Monday. I'm looking forward to it with some trepidation. It was for such a short time, such a long time ago, that we knew each other. On which note I'll sign off for the evening. I go back to the theatre in a few minutes to the first preview. I'll report on it either later tonight, or tomorrow morning. When I'm either drunk or hungover.

*Later*

The first preview went off well enough, under the circumstances. The play seemed to hold up strongly, the audience was absorbed, laughing a great deal and also seeming, from time to time, to be touched. The key moments certainly worked better than at the Long Wharf or in London. But the set is an utter disaster. The actors remain dwarfed by the monumental walls and the vast stretches of brown. One of the designer's most ghastly mistakes is that he's used the same door for the two rooms, although the first room, in Cambridge, is back in the sixties, and the one in London goes up almost to the present. But in each room we have the same door, an *enormous* door. The architecture of the stage is such that your eyes go to it immediately, and you are immediately convinced that you are, even after the most elaborate, ponderous and time-consuming set-changes, still in the same room.

The other problem is Kris Tabori. He played the funny bits 'funnily' and the serious bits 'seriously', over-emphasis everywhere, back to Lee J. Cobb, in fact. Now Lee J. Cobb was a great actor, everything he did coming, or seeming to come, from something found and truthful in his own nature. But Kristoffer Tabori was giving a mere imitation of Lee J. Cobb, announcing the mood in every scene with his first line, leaving himself absolutely nowhere to go – Lee J. Cobb always had plenty of places to go. It was as if Tabori couldn't trust the text to make itself understood, or the audience to understand it. He was directing himself, as a policeman directs traffic. Now this way, now that. Go. Stop, watch the lights.

Still, there was euphoria at the interval, and euphoria after the second act, Joe grinning jubilantly, Sam Weisman stamping ferociously about proclaiming that we had a hit, 'a monster hit, a fucking monster!', on our hands, though as the auditorium seats only ninety-nine it seems to me that it will be a very small monster of a hit, fucking or otherwise.

But being the Matrix they weren't content to leave the evening at that, in a blaze of celebration and some formal pronouncement to the effect that we'd all meet tomorrow for a general note period, followed by specific notes, followed by rehearsals. Instead Joe and Sam Weisman, in their weird, implacable devotional style – perhaps it's the house-style – insisted on holding a post-mortem on the props, and where they should be placed. It became increasingly byzantine, this conversation, moving from a consideration of the props to even smaller considerations, until Wayne Alexander insisted on discussing the question of whether he should have marking tapes to illuminate the keyboard of his typewriter in the dark, so that he will know exactly where to put his fingers when he begins typing at the beginning of Act Two, just before the lights go up. The idea that Wayne Alexander needs to have the keys he is *pretending* to tap illuminated with tape seems to me preposterous, at least as a subject for a debate that lasted a full twenty minutes, at getting on for midnight.

Driven by all this beyond endurance, I seized Nathan Lane and hurled him into the lobby, where he was gathered up by a friend – a tall, dark Jewish girl in her early thirties from New York, who comes up periodically to Los Angeles to turn a buck or two as a warm-up comedienne for situation comedies on television. The three of us went off to Joe Allen's, where I had a very large Scotch, a piece of pecan pie and a large espresso, while they dealt out to each other spoonfuls of various salads and ordered each other drinks. The warm-up comedienne lady had seen the show at the Long Wharf, felt that the version here went deeper, but also felt that the set was a catastrophe. As we'd asked for her opinion, we had to tolerate her giving it to us. She went through the cast, plus-ing and minus-ing in terms of the Long Wharf production, while the Joe Allen waiters kept skirmishing up with offers of more food, drink, etc., until I suppose after one in the morning, virtually the last ones in the place, we left, the stand-up comedienne driving Nathan and myself back to the Magic Hotel – where I am now, dictating this. I wish she hadn't confirmed all my fears about the set, I'd hoped my reactions were special to myself, paranoid, and that we'd got by. But we simply can't have two different sets creating exactly the same atmosphere in different places and times, especially after we make such a fuss about changing them. The problems with the actor, Kris Tabori, will probably be corrected by a serious conversation or two; but the problem of the set won't be corrected by just conversations, however many of them we have, however serious. Really, we should begin by ripping it down and reconceiving it.

Before dictating this I phoned Beryl – 2 a.m. my time, 10 in the morning her time – to be told, among other things, that Hazel has become almost completely incontinent, seeming to have developed a method of eating and crapping simultaneously. When ushered into the garden, where in her prime she dropped turds at random, she now merely stands sniffing abstractedly for a brief moment, before hurrying in to mess up the kitchen floor, her nose buried in a dish. I can't bear the thought of anything happening to her, even though I know it will and must, as to all mortal creatures, so what I mean is that I can't bear the thought of my life without her. She sits under my desk or lies on the sofa gazing at me with sheer reverence when I write, and has been my friend and confidante for sixteen years now.

## Sunday, 2 February

Lunch by myself at Musso and Frank's. Read the English newspapers, three days behind, and ate mushrooms on toast, or tried to. They were disgusting, actually. They have no idea about mushrooms, Americans. They think that you have to pour vinegar and wine over them, when all a civilized eater wants is for them to be fried in butter with a little bit of garlic, some salt and pepper added – true mushrooms on toast. If the toast's OK. But at Musso and Frank's the mushrooms sprawl across the thick, sweet toast, lapping around its edges, smothered in wine and vinegar. And beside it is another plate of mushrooms on sweet thick toast, so that if one runs out of the first load, one has a second load to turn to. Though the prospect of running through the first load and wanting more must surely be remote, even for Californians.

Sam Weisman arrived while I was toying with my coffee, drove me to the theatre. We talked about the actors, the costumes, the props, and above all, the set. Although he hates it too, he doesn't think anything can be done about it. When we got to the theatre, we had a talk with Kristoffer Tabori about the part of Stuart. I put down various cards about my understanding of the character, that he is so much at home in the English language that he never feels the need to colour his words with 'meaning' and 'intention'; that he is always poised, calm, only breaking down once in the play, in a moment of extreme crisis. Tabori nodded thoughtfully through all this, and I left him with Sam Weisman to do some specific rehearsing, while I went along to the office, and found Joe on the telephone, looking odd. He hung up, terminating his conversation abruptly, and said he didn't feel well. He seemed rather puzzled by this. His eyes had a slightly dreamy, almost vacant look, as if he'd been drugged. I suppose he's suffering from a combination of fatigue and tension, the feeling that things are almost there, but aren't quite – it's characteristic of the Matrix that although we've had *two* public previews, everyone has behaved as if both were an official First Night, instead of viewing them as mere extensions of the rehearsal period, a time to learn through an audience.

I went next door to the Café Melrose for a glass of wine. Joe joined me a few minutes later, to talk about the set, Kristoffer Tabori, Wayne Alexander, this actor, that actor, how it had gone last night, how it had failed to go, all this with his usual energy but still slightly unfocused, although he did manage to ask if he could be guaranteed some participation, should the play be produced in New York. I said that of course he would be – I do think he's a terrific producer, given the limited resources he has to work with, although I also think that as a producer he continues in many respects to be an actor playing the part of a producer, and is sometimes in need of a good director.* I went back to the rehearsal, where I immediately found myself in another altercation with Wayne Alexander about a line that *I* felt he was delivering as if he'd learnt it, that *he* felt he was delivering as if it were spontaneous. 'I don't understand what you're saying,' he kept saying. 'It was spontaneous. It felt spontaneous.' 'But it sounded,' I kept saying, 'rehearsed. As if it had been rehearsed.' Back and forth we went, he getting pricklier, I more ponderous, Sam Weisman saying nothing, watching with a kind of vacant impatience until we got back to work, then broke for a pre-preview meal and rest. I dashed off for a drink with Antonia Pinter's daughter, Natasha, to exchange views about Los Angeles, then back to the theatre just before the lights were due to come up, to find the actors hanging about looking listless, accident-prone, riddled with anxiety in the Matrix manner. I went next door to the Café Melrose, ordered a glass of wine, where I was joined by a Joe even more frantic and unfocused than before, wanting to talk, though it wasn't clear about what, he was so fretful. He sat down, got up, sat down, got up, finally sat himself down for about four long minutes before getting up again and

* Which reminds me that Joe's production company is officially (and ominously) entitled 'Actors for Themselves'.

going out, saying he'd see me in the theatre. During all this he scarcely spoke. It was as if Joe – the fertile-minded, imaginative, joke-making Joe – had been abruptly drained, while his body continued to behave with remembered energy. It made me uneasy.

I got into the theatre just as the play was starting. At once it was obvious that we had a rather different Kris Tabori on stage, much more in control, much calmer. As he's got natural presence he therefore became vastly more eloquent than when dramatizing every line with his body and his voice. There were the usual technical problems and of course I found myself from time to time staring angrily at the set, particularly at the double-duty door.

At the interval I nipped into the Melrose again to stay out of earshot of the audience, then went back to the office just as the second act was about to begin, to find Joe and Sam sitting silently in an atmosphere of strain, as if they had been having, or were on the verge of having, a row. I stared at them both, then hurried out into the auditorium for the second act, fixing my attention on four old ladies in the front row, on whose faces there wasn't a flicker of surprise, concern, amusement, interest of any kind. I suppose they'd only come back from the interval because they had ordered their limo to return at the end of the play. Just before the change to the Epilogue the audience burst into what I would have taken as heart-warming applause if I hadn't known that a few seconds later – quite a few seconds later, as a matter of fact, because of the elaborations of the set-change – the audience was going to find itself back in a strikingly similar room, with all the actors assembled, and the Epilogue still to get through. They took it on the chin, when they at last discovered that the play was going on past the point at which they'd complimented it for having finished.

So that was that. I scurried, as is my wont, around to the office, to find Joe and Sam already there, having a row – the row that had presumably not quite started, or that I had interrupted, at the interval. Joe was not only shouting at Sam Weisman but – between sentences – also shouting at the stage-hands for their incompetence. It was the first time I'd ever seen Joe angry, really angry. Sam kept intervening, ordering Joe not to shout at the stage-hands, they were doing their best, which of course further incensed Joe, who has had to spend, as he loudly pointed out, the last month or so attempting to pacify everyone with whom Sam has come into contact – having Sam now publicly telling him to calm down and to behave with better manners was more than he could endure. Sam actually developed a very good line in the middle of the row, sitting down and smiling gravely at the folly of mankind, or more specifically Joe's folly, which had the (desired, I assume) effect of enraging Joe even further, until Sam suddenly got up, said he had to get to his television studio to look at some stills, and went, leaving Joe fulminating into emptiness. Then, noticing me, he began to fulminate in my direction, though not precisely at me, saying that the work 'you guys' had done on the first scene had turned it into a pile of shit. And the whole play goes down the toilet. 'And the whole play goes down the toilet!' he bellowed. I always find it very hard to be angry with Joe when we're face to face, and even in these circumstances, melodramatic though they were, I found myself trying to pacify him. I dimly understood, I think, that his fury had in some way to be spent. He went on lashing out at Sam and myself (this package deal was rather hard to take) like a minor heavy in a Clint Eastwood film, every other sentence containing 'fucking' and 'fuck', with 'shit' bobbing about on the surface as well. He didn't so much calm down as wind down. He stared at me blankly for a moment, gave a feeble laugh, offered to drive me to Joe Allen's, then was overwhelmed by a fit of the shakes. He stood in his office shaking, looking extremely perplexed by the shaking, saying he couldn't understand what was the matter with him. Chip Estees and I got him to lie down on the sofa, and covered him with a blanket. He continued to shake and tremble under the blanket, looking utterly befuddled, while I phoned Pepe to come and fetch him.

I wasn't really as worried as perhaps I ought to have been because I felt that the shaking and the trembling were intimately connected with his rage, as if a very strong tempest had passed through his body, leaving his will unable to deal with the complete exhaustion that followed it. I got the stage manager, the young guy with the wispy beard, to drive me to Joe Allen's, where Nathan, already ensconced, had his own drink in his hand, and another on the table, waiting for me. Before I could tell him about Joe, the door swung open. Sam Weisman stood there, framed in it, like some kind of goatish gun-slinger from an old B-movie. His eyes scanned the room, he picked out our table, over he came. Nathan and I, who had been going to spend the evening celebrating his birthday – it was his thirtieth – along with old times past and old times to come, found ourselves instead having to deal with an absolutely obsessed director, who wanted to talk about the set, and how he was determined to make its changes work, some awkward moves and how he was going to change them to make them work, on and on and on, until I was too drunk to listen to him properly. Nathan sloped off, gesturing that he was going to the lavatory, came back again, then after five minutes, glancing out of the window, said, 'There's my taxi.' I said, 'Your taxi?' He said, 'Yes, my taxi. Somebody I want to see. I'll drop you off at the Magic on the way there.' I began to say, 'Yes, fine,' but Sam Weisman cut across – he being in full flow – and said, 'I'll take him home, I'll take him home. Don't worry about him, I'll look after him, you go off, Nathan!' Nathan went off, I don't know where to but I hope to someone with whom he had a night of passion.

I sat on with Sam Weisman, my concentration gone, my focus gone, sat with my chin on my fist, staring dully at him as he talked very emotionally about all the things he intended to do, to the set, to the blocking, to make the production work. Joe Allen's cleared, the restaurant was empty, the kitchen was closed, the bar was closing, the waiters were desperate to get rid of us, and I only wanted, it was all I wanted, to get back to the Magic, and into bed. But Sam Weisman talked on until, in the middle of a sentence, he got up, said, 'Listen, I'm very tired so you'll have to find your own way home, I can't make it, I've got to get home myself so see you,' and went off. I went to the bar where I asked for a taxi. 'The guy here wants a cab,' one of the two remaining waiters said. 'Well actually not a guy,' I said. 'It's a gentleman here asking for a taxi.' There was a pause, then some merriment between the two of them at the proposition that the guy who wanted a cab was actually passing himself off as a gentleman who wanted a taxi, though a taxi arrived almost at once, and I was brought here to the Magic to end my day by reporting all this into the tape-recorder.

## Monday, 3 February

Awoke at ten thirty this morning, a rest day and therefore no rehearsal. I lay in bed, rather numbly, unable to get going until I forced myself to the telephone and called Joe to find out how he was. He sounded a bit enfeebled but said he felt he was OK, really. Then Nathan phoned to say he was going out to lunch, would I like to come with him? I said yes but explained that we couldn't have lunch, as I'd already arranged to have lunch with Rick Quinones, the guy I'd last seen twenty-nine or thirty years ago in Clermont-Ferrand. Nathan and I strolled down to Musso and Frank's, sat down at a table and ordered a drink. I kept checking people as they came through the door, occasionally thinking I half recognized Rick Quinones, until suddenly at exactly one o'clock I looked up and there was a man, whom I'd last seen beardless and with quite a head of hair, coming through the door, almost bald with a beard. He came over to the table, I introduced him to Nathan, who then withdrew to another table, leaving us alone to talk. The last time I'd seen him he'd also been with his beautiful and pregnant wife, and now I learnt that not only was Laurel dead from cancer, but that the son with whom she'd been pregnant had been killed, a month before Laurel died, in a car crash. We talked our way through that, all the way back through our respective careers as university teachers, to what we wanted to remember about Clermont-Ferrand, the friendships formed between the English and Americans, various incidents, as for example Laurel's telling me that they were having trouble getting to sleep at night as their mattress seemed to move under them – they later discovered that a couple of large rats were nesting in its stuffing. We began our lunch at one, ended it at five, not long enough to cover so much time, so much life, so much grief. He drove me back to the Magic, accompanied me to my rooms, looked around them as he pulled at his beard, left, leaving me on the sofa, in tears at the memory of Laurel, triumphantly pregnant, resembling in fact a large and proud robin, two deaths ago, thirty years ago, in Clermont-Ferrand.

I think I would have sat on there for hours if Nathan hadn't phoned from his room on the other side of the pool to say he was going to have dinner with his audience-warming comedienne friend, would I like to join them? She picked us up at about seven, and drove us to an Italian restaurant in Melrose Avenue – near the theatre, in fact – where we ate extremely badly. We were joined by Ted Larkins, to whom nothing had happened professionally since he'd left the company. Conversation was rather strained. There we were: Ted Larkins and his replacement, Nathan Lane; the author who'd done the replacing; the warm-up comedienne who, though chattering brightly, seemed to have her mind on other things; all sitting side by side with bad food in front of them. Suddenly the warm-up comedienne said, 'I've got to go,' and rose to her feet. 'What?' I cried. 'Where?' 'To a club,' she said. 'What club?' She replied, 'Just a club,' but she had to get to it straight away, rather as if she had an appointment with her doctor. 'Well, it sounds very interesting,' I said. 'Let's *all* go to this club.'

So Nathan and I, minus Ted Larkins, who suddenly discovered a previous engagement, clambered into her car, and were driven smartly to the club, a mere few minutes from the restaurant. She parked the car in the car-park, and we ascended in an elevator to a disco, where a few men were dancing with each other, one man dancing alone in the middle of the floor, others huddled together, not so much dancing as responding to the music with their feet and torsos while engaged in private conversations – they were dressed in jeans and vests, and they danced extremely closely, touching each other as they jogged up and down. We went on through, past this lot, into an enormous room with a bar where there were about seventy or eighty people sitting on stools at tables, at the end of which was a stage with a microphone. Nathan's comedienne friend walked on up to the stage, picked up the microphone, and went straight into a number about what it was like to be a Jewish New York princess loose in Los Angeles, a comic monologue in fact, for which she was being paid, Nathan whispered to me, nothing. She was doing it to be *seen*, in the hope that her name would be passed on to agents and producers who'd get her into television series. Nathan and I, full of drink and friendship, thought she was very funny indeed, rocking with laughter on our stools, and signalling congratulations every time the audience appreciated one of her jokes. When she'd finished we went on to Joe Allen's, where we had a few more drinks, until Nathan rose, saying his taxi had arrived 'to take him on' – really, I don't know how he arranges these taxis; this time he seemed to have done it without even leaving the table – and tumbled off into the night. The comedienne and I had coffee, then she drove me back to the Magic. I tottered in, treading across the Astroturf, made slushy by recent rain, and wove my way up the stairs to my flat, pitched myself into bed.

## Tuesday, 4 February

Met Phyllis Wender, my New York agent, at the Café Melrose, just before the preview. We took our time, sipping glasses of wine, as I'd discovered that we were going to go up late – the handle had come off the double-duty door, so it could be neither opened nor closed properly. We drifted into the theatre half an hour late, a few minutes before the play began. It got off to a good start, and remained good throughout the first act, Kris Tabori and his wife being especially simple, direct and therefore touching. The only actor who had lost it a trifle was old Nathan, who'd gone metaphorically right back to the large auditorium at the Long Wharf, booming and rasping his way through his scenes as if unaware of how close he was to the audience. Something went wrong with the timing of the lights-down at the interval – we went to dark very abruptly, as if merely ending a scene rather than the act. The audience, not knowing the play and therefore not knowing that they were free to leave for a cup of coffee (all the Matrix can provide), remained in their seats. Knowing better, and anxious as always to avoid hearing the audience's comments, I made my way up the aisle in the pitch black, my hands held in front of me and so inevitably jammed my fingers straight into Sam Weisman's eyes, at the head of the gangway. I heard him barking with both rage and physical distress as I swivelled smoothly around him, down into the hall, and out to the Café Melrose, trusting that he hadn't identified his assailant.

The second act went as well as the first, though the set changes are, of course, interminable and the Epilogue struck me as a bit ponderous – probably the fault of the writing. After the show I raced up the aisle and into the office. Phyllis came in a few seconds behind me, and then Joe came in, having recovered from his hysteria, flu, breakdown or whatever it was, but looking distinctly lighter and yellower. He was in characteristic form, demanding that I should stay on to help him with the press photocalls for the pictures that would accompany the reviews.

I refused point-blank, and went off with Phyllis to Joe Allen's, where we were joined by Michael McGuire, an old friend of mine. I first met him during rehearsals of *Quartermaine's Terms* in San Francisco.* He'd been brought in as a replacement for the part of Windscape about a week before we were due to open. Now Windscape is a solid, cheerful, dedicated teacher of English to foreigners, of the English English and middle class, academical with

* The following, rather extensive account of my relationship with Michael McGuire is, I hope, justified by his dramatic reappearance in the last section of this book.

it. What we had in Michael McGuire was a thin, almost cadaverous Midwestern American, wearing high-heeled boots, and with a nasal, Midwestern accent. Not so much a non-Windscape as an anti-Windscape. Or so I thought. But what became clear very quickly was that he was a highly intelligent man, and a real actor. Within a few days he'd not only learnt his lines – there are a lot of them – but he'd moved closer and closer to a Windscape that made complete emotional sense. By the First Night his accent was impeccably English, his Windscape entirely his own. And all this achieved in really desperate circumstances. We also hit it off offstage. Having spent most of his adult life drinking very heavily, he'd given up drink, but he still had the conviviality, the *esprit* of the drinker – to such an extent that though he merely sipped genteelly away at Perriers and club-sodas, I always remembered him as a chap with whom I'd shared many bottles of whisky. In fact, what I still recall most vividly and with most affection about San Francisco were the late nights he and I spent with Jack McQuiggan, who was overseeing the production – he had produced the play in New York – and who was, like Michael, an ex-drinker. We hung out in a deeply sleazy hamburger joint, Michael tippling away at his bottles of water and chain-smoking, Jack, an ex-chain-smoker, knocking back the coffees, I chain-smoking and at my whiskies; all three of us shouting out anecdotes and rocking with laughter until two or three in the morning.

The next time I bumped into Michael was when I came over here six weeks ago, to help cast *The Common Pursuit*. He's an old friend of Kristoffer Tabori's – no, that isn't right. Kristoffer Tabori isn't old enough yet to have old friends – he was Tabori's mentor and protector when Tabori first started out as an actor at the age of sixteen or so, when Michael was in his early thirties or so. Tabori and Judy Geeson invited him to dinner so that he and I could renew our acquaintance. Since San Francisco he'd given up smoking, which made him (like Jack McQuiggan) an ex-alcoholic ex-chain-smoker. He'd also separated from his long-term girlfriend. He said he was depressed – 'liberated but depressed' – by all this cutting down in his life, but within minutes he was telling a story, yelping with laughter, the same old Michael. A few days later – he'd acted at the Matrix, and knew Joe Stern – he came in to help us with auditions, reading the most unlikely parts, twenty-year-old Cambridge undergraduates, for instance, in his flat, nasal Midwestern accent, but still making enough sense of the lines to give the actors who were actually up for the parts of twenty-year-old Cambridge undergraduates a genuine understanding of what was expected of them.

And now there he was in Joe Allen's this evening, standing at our table, still elevated by his cowboy boots, sucking his chest in and throwing his arms out as he talked passionately about what he'd seen on the stage of the Matrix. I pulled him down into a chair, and allowed him to soliloquize flatteringly on and therefore *intelligently* on, until he expired into his Perrier or club-soda on a final few compliments. Exalted, I decided the stage was mine. I launched into a monologue about my immediate future as a playwright, my future as a playwright after I was dead, the state of acting in Los Angeles (cutting off any interpolations from Michael, who laboured under the double disadvantage both of knowing far more about the subject than I did, and of being completely sober) until Phyllis drew my attention to the fact that (yet again) Joe Allen's was beginning to clear, and that I was yet again among the last to leave. Phyllis and I accompanied Michael to his car, one on either side of him, in a rather bizarre role reversal – after all, we'd both been drinking and he hadn't. He clipped along contentedly between us, embraced us both, climbed into his car, drove off to the far Los Angeles canyon he lives in. Phyllis and I then tumbled into her car. Phyllis is about my age, I suppose, a small, neat, methodical lady with a frequent and exceptionally pleasant laugh. Most of all she resembles a successful High School teacher – perhaps, more accurately, a Principal – and is a very sharp agent indeed. Now Phyllis is a New Yorker, doesn't know Los Angeles particularly well, and didn't have a road map to refer to, yet she drove at exceptional speed, unnerving speed, up and down streets she'd never travelled before, depositing me by instinct, it seemed, at the doors of the Magic, then drove off into the night. A pretty good evening, as evenings go in Los Angeles. At the Matrix, anyway.

## Wednesday, 5 February

Did what I normally do when I'm free in the morning. Pottered about the flat, watched a bit of television, listened to some music on the radio, tried to do a bit of reading, then shambled down to Musso and Frank's, where I had an altercation with the elderly guy, the bespectacled figure who looks rather like a dentist to the Mafia, who refused me a table on the grounds that tables were for two and I am only one. I pointed out that I'd booked (true), and that I was going to be joined by a friend (a lie) but this old Mafia dentist figure, who's seen me virtually every day since I arrived in Los Angeles, first of all insisted on my telling him my name, which he made an elaborate show of finding confusing and making me spell, then pointed me to a swivel stool at the counter, where I could wait, he informed me, until my friend (actually he said 'fran') came. I've come to hate the counter, because it's quite obvious that anyone sitting at it is by himself, somehow for ever unpartnered, and I can no longer bear to add myself to this poignant line-up of swivelling solitaries, but instead of engaging him in combat – the demons for once being passive – I plodded to the bar and found myself facing a guy who was the image of benevolent authority. I explained that I needed a booth. He immediately conducted me to one. I've no idea where he is in the Musso and Frank's hierarchy. He may not work there at all. But the fact is, he escorted me to a table, and I read my papers, comfortably if rather slowly and carefully as a dyslexic might, actually mouthing some of the words out loud. I spent hours studying the cricket columns.

In the evening I went along to the theatre, arriving in good time for rehearsals. I gave my notes, worried aloud about the Epilogue, complained about the set-changes, etc., usual sort of stuff. Except nothing is usual in the Matrix. There is now an atmosphere of frenzy in the auditorium that increases the moment Sam Weisman begins to speak, and will obviously never abate until he's no longer on the premises. It doesn't matter how intelligent he is about the previous night's performance, the actors sit there enduring his notes while making it clear that they can't stand him. And the most astonishing thing is that he goes on, implacably, grindingly, giving his notes, quite unaware of what the actors feel about them and him. About them because of him.

The preview went OK, though Kristoffer Tabori had slipped back to his pantomime performance. Such an odd thing because he's very effective when he's calm and still – the more he 'acts' the less effective he is – and yet there he was, after his wonderful performance on Tuesday night, going right back to it all, as if anxious to show the audience that he is determined to give them their money's worth. It depressed me deeply. After the show

Nathan and I went to Joe Allen's. We were having quite a jolly evening when the door opened and in came Sam Weisman, to join us.

## Thursday, 6 February

Nathan and I went to Musso and Frank's for lunch, and found bedlam. Not only was every table taken, even the counter was packed, with a crush of people jamming the entrance, desperate for any kind of seating. There was nobody in attendance, the Mafia-dentist who generally stands guarding the route to the tables and counter had vanished, presumably having given up. People were just milling angrily about, hungry. We went back along Hollywood Boulevard to the Hamburger Hamlet, which would have been tolerable if it hadn't been crudely segregated – non-smokers being conducted to a light and airy room, smokers consigned to a dark chamber in the back, with grubby booths, like a speakeasy. We talked, as we so often did, about the good times in New Haven in the raw and brutal cold, as opposed to the bad times in Los Angeles in the balmy sunshine, recalling the train from Grand Central to New Haven, and back again, arriving at Grand Central at two or so in the morning, anything from an hour to an hour and a half late, all of us slightly to extremely drunk from Michael Countryman's hip-flask full of whisky, and then the trudges through the snow for cabs, then back to New Haven the next day. Nathan went on to complain about the lack of any kind of theatre community in Los Angeles, the obsession here with films and television, the sheer sunshiny dullness of the place.

After rehearsals I went off to meet Natasha Fraser, treated her to a glass of the Café Melrose white wine, escorted her to the theatre, where she met up with two young and attractive (girl) friends of hers. It went, the play, just about OK, no better than the previous preview, no worse, though once again Kristoffer Tabori's tendency to posture was troubling. Natasha and I went off for dinner, over which we gossiped about the performance, then she drove me to the Magic. And I thought as we drove back that here I was, at the sort of age when I escorted to dinner girls whom I'd first known when they were ten or so. But then, I further ruminated, these girls had also reached the age when they were escorted out to dinner by middle-aged men they'd first known when they were ten or so, and that they, in their turn, would one day be escorting out to dinner boys of ten or so – no, that can't be right. Forget it.

## Friday, 7 February, First Night

After breakfast I phoned up all the actors and gave them my notes. I've taken to doing this as a regular morning activity; first breakfast, then phone the actors to discuss their performances. A number of them informed me that they'd had enough of the Matrix, they'd never work there again, they resented Joe for his continual interferences, Sam Weisman for his manner. They didn't say how much or why they resented me, although I expect they do. Sat in a torpor on the balcony for a few hours, a bottle of champagne to hand, then off to M. & F. for lunch.

Most of the afternoon I spent crouching by my bedroom window, staring through a gap in the curtains at a man sitting on a bench, across the road from the hotel. Tall, ginger-bearded man, about thirty, wearing a tartan shirt, tight jeans, cowboy boots, with an enormous knife strapped to his left buttock. He followed me back to the Magic from just outside Musso and Frank's – the second time he's followed me. The first time, a few days ago, in the early afternoon, also when returning from Musso and Frank's, I found myself standing beside him at a crossing. When the lights changed he waited for me to get ahead, then settled in behind me. I could hear his boots tapping along in time to my own tread, which I kept measured and confident, at least until I got to the hotel steps, up which I shot like a whippet, if you can imagine a portly, forty-nine-year-old whippet, on two legs and with poor wind. That time it didn't occur to me to check whether he lingered on outside, keeping watch. But today the whole business seemed even more deliberate. When I came out of Musso and Frank's he was coming towards me on the crowded pavement. His face registered nothing, but I sensed him turning, settling down behind me again, and once out of Hollywood Boulevard, on the deserted street – Orange Street – that leads up to the Magic, I could hear his boots again, tapping rhythmically along. Again I whippeted up the steps into the lobby, but this time I turned and watched him through the glass doors. He crossed the street to the bench, sat down on it, folded his arms, and stared towards the hotel – or putting it in more personal terms, stared towards *me*. Of course I can't see the bench from my sitting room or balcony, but I can from my bedroom. Hence my crouching there, peering through the curtains. He must have spent several hours virtually immobile, and eventually left when I wasn't watching him. Given my behaviour it's no good pretending that I don't find him, the thought of him, the *image* of him following me back to the Magic, then sitting outside on a bench in the sun as if waiting for me, quite unnerving. He corresponds almost exactly to my vision of the ruffian on the stair, in the W. E. Henley poem.* On the other hand he might simply be a sort of stray, who likes a bit of company when roaming the streets – pedestrians lead a lonely life in Los Angeles. But why the knife? Can it possibly be legal, even in a town like Los Angeles, to go about publicly with a knife that size clamped to your buttock?†

At about six I phoned for a taxi, then hung about on my balcony, keeping an eye on the lobby. The sunnies there sometimes forget to ring you up to let you know that your taxi's arrived. On one occasion, a couple of evenings ago, they actually sent the taxi away, on what grounds I couldn't fathom. Perhaps that I don't exist. Or was curled up with a cat, and shouldn't be disturbed. This time I spotted the driver going to the desk, so I scooted down while he was still on the premises. He and sunny were having a pleasant conversation, though clearly not on the whereabouts of the prospective client – at least I hope not, as there was a lot of head-shaking laughter, and exclamations of 'you don't say!', etc. I got to the Matrix at six thirty, an hour and a half before lights up on our official First Night. I zipped up the road to Antonio's for a drink and a song in my face, then sauntered fairly calmly back to the Matrix, where Joe informed me I'd have to stand through the performance, as all the seats had been allocated to critics.

According to Joe the word of mouth from the previews has been 'terrific, just terrific', which is not always to the advantage of a First Night, as critics like to think that they generate the word of mouth, and certainly don't like to think that they're being usurped by it.‡

* Madam Life's a piece in bloom
Death goes dogging everywhere;
She's the tenant of the room,
He's the ruffian on the stair.

† I wasn't able to put this question to him as I never saw him again.

‡ A New York producer, who knew his show was a bummer, was astonished to read rave reviews after the First Night. 'Now,' he is reported to have said, 'all we got to do is stop the word of mouth.'

So it's not surprising really, that I detected pockets of resistance here and there, some ostentatiously unimpressed expressions on the heavily sun-tanned faces. Nevertheless I thought the show was good, really very good, and afterwards hurried around to the dressing-rooms (some of which are merely alcoves with coat hooks) to dish out thanks to the cast, each one in turn. For the first time in my experience of the theatre I felt this was merely a ritual. No, worse. A courtesy. I suddenly realized that though I liked this actor, respected that one, I had no sense of intimacy with any of them. Except for Nathan, of course. Him I gathered up and bore off in a cab to Joe Allen's, where we were joined by friends of his, a husband and wife who failed to observe the First Night conventions, and talked about the play and the production only in qualifying details – what they felt wasn't clear in a scene here, what went wrong in a scene there (Act One, Scene Two). We were interrupted by Sam Weisman, who burst through the door, stood for a moment checking out the room, waved to us that he was coming to our table, then sped past us with a late swerve, to join a clutch of people at a large table at the end of the room. Friends, I assume. Or anyway, people with whom he has some acquaintance. While he rampaged amongst them, stabbing his fist into the air with triumph, I went to the bar, ordered a taxi, came back to the Magic, where I now am, out on the balcony, dictating this.

Another First Night gone. The third for *The Common Pursuit*. I don't remember the previous two. Soon I won't remember this one – though perhaps I'll remember the next, which is tomorrow. I don't quite know why there should be two official First Nights at the Matrix, except of course that as you have to say everything at least twice here, why shouldn't you have to do everything at least twice, too? It's a still night, very quiet for the Magic. Most of the lights are out. No televisions or radios on, that I can hear. Perhaps all the other guests are in bed but awake, listening to my low, disappointed drone, occasionally quickened by a spasm of spite, as I talk on the balcony into this machine.

## Saturday, 8 February

Got up just in time for lunch at Musso and Frank's, over which (though what, I don't recall) I read the English papers. Came back, listened to some music, then went to our second First Night. All the critics that didn't come (couldn't get in?) to our first First Night had appropriated every seat in the auditorium. This would seem to mean that there are nearly 200 theatre critics in Los Angeles. More than enough, when you consider that there aren't many theatres, and that very few of those are visited by plays. I shambled around the dressing-rooms, looking shy but dishing out notes to the actors, then went up to Antonio's for a drink. A drink and a half (a double and single, to be technical. An Antonio double is about the size of a London sextuple) – two songs smack in the face, and a platter of hors-d'oeuvres that were simultaneously fiery and heavy. Rather like the songs, come to think of it. Then back to the theatre about ten minutes before the show began. I had to stand at the back again, as a critic, a small bearded woman wearing bombazine and shades, was in my usual seat.*

The show was the best it's ever been, controlled, intelligent, sensitive. I could have made forty notes about the performances, but then at a certain stage of a production one could make forty different notes every night. On the next night the actors themselves would have corrected those forty, while doing forty other things one could note. The real point of continuing to give notes is to make sure they don't become stale, lurching by degrees into habits that usually manifest themselves early in rehearsals, from the something intractable that is in all our natures. Nevertheless I was delighted with the play and with the production, as was the producer and the director, though they were also apprehensive, having observed that the theatre critic for the *Los Angeles Times*, one Dan† O'Sullivan, sat cold-eyed through the evening, apparently totally uninvolved. I said that perhaps he was merely on heavy medication. Or had a hearing problem. Or was bored.

We went on to Joe Allen's, where I found myself at a table of about fourteen or so, Sam Weisman on my left, Joe Stern on my right, both still glumly assessing the reactions, or rather lack of reactions, of Dan O'Sullivan. As I'd already offered my analysis I left pretty quickly for the Magic, where I am now, dictating this.

* Sheer fantasy. My usual seat was occupied by a moustachioed man in swimming trunks and shades.

† It might have been Don. Don O'Sullivan. But for some reason I think of him as Dan. Perhaps because it's his name. Dan O'Sullivan. But now it comes to it I'm not too sure of his surname either. It could be Sullivan without the O'. Possibly Don Sullivan then. For the purposes of clarity I've decided to stick with Dan O'Sullivan.

I can't WAIT to get out of Los Angeles, away from the Matrix to Dallas, and then, after Dallas, home. I only hope that somewhere else, but preferably in New York, *The Common Pursuit* will continue its new life. If only to justify the way I've spent the last six weeks.

## Sunday, 9 February

I was awoken at about eight this morning by a marital quarrel, full-throated, in the rooms next to mine. I gathered that the man had come back about an hour before, with the woman up waiting for him, demanding to know where he'd been. As their voices were blurred with rage and emotion, I couldn't get the details, though I did catch the following exchange:

From him: 'You've ruined my fucking life.'

From her: '*You've* ruined *my* fucking life.'

They went on for about an hour or so in this vein.

Had lunch with Kristoffer Tabori. He talked for the first time about what it had been like to go from director to leading man, and above all what it had been like to be directed by Sam Weisman, who hadn't consulted him when he took over on any aspect of the production. I took the opportunity – frankness being our agreed mode – to say that I had always believed it was a mistake for him to cast his wife, especially when the playwright was going to be around. He agreed that it had been a mistake, one he intended to avoid in the future, but added that he was certain she was by far the best Marigold available in Los Angeles. I couldn't argue with that. I think her performance, which I realize I have scarcely discussed in these reports, is quite superb. Simple, direct, unaffected. The other performance I haven't discussed is Chris Neame's as Peter, mainly because from the moment he got it right there was little to be said – he is the definitive Peter. If the play goes to New York, I would like to cast Kris Tabori, Judy Geeson, Chris Neame and, of course, old Nathan from the Matrix production, and get Michael Countryman and Peter Friedman from the Long Wharf production to play Martin and Humphry. Not that I think John Delancey, who has great presence, or Wayne Alexander, who is a very skilful actor, are bad, but I believe the other two would be definitive in the way that Chris Neame is definitive. Kristoffer Tabori and I also agreed – we spent a lot of time citing examples – that the Matrix production lacks fine tuning. Plenty of cues are either being rushed or not picked up quickly enough. I didn't say, my frankness not extending that far, that his own performance required considerable fine tuning and there are still moments when he is ponderous, explanatory, and even melodramatic. It was a very friendly lunch.

When I got back Joe phoned. He had nothing particular to say, just wanting to make contact. He sounded slightly depressed, so I suspect he has picked up something about the *Los Angeles Times* review which he doesn't want to divulge, for psychological reasons presumably. I can't say I give a damn, as long as it doesn't affect the run of the play. I shall be in Dallas when it comes out.

## Monday, 10 February

Last night was my last night ever, I trust, at the Matrix. Before the show I dispensed a few subversive notes to the actors, and then up to Antonio's for a quick large Scotch on ice, then back just ten minutes before the show came up. At the interval I hustled into the Café Melrose, also for the last time, and had a quick farewell cuddle with the Japanese (actually I'm still not sure of their nationality) daughter of the owner, who has waited on me these last six weeks. Then went back for the second act, which I thought was in excellent nick. There was a party in the theatre after the show – really, I suppose, a postponed First Night party. Anyway, it was typically First Nightish in that people one doesn't know and doesn't really want to talk to come up and talk to one knowingly. After an hour or so of just cruising about with glasses of bubbly in my hand, I made it to Joe Allen's, where I was joined by Kristoffer Tabori and Judy Geeson just after I'd phoned for a taxi to take me home. I sat with them for about five minutes, then Nathan Lane arrived with the warm-up comedienne. Nathan escorted me outside – I think I rather needed an escort – put me in a taxi, and back I came. Joe is picking me up tomorrow morning to take me to the airport, and then I shall be away from Los Angeles at last, though not comfortably or easily as I shall have to drag with me all my First Night gifts of bottles of champagne and bottles of malt whisky. And I shall be wearing heavy trousers, a thick shirt and carrying my raincoat and my sweater. Dallas is just as hot as Los Angeles apparently, if not hotter. I shall also be very tired, as I am now.

# 3

# Sitting on the Right Hand of God, or Was It John Wayne?

## Tuesday, 11 February 1986

I'm reporting into my machine from Room 328 of the Hyatt-Regency, or the Regency-Hyatt Hotel – I can't remember which way round it is – in Dallas, where I arrived yesterday evening. I spent part of yesterday morning (about ten minutes) packing, and the rest sitting on the balcony in the sunshine, finishing off a bottle of champagne and taking a long, dazed leave of the Matrix, Los Angeles, the Magic. Now and then I told myself that I ought to phone people – members of the cast, and so forth – to say goodbye, but somehow couldn't bring myself to do it, lacking both the natural impulse and the will. Nathan popped in and joined me on the balcony, but for once there didn't seem much for either of us to say. We looked down at the pool together, made a few comments on the personnel around it, he drained off his glass, then left. I lingered on until a few minutes after Joe was due to arrive to take me to the airport, then pausing only to stare at the winking video – I was leaving it to the fates, or Chip Estees or Donna from the video shop to deal with – I trudged for the last time out of the apartment, down the steps, around the pool, into the lobby where one of the sunnies was waiting for me with an enormous telephone bill. Presumably he was saving it up until a few minutes after I ought to have left in the hope of witnessing a final tantrum. It took ages to sort out, of course. They have computers at the Magic that are slightly slower than most human beings but might be faster than most Californians. We were still at it when Joe arrived, bearing with him twenty-five posters which he wanted me to sign and proposed to sell in the foyer of the Matrix. This seemed to be a more imperative piece of business, as far as he was concerned, than getting me out of the Magic and to the airport in time for my plane. I signed several on the counter – Sunny sunnying interminably about with my American Express card, actually losing it for a few minutes – and the rest in the car. Joe had to drive at such speed, darting around corners into short-cuts, that I have a suspicion that my signature will look like the work of a man unused to writing his name.

On the way we discussed the experience of the last six weeks. I said that my main feeling was that no production of a play, even one by me, was worth all the pain we had gone through. To my surprise, Joe agreed and went on to prognosticate yet again a poor review in the *Los Angeles Times*, saying he suspected that the critic, Dan O'Sullivan, would fail to allow himself the full experience of the play, taking it on instead as some kind of intellectual challenge. I said – I don't think it was much comfort to him – that my plays tended to get that kind of treatment, as the reviewers always seemed to think that they had in some way to square up to me, though more so in London than in the States, perhaps because my characters came from the sort of world London reviewers themselves inhabited. It was a kind of 'who-does-he-think-he-is?' syndrome. So we chatted, the usual kind of chat between a playwright and producer (except that we really do feel very comfortable with each other) all the way to the airport. When we got there I had to change my ticket. Joe had got me another of his cheapos, which this time seemed not even to be valid. He was parking the car and thus missed out on the acrimonious exchange at the counter which culminated in my handing over my American Express card. We walked to the gate together, touched each other on the arm, and then I was in the plane and off to Dallas for *Dog Days*.

I spent the journey in a kind of doze, an unpleasant doze actually. I was very tired, unable to think coherently, unable to read, without even a glass of champagne as there was no champagne about, even though I was travelling first class. I felt very bitter about this as I had been looking forward to two and a half hours cocooned in luxury, champagne in my mit. Stephen met me at the airport and drove me to this hotel. I must have asked all the correct and courteous questions, as he talked about how the rehearsals were going, but I wasn't really listening to him or to myself, I was still somewhere quite different, in fact still at the Matrix and *The Common Pursuit*. I did, however, manage to take in the Dallas skyline – enormous slabs of office buildings and hotels rising into the air in different forms, some of them seeming actually to be one-dimensional. It isn't unattractive, in fact it's rather stunning. The Regency-Hyatt or the Hyatt-Regency turned out to be one of these slabs, made out of marble, glass and concrete, quite graceful and certainly one of the most modern-looking buildings I've ever seen, let alone been inside of. The lobby is like an enormous shopping arcade, with restaurants, cafés, bars, shops and fountains, the whole enclosed in glass, with an escalator to take you to the car-park below and glass elevators to take you to the forty or so floors above – the antithesis of the Magic, in fact, with its small swimming-pool surrounded by Astroturf, and its minute lobby.

But in spite of its atmosphere of opulent high-tech efficiency, it took me nearly half an hour at reception to check in. Apparently a convention had just arrived and the computer had either broken down or was very slow, we couldn't make out which. The clerks were infuriatingly friendly, meeting my increasing impatience with bright smiles and warm Texan drawls. I was finally given the key to a room by a pretty blonde clerk (female) and as I turned to leave, was given the key to another room by another clerk (male) – the computer having booked me in twice. As I now had two rooms to choose from, one on the twenty-seventh floor, one on the third floor, I asked the second clerk which one he recommended. He plumped for the twenty-seventh, 'because it has a view'. So up we went to the twenty-seventh. As the elevator stopped at every floor, I had lots of time to summon up a memory of that film, *The Towering Inferno*, in which a hotel much like this one blazed to the ground. I found the film deeply satisfying at the time, being almost completely on the side of the fire and regretting only that it didn't manage to make a clean sweep of all the special guest stars, but in the elevator, climbing up in staccato bursts, like a maimed helicopter – they talk of 'riding' the elevator here – with my natural terror of heights somehow intensified by the receding and diminishing shops, bars, cafés and fountains in the lobby, the people turning into brightly coloured specks, like a nasty rash, and surrounded by threateningly affable Texans, most of them tall, all of them fat, I found myself not only recalling the film with deep distaste, but also on the very edge of a scream – I think I was actually in the grip of two terrors simultaneously, agoraphobia *and* claustrophobia. I knew, before we even saw the room, that the twenty-seventh floor was not for me, especially as the view it provided was not for me either – consisting of the most ghastly combination of flyovers, spaghetti junctions and car-parks that I've ever seen. Back down we went, I riding with my eyes firmly shut, to the lobby, where after a bit of a wait and altercations rising therefrom, I got the key to the third floor room – 328 – from which one can actually *walk* to the lobby. The room itself is identical to the one on the twenty-seventh floor, functional and comfortable, with an enormous bed facing a television set. Except in smell. Twenty-seven had no smell. Three-two-eight smells distinctly marshy, as if fetid waters have recently passed through it. Also, being up to date in all its details, it has windows that can't be opened, and an air-conditioner that howls lightly while chilling you to the marrow. Oh Magic, my Magic . . .

I ordered up a fridge, a complicated business, naturally, involving much discussion with hostesses, engineers, stewards, clerks. When it arrived, I installed in it all the champagne that I'd lugged from Los Angeles, so that it would at least be cold, then opened one of the bottles of Glenfiddich, had a few drinks, lay down on the bed, phoned Beryl, passed into a light coma. From which I was disturbed by Stephen, returning from the theatre to take me out to dinner.

I was, of course, wretchedly tired from my six weeks at the Matrix and from the airplane journey, and quite drunk from airplane wine and large, self-administered malts. The last thing I wanted was to go out to dinner. But out I went, with Stephen and his assistant, a chap called Michael Yorda, who is half German, half Cherokee Indian, and on a first, blurred viewing, very pleasant – at least he took the cheque Joe had given me to cover my Los Angeles expenses and said he would give me cash for it, which seemed to me a very pleasant thing to do. The truth is, the pitiful truth is, I don't remember much about the evening except the bad bits, like having to focus on three or four versions of Stephen and Michael Yorda, trying to force the restaurant to settle down while I got food from my mouth to my stomach, then wavering to my feet, demanding to be taken back to my hotel, where, fortunately after I'd made it to my room, I was attacked by the squitters. A savage bout. Went to bed but – Dallas is three hours behind Los Angeles so my system is out of kilter – though I felt very tired, and was drunk and comatose, couldn't get to sleep. Instead I lay fretting and fuming about the Matrix and *The Common Pursuit*. Then when I did get to sleep at last, at about five in the morning, Stephen woke me with a call from the lobby five minutes later it seemed, though in reality it was a quarter to ten, time to go to the rehearsal – my first rehearsal – of *Dog Days*. I told him I simply wasn't up to it, bad night, squitters, monomania, etc. – almost the first time in my life that I've skipped a rehearsal as an author, and on this occasion I'm also meant to be the director, co-director, anyway. We arranged to meet at lunch time, for a run-through in the afternoon.

I went back to sleep, was awoken by Joe, in an absolute frenzy because O'Sullivan, the reviewer for the *Los Angeles Times*, had come up with a review that was exactly as Joe had predicted: ponderous, dull, telling the whole story of the play, recounting every twist, however minor, of the plot, analysing every character in clotted detail. It wasn't exactly an unfavourable review – did he want me to read it? (I didn't.) It paid me compliments which it then dumpily qualified; the trouble wasn't that it was unfavourable, but that it was boring and unhelpful, the most boring and unhelpful review he'd ever read. And sedentary. A sedentary review. He was particularly incensed because O'Sullivan had gone out and bought a copy of the London version of the play, and quoted a line from that text – a line I'd hated so much that I'd cut it *before* we opened in London* – as proof that the London version was better. At which point I, who'd gone in for soothing Joe, became incensed myself. I mean, here is this chap O'Sullivan, who'd read but not seen the London production, preferring its text to the text of the Matrix production, which he'd seen but not read – and adducing as evidence a line that hadn't even turned up in the London production. Since the London production I'd worked on the script for the Long Wharf, worked on it again in London before the Matrix production, worked on it in Los Angeles while casting the Matrix production, and worked on it during rehearsals of the Matrix production, and if I knew anything in my bones, *anything*, it was that the current version of the play is vastly superior to the Long Wharf version, which in its turn was vastly superior to the London version. And yet O'Sullivan, with a lax, no, imbecile clatter of his typewriter, negates all those weeks of work . . . And so forth. So forth. So forth. Normal sort of response on receiving news of a review. The other main review was very good for the play, less good for the production, going after Kristoffer Tabori especially, but was at least, Joe said, written with a certain liveliness, and would make people want to go and see for themselves. So back to O'Sullivan –

* The first Methuen text, which was published to coincide with the opening of the play, could not therefore include cuts and changes made in rehearsals or previews.

various other critics had phoned Joe to express their indignation, Joe himself was going to phone him up and have it out with him for being so boring, what did I think about writing in a complaint myself? I said I really didn't see the point, nothing I could say would stop O'Sullivan from being O'Sullivan, he might even enjoy opening what he'd no doubt call 'a dialogue' between us, and besides, it sounded like the usual sort of review, *my* usual sort of review. He agreed, reluctantly, and then went on to admit that it probably didn't matter too much, as the show was an established success, the word of mouth was 'great', and on that note – in rather high spirits, actually – he hung up.

I lay on in bed, obliterating all thoughts of tossing lumps of O'Sullivan to the hounds for their breakfast, and didn't, finally, drag myself up, out of my room, and down to one of the smaller hotel bars until one in the afternoon, that bar and that time being where and when I'd arranged to meet Stephen. A mistake, as it turned out, as that particular bar doesn't open until four in the afternoon, which seems to me a most eccentric hour for a bar to open, being the only time in the day when I don't want a drink. So I went to the main bar, which is right out in the concourse, in the open, ordered up a glass of champagne and some smoked sausage, and kept an eye open for Stephen, already late by my reckoning. In fact, he arrived an hour later, at two o'clock, checking my indignation – 'The hours of my life I've wasted by being on time,' I quoted* – with the assurance that I'd got it wrong, he'd explained on the phone that though he'd break rehearsals at one, he had other theatre business to attend to and wouldn't get to the hotel until two. Actually I'd enjoyed my hour in the lobby, watching the men in their stetsons and boots, the women in their furs. Furs. To combat the air-conditioning, I suppose, as it was hot and humid outside.

We drove down a number of ugly streets, to a rather nice section of town – the *only* nice section of town, Stephen informed me – where the theatre is. He introduced me to the stage management, the lighting designer, the set designer, etc., and to the actors, and then we crossed the street, cut through a parking lot, and went into the large rehearsal room, situated on the ground floor of a mostly unlet office block. Stephen started the run immediately. It was a bit

* Bernard Malamud.

tight and choked – the four actors were evidently nervous – but I was more pleased with the play than I'd expected. It struck me as an odd piece, written by a self (fifteen years ago) that I am no longer in touch with, but it has its own character all right. Anyway it certainly isn't the nasty little specimen I'd worked myself up into hating in London and in Los Angeles.

We broke at about five thirty, and went to an Irish bar around the corner for a drink, where we were interrupted almost immediately by the theatre critic of one of the Dallas newspapers, also called Dan, as in O'Sullivan, whose second name I didn't catch. He was youngish (i.e. younger than me) and leanish (i.e. leaner than me), saturnine, serious and seemed to be favourably disposed, claiming to believe, without serious prompting, that there was a general critical consensus to downgrade my work, a conspiracy almost, of which – he assured me – he wasn't part. I had a sudden vision of this conspiracy, literary-looking men in capes, scuffling at midnight through the streets to anonymous bars where they laid their further plots to downgrade me – it made complete and satisfying sense. He went on, though, to make it clear that he was familiar with the text of *Dog Days* – he'd read it several times – believed that it was a good play *in embryo*; but was alarmed to discover (from me) that I'd cut the Prologue and the Coda, in many ways his favourite scenes. He hoped, very much hoped, that I could transform the embryo into a mature adult, though sombrely hinting that I might have hampered myself somewhat by lopping off its head and balls.

After the interview Stanley Wilson (playing Peter), Karen Ratcliffe (playing Hilary), Stephen and I went to a nearby Italian restaurant called Lombardi's for dinner. I didn't enjoy the occasion much as I was still tired, gastricly shaky, and full of Scotches imbibed before and during my session with Dan the Critic. I got a taxi back to the hotel, slouched into the bar for a last malt, then came up here, lay down on the bed, fell asleep. I woke up half an hour ago, and began dictating this. I'm now lying full-length on the bed, still dressed, the tape recorder still to my mouth as I watch a girl undressing in a slow, unstately fashion. She's now caressing somewhat dappled breasts, which she is thrusting at me. So this is the sort of thing that goes on, on television, in the Regency-Hyatt or Hyatt-Regency in Dallas. In room 328, anyway.

## Wednesday, 12 February

Slept badly. Was woken at seven by music from what I took to be the radio or television in the next room. Lay in bed cursing this extraordinary hotel, with its high-tech wizardry and its transparent bug-like elevators, that yet can't provide sound-proofed rooms for their guests. Cursed also the people next door for playing their radio or television at such an hour, heaved myself out of bed, put on minimal togs, left my room with the intention of beating on the door of theirs, and discovered, by looking over the rail of the passage outside my room, that the music was coming from the lobby – there was a chap at the bar playing the piano. There he was, in a suit, playing the piano, at seven in the morning. So porno films at midnight, piano-players at dawn, at the Hyatt-Regency in Dallas, Texas.

When I went down to have breakfast at ten, the pianist had gone. Presumably home to bed, for a decent morning's sleep. I sat at a table, sipping coffee, contemplating the amazing lobby, my eye tracking one of the transparent bugs sliding up the wall, the people in it looking like the bug's innards, and then tracking up past the last stopping place of the bug, right up to the ceiling, where there is a network of iron rafters, and saw – I nearly threw up – a child sitting on one of the rafters, playing with a balloon before popping it. I couldn't get myself away from him – I kept trying to fix my eyes on my coffee, but they lifted immediately to this diminutive figure, a hundred feet or so above me, on a strip of metal, playing with a balloon, popping it, scampering on his buttocks to another balloon, reaching out for it, cuddling and patting it, popping it, then off after another one – there were about twenty balloons bobbing about up there, in all. My main impulse was to bellow out warnings both to the boy and to officials down below, but deciding that this was after all Texas, and I hadn't yet had time to acquaint myself with the customs, I inquired casually of the waitress who that was up there, doing what, eh? He was the window-cleaner, she said. Clearing out the balloons that had drifted to the rafters during some festivities down here last night. And of course he wasn't a child, he was a grown man, attached to the rafters by ropes and a pulley I couldn't see from where I sat.

Stephen arrived. We went to the theatre and I began the day's rehearsals, the plan being that Stephen should absent himself until

I'd had my way with the actors. We spent the day working from the top of the play. It is the first session in the theatre that I've actually enjoyed since arriving all those weeks ago in Los Angeles. The actors were eager to get on with it, seeming vastly to prefer work to conspiracies and explosions, while I enjoyed exploring the play, finding myself obliged to direct it as if it had been written by somebody else, which in a sense it was. I couldn't *remember* any of the intentions in the lines, which therefore had to be found as if for the first time.

Stephen suggested that we all go to a show in the evening, but I couldn't face it, feeling tired and limp. I came back to the hotel, lay on the bed, and watched on their cable television one of the foulest films I've ever seen – *Deathwish III*, with Charles Bronson – about a pack of hooligans beating up people in a run-down residential neighbourhood in an unspecified American town, and then being beaten up in their turn by Charles Bronson. The director scarcely bothered to motivate the violence. I was so drugged with fatigue – I had a large Scotch in my hand, needless to say – that I kept slipping into a doze and swimming out of it, to find Bronson smashing somebody's face, or somebody smashing somebody else's face which would then be Bronson's excuse for smashing his face – these unspeakable images no doubt woven into the fabric of a nightmare. I went down, had a pleasant, solitary dinner, reading Sidney Sheldon,* came back and read some more, turned on the television set, immediately fell into a doze again. Woke at midnight, tried to sleep and couldn't, kept on reading until two or three. It must have been three, I think, when I turned my light off. Was woken again by the bloody pianist. 'Shoot the pianist' is becoming my slogan. As we all know, guns are easy to come by in Dallas.

## Thursday, 13 February

Another normal and sensible working day interrupted only occasionally by the alarming behaviour of our non-Equity actress,† Cindy Vance. It's irritating enough that our rehearsals frequently have to be organized around her drama-school timetable – she

* I hope that this was a different Sidney Sheldon from the Sidney Sheldon I was reading in Los Angeles.

† The New Arts Theatre had a deal with Equity which allowed them to use one non-Equity member in every so many productions.

either can't or won't come in when she's got a workshop, seminar, whatever – but what makes it worse is that nobody seems to have taught her any of the basic acting stuff.* She certainly hasn't been taught, or anyway hasn't learnt, that the simpler her performance the more effective it will be. She delivers almost every sentence either quaveringly or with a trill of laughter running through it (thus rendering the words incomprehensible) and accompanies it with gestures of the hand, twitches of the shoulders, tappings of the feet – quite hard to take, especially as she has a brazenly democratic attitude to the rehearsal process – the consequence, I suspect, of a confidently Republican upbringing. At one point she stopped in the middle of the run of a scene, to denounce my placing of her – 'I don't like this. I don't feel comfortable doing this. I'll do something else here' – leaving her accomplished and professional colleagues (Stanley Wilson and Michael Rothaar) dangling while she tried out a series of new positions that bore no relation to the purpose of the scene, or to the positions of the two other actors involved in it. I stood, dumb with disbelief, watching this, then heard myself croak out that 'we'll get on with it, shall we, from where we were when we stopped, all right?' and waved Stanley Wilson and Michael Rothaar back into action. I thought that that would be the end of *that*, but a mere few minutes later she introduced without warning a piece of business that was neither in the script nor had been hinted at by either of her directors.

I broke rehearsals immediately, went for a brief but brisk walk around the room, out of the door, along the corridor, back into the room and around it once again, attempting to calm myself down by telling myself that after all Cindy Vance was a mere girl (actually in her mid-twenties, and working for her MA degree – so not a mere girl, merely an unqualified actress playing a mere girl), jolly lucky to have her, important not to create an atmosphere by losing my temper, etc., and finally returned to the group to find Michael Rothaar and Stanley Wilson sitting apprehensively to one side, while Cindy Vance, bubbling with good spirits, demonstrated some aerobics, or gymnastics, anyway some sort of relaxing exercises that she said everybody – presumably she meant *me* as well – ought to take up. But there must have been something about me – perhaps simply my cheeks, swollen and empurpled with suppressed rage –

* An echo here, I now detect, of Sam Weisman.

that had an effect, because from then on the rehearsal proceeded without Cindy's improvising new business or rearranging the blocking. By the end of the afternoon I'd got her to play her scenes with her hands, metaphorically, in her pockets. The next time she can manage to squeeze in a rehearsal I'll try to find the equivalent to a pocket for her voice. I have an idea that she's quite talented, and will turn out to be rather good. Patience. Yes, patience. That's all that's required, really, for harmony and progress.

After rehearsals Stephen drove me back to the hotel, where we had dinner in a restaurant perched at the top of a tower. In fact, having a restaurant perched on its top seemed to be the tower's sole reason for existing. The glass-sided elevator that took us up to it was run by a young woman called Marj, according to a button on her lapel, who pointed out vertiginous views of some of Dallas's car-parks. I felt pretty sick by the time we stepped into the restaurant which turned out to have a revolving floor and glass walls, so that after a girl called Robyn ('Hi there, I'm Robyn and I'm going to look after you') had led us to a table, we could by degrees take in vertiginous views of *all* the Dallas car-parks, which seemed to be the sum total of what Dallas amounts to, at ground-level seen from high above. I still hadn't recovered from my elevator nausea when Stephen began to succumb to a nausea induced by the revolving floor. Not an altogether successful dinner, in fact, for all of Robyn's epigrams and *bon mots*, but we hung on there for hours, lacking the will to escape.

Back in 328 I slotted a tape of *Criss-Cross* into the video – I'd brought the tape from Los Angeles; the video had been hired for me by Karen Ratcliffe (our leading lady) and installed, in a matter of minutes, by the hotel electrician – lay down on the bed, to watch it.

I woke some time after midnight to find myself fully clothed on the bed, the tape humming in the video and a sinister crackling sound coming from the screen across which dots and blobs were racing. I wound the film back, put myself slowly to bed, fearful that I was going to fall asleep while still standing, turned off the light, and promptly became wide awake. By three in the morning my mind was humming along familiar tracks of resentment, some of which led right back to childhood, and a swine of a prep-school master called Mister Brown, who used to beat me savagely and regularly for reasons so arbitrary that he eventually stopped bothering to offer them.

## Friday, 14 February

A good morning's work, Stanley Wilson (our leading man) finding charm and humour in the perilous long scene at the beginning of the play. At the break I took him out to lunch – I gather that he's currently a trifle short of funds – and talked, gossiped, really, about his part. It was very pleasant and relaxed, perhaps too much so, as the wine I allowed him to consume induced a very different mood in the afternoon. No charm, very little wit, but a great deal of snarling ill-temper interspersed with bouts of melancholy. I was struggling to recall him to his pre-lunch lightness when the door burst open and a rather plain girl, short and stocky, strode in. She was wearing high-heeled shoes, tights, a little skirt, and above her waist, on her bosom and her back, two red, heart-shaped cushions. She was also carrying about thirty balloons. 'Which one of you gentlemen is Mr Rothaar?' she demanded. I pointed – as did Stanley Wilson, Karen Ratcliffe and Cynthia Vance – at Michael. She advanced on him, tunelessly singing a song of love, even of adoration. She sang several further songs, her face pressing closer and closer to his, told him three dreadful jokes, pressed the balloons into one hand, a telegram into the other, kissed him on the cheeks, and left. Throughout it all Michael stood there with his jaw dropped – this is a literal description. His jaw fell away from the upper part of his face, and stayed down. But there was something else in his look, his posture – a kind of awkward, shy pleasure at having been remembered on Valentine's Day, I suppose.

When I popped into the theatre later I found a message from Joe, asking me to phone. I caught him at the Matrix, positively jubilant. He told me that he was thinking of coming to Dallas to see an early preview, how was I, how were the rehearsals going, and then got to his main course which was that everything was humming in Los Angeles, *The Common Pursuit* was a big hit, sold out for days ahead, and that all the reviews except the two that he'd phoned me about the last time had been 'raves'. He also said that O'Sullivan of the *Los Angeles Times* had been besieged by telephone calls and letters. When Joe himself had rung him up to remonstrate, he had replied that he was very proud of his review because 'he had conducted the analysis on a high intellectual level'. On the other hand some guy had phoned the theatre to reserve tickets – quite a few tickets – and when Joe had asked him why he had decided to bring a whole party, had said that anything that O'Sullivan wasn't passionate about was for him.

I went back to Lombardi's to have a drink with Stanley Wilson who dropped me at the hotel after initially mistaking the route and driving off across a bridge that threatened to carry us to somewhere even more Texan than Dallas. We went at least twenty miles out of the way, and when I finally made it to 328 I discovered that the video had been disconnected – all the wires were out – and none of the lights worked. I phoned down to the chap who'd installed the video. He came up, reinstalled it, got the lights working, and informed me that as my fridge was connected to one of the light plugs, it functioned only when the light was on. For hours during the night, therefore, the fridge stopped freezing and all the food – not much food, some grapes and a strange bowl of something that looks like gelatine which the management sent up with the fridge, compliments of the house – had been rotting away. Which explains the smell. I'd been beginning to wonder whether it might be coming from my feet, as I haven't changed my shoes for something like six weeks.

## Sunday, 16 February

I was woken before dawn by a nightmare to do with the safety of my family. I phoned home to make sure everyone was all right, and got Lucy, back from school for the weekend, who was extremely cheerful and I think a mite perplexed to hear a kind of grave but unexplained undertone of worry in her father's voice. When I spoke to Beryl, she asked me not to phone again at six in the morning Dallas time (midday London) as my voice was sluggish, and the pauses between my sentences were rather taxing on the attention. I coasted back to sleep and had another nightmare or dream, it was part nightmare, part dream. I was trying to get into a memorial service at the Albert Hall (Beryl had told me that there had been a memorial service that morning for Philip Larkin, and that she'd seen Harold right in the centre of the congregation on television) but the auditorium was packed. I finally managed to climb up to the top tier and was walking along it on the outside when I brushed against a boy who was standing on a kind of plank, so sending him tumbling to his death in the crowd below. I think I was identified, and also identified as being drunk, which I might or might not have been – how does one know in a dream? – got back out into the street, above all being shaken by not being shaken at having caused a death. Suddenly something zoomed into the ground – it was a kind of disc – a turret shot out, some stuff was puffed into my face and I sort of froze. My face froze and I froze. People screamed, ran to call the police. An old-fashioned bus with rocket-like exhausts arrived. I was escorted aboard, shown to a small room with a chair in it, and was told by two very pleasant men that I was being taken off to a planet, whose name I can't recall, to serve three and a half years in the penitentiary there. I began to expostulate – in a deeply depressed way, because I knew that somehow this was my proper fate – that I should surely let my family and friends know what was happening to me. They explained that this, on the whole, was not allowed. They were perfectly affable. We sped off through the air and I said, but I can't spend all my time sitting in this room on this seat. They said not to worry too much, some kind of gas would render me unconscious for most of the journey, and that anyway I would find my three and a half years of servitude in a penitentiary extremely pleasant ones as they were going to call on my particular gifts as a writer and a teacher, had I ever thought of doing the lecture circuit in America? – this is all absolutely as it went – because I could make an enormous amount of money. But they also kept on saying at interludes, as I recall, that three and a half years was a very long time, I must have done something serious. They couldn't imagine why somebody of my nature and status should be serving three and a half years in a penitentiary on this other planet. I didn't formulate it then – because of the wisdom of their manner – that it seemed to me an impertinence to impose their penal or moral code on aliens. After a while we had to stop to pick up a baby with a deformed skull, who was put down beside me. I couldn't think what its offence might have been, or was it perhaps going to this other planet's casualty ward? We also stopped for refueling somewhere where Marlon Brando was acting in a film. We went for a walk down the street in which there were humming-birds and squirrels singing, as in one of the old Walt Disneys.

There the dream ended. But it hung around inside me, in my nervous system it almost seemed, so that all my perceptions were slightly odd, even in rehearsals, which began at midday. The scenes we worked on struck me as quite unreal, as did the actors, the props, the walls of the room. But I plugged on, plugged on, stopping scenes, starting them, running them through until everything gradually slipped back into a kind of sense, and I began to enjoy myself again. By the time we broke, at seven, I felt fairly normal, anyway no longer dream-ridden, nightmare-haunted, whatever it was, and by the time I was in Lombardi's settling into the malts, I felt comfortable, tired and pretty good. Stephen came in, looking alarmed, to say he'd been waiting in his office, had I forgotten the party? I said I didn't know anything about any party, except the small one I was holding by myself, of course. He said I had to come, we had to leave now. This minute. 'Not on your Nelly,' I said. Hard day. Needed a rest. Another drink or two. Quiet dinner. Video. Sheldon. Early night. He explained, slowly, gravely, not to say imploringly, that the party was being given by rich patrons of the theatre, that I was the guest of honour, that my absence would give enormous offence.

Off we went, to the upper and monied reaches of Dallas, where the houses were enormous, some of them the size of little castles, but the surrounding countryside was parched and drear. We arrived late, having started late and then getting lost on the way, and I didn't realize until I was through the doors and inside the massive living room, packed with dinner-jackets and long gowns, that I was still in my rehearsal clothes, scruffier even than I'd been at Roddy McDowall's dinner party, and no doubt flushed both with ill-temper and the couple of drinks I'd already downed. Somebody – I suppose the host, though it could well have been a waiter – pressed into my hand the largest glass of Scotch I've ever seen. In fact it looked like a glass of lager. I swayed at the very sight of it. Around me the dinner-jackets and long gowns clustered, engaging me and each other in conversation of exotic banality – I mean the subjects were banal, but the accents and vocabulary were exotic. I expect I cut a pretty disturbing figure back at them, down at heel, gruffly monosyllabic, my tankard of whisky dwindling by the second.

The only person – a middle-aged woman – with whom I managed to have what seemed to me a reasonable conversation turned out to be from New York and Jewish, running a large theatre in a nearby city, or was it state, but before we could settle properly into comparisons and gossip she was elbowed aside by a strange-looking and adhesive Pole, who'd just escaped from Gdansk. He had been a teacher of theatre there but now, by routes too complicated to fathom, was lecturing in a college in Dallas. Frankly, though I would wish no one in Gdansk who doesn't want to be there, I did wish that this particular chap hadn't made it all the way to Dallas – couldn't he have been stopped in Mesquite, a place outside Dallas that I don't like the sound of? It wasn't only that he was boring, noisy and mainly incomprehensible, but also that he covered me with his spittle, some of which got into my whisky. Which I drained off anyway. At that point Stephen reappeared, took in my swaying figure; my large, ominously empty glass; my frenzied companion, then summoned Stanley Wilson and Karen Ratcliffe, and got us back to a restaurant near the New Arts, *not* Lombardi's. I began to go very fast. I was both exhausted and drunk. I have a dim memory of attempting to describe my dream, a dimmer memory of being deposited back at the hotel, but have no memory of what transpired in my room. Whether I watched *Criss-Cross* or what.

## Monday, 17 February

Stephen phoned me before I was properly awake to remind me that we were expected to give a couple of talks – one at lunchtime, one in the evening – to students at a college with a Shakespearian-pastoral name, Arcadia perhaps, outside Dallas. I said I'd have to cancel, too busy with rehearsals, etc. He said, 'Today's Monday. No rehearsals.' I said, ah, well in that case I'd spend the morning in my room meditating, in the afternoon perhaps a stroll downtown, where I'd chat with the natives on such subjects as Karl Marx and transsexuality, while poking mild fun at their accents and clothes. He said, 'They're paying you a lot of money for these talks. It's an hour's drive. I'll pick you up at 11.15 on the nose,' thus allowing me a mere forty-five minutes to bath, shave, get dressed, drink some champagne. In twelve minutes flat, spruce and thirsty, I sped in a dignified way down to the bar, where a splendid-looking Indian or Pakistani, polishing glasses behind the counter, greeted me as follows: 'Hello there, how are you today, nice to see you, sorry I can't serve you yet, bar doesn't open until eleven.' I sped back up to my room, paced about fuming – in both the English and the French senses – until one minute to eleven, then sped back down to the bar, arriving just in time to see the Indian or Pakistani strutting rapidly away from it, off across the foyer.

I sat down at a table and fixed my concentration on the only other customer, a small, thin, middle-aged man with spectacles wearing civvies (i.e. no stetson, no high heels, just a business-like suit, black shoes) who was working his pocket calculator as he checked through some accounts or something. At seven minutes past eleven by my watch the barman returned, carrying a tray of money, which he then organized into his till, patting the different denominations into their compartments, rolling the coins into their troughs. When he'd finished he turned to the computer-accounts chap, listened closely to his order, and to my amazement strutted rapidly off again, his figure dwindling into the lobby's distant reaches. Four minutes later he returned with a pot of coffee, presumably fetched from one of the many places in the lobby that serve it, placed it before the computer and accounts bugger, then took my order for a glass of champagne – two glasses, actually, as they're diminutive at the Hyatt. Of course he had trouble opening the bottle, trouble locating the glasses, trouble slicing the strawberries, trouble getting the strawberries to perch on the rim of the glasses, trouble remembering who it was he was going to all this trouble for, finally bringing the drinks to me at the very second that Stephen arrived to take me away from them. I swilled them down on my feet, then jogged across the lobby, down some corridors, around some corners, into a lavatory all of whose urinals were blocked except one which, I'm proud to report, was the one I chose to pee into, jogged back to Stephen waiting at the car exit, and off we went, through the sleaze of downtown Dallas, through one of its wasteland suburbs, along a freeway and on to a ribbon road and eventually off that into a car-park that encircled the Arcadian-sounding college like a moat. A pleasant lady of about fifty in a white suit greeted us at the reception bunker, and guided us to a younger woman, small, dark, intense, who claimed, as she led us towards the lecture room, to be familiar with all my works.

In the car Stephen had told me that we would be addressing a smallish group, almost a seminar, of two dozen or so. Waiting in the vast hall were something like two hundred people, sitting or standing in rows around a stage on to which we were led. There were no chairs, no table, only the small, intense woman who was now holding a microphone. She spoke into it, droning and garrulous, sketching out a theological scheme in which Harold sat plumb at the top as God,* I down on his right as either Jesus Christ or the Holy Ghost, I couldn't quite make out which, though I suspect that if I hadn't been present in the flesh I'd only have scraped in, if at all, as one of the minor prophets. She then handed me the microphone, informing me that when I'd finished speaking I was to hand it to Stephen, then informed Stephen that when he'd finished speaking he was to hand it back to me, which meant that in the unlikely event of our dialogue turning snappy, we'd end up passing it back and forth like a couple of old-style comics in a radio skit. I led off by saying here we were, Stephen and I, nice to see them all, wasn't it, Stephen? Had they any questions, be happy to answer them, wouldn't we, Stephen? The first question – 'What do you use to write with?' – wasn't the most stupid; the second – 'What about your personal life?' – wasn't the most impertinent. It went on and on, the questions so valueless that eventually we took to answering on a kind of rota system, doing ten minutes or so each, without concern as to which of us was being addressed.

After well over an hour, the small, intense lady, who thought (and almost certainly still thinks) that Harold is God, took the microphone back, introduced us all over again, then closed down the proceedings by inviting us through the microphone, and therefore publicly, to a brown-bag lunch. Stephen, whose mind can work with the speed of a cornered rat in this sort of situation, explained smoothly that, alas, we had to get back to the theatre where there was a crisis over the set, but we'd have everything sorted out before our second session in the evening. 'Now there's a little problem there,' she said. 'Our evening session won't be in here, it'll be in the large theatre, there are always two or three times the number in the evening, about, well four or five hundred you'll

* Evidence that Harold's status, if not actually divine, is unusually high in the order of things was provided shortly after my return to London. We were having dinner out *à quatre* – i.e. with wives – when we fell, late in the evening, into a dispute. A rather fierce dispute. It was still unresolved when Harold declared himself too tired to continue. I offered to call him up a taxi while calling up one for myself and made a specific point to the dispatcher of demanding my taxi immediately, the one for Mr Pinter to follow in due course, without urgency – 'in twenty minutes or so would do' – my plan, of course, being to exit with dignity, rather than to be exited from by a dignified Harold. It was hard to believe it, therefore, when his taxi arrived almost before I got back to the table, while mine turned up in not much under half an hour. It's just possible that there was nothing miraculous about this – taxis no doubt preferring to go to Holland Park than all the way up to Highgate – but at the time it felt like an intervention of some sort.

be talking to, I won't be there myself, I've got other festival duties. But somebody will look after you. Thank you, thank you so much, hope we meet again some time.' So back we went, Stephen and I, around the car-park, down the ribbon road, on to the freeway, through the sleaze, past the Wendy Inns and hamburger joints and wasteland to the New Arts, where we did indeed look in on the set – in the earliest stage of construction and therefore virtually indecipherable – and then to Lombardi's for a leisurely meal, over which we tried to guess at the contents of a brown-bag lunch, then back I came to the hotel for a brief nap, and then back we went, Stephen and I, through the sleaze and wasteland to the freeway, on to the ribbon road, into the moat-like car-park of the Arcadian college.

We were met by – actually I don't know who the hell we were met by. I don't have the slightest recollection of anything about her but a mop of ginger hair and pendulous green slacks, seen from behind as she led us off to the lecture hall – not the larger one we'd been warned about, but a much smaller one, classroom sized, in fact, where we found ourselves confronted by rather fewer than the five hundred we'd been dreading. Four hundred and ninety-three fewer, to be accurate, as there were seven people in the audience.

## Tuesday, 18 February

Stephen collected me at ten o'clock, and drove me to a local radio station, where we were scheduled to give a joint interview. The station was located in the usual devastation of vacant lots and car-parks, in which Stephen got lost, driving out of them on to a motorway that led back several minutes and miles further on into what looked like the section we'd driven away from. Arrived late, therefore, having parked in a patch of marsh (the result of overnight rain) and then having had to pick our way through partially cemented paths into a deserted lobby. We pressed a buzzer, banged on the counter, shouted hellos, then wandered down a corridor to a small studio, where a tall man with a grey beard was waiting for us. He beckoned us in through semi-opaque windows, then sent Stephen straight out again, saying he didn't want him to be in the interview. Stephen went back to the lobby. I asked the greybeard if he minded my smoking. He said yes, he did mind. I said, 'Sorry, but I smoke, OK? What about you?' I asked the engineer. 'Do you mind?' 'Yes,' he said, 'I mind. But thanks for the courtesy of asking.' 'Not at all,' I said. 'Not at all.'

The engineer went behind his partition, the greybeard tested his mike, I lit up a cigarette, the interview began. It went on for twenty minutes, stopping when the engineer signalled despair to the interviewer. Apparently my voice had been so faint, so enfeebled and vitiated by life in first Los Angeles and now Dallas, that almost nothing I'd said had been audible. Start again. Greybeard took me through exactly the same questions as before, though introducing me in strikingly different terms. The first time round he'd described me as the most prominent playwright in the country (my country, I assumed he meant). The second time round he introduced me as 'one of the more prominent playwrights'. So, in the course of two virtually identical interviews, I'd succeeded in having myself substantially downgraded. We then plodded through the same set of questions, getting halfway to where we'd been the first time, when the door swung open and a man, also with a grey beard, wearing laundered blue jeans and an odd jacket – I don't remember what was odd about it, I just remember noticing that it was odd – and with a clutch of keys dangling from his belt, staggered in. Greybeard ordered him out. Alternative greybeard stood in the studio shouting defiance, then turned, and went out, around to the semi-opaque window, through which he mouthed abuse. Greybeard mouthed abuse back at him, then told me to ignore him – 'Just a guy who runs a local bookshop. He buys advertising time, thinks he owns the place. Let's get on with it, eh?' But there was nothing to get on with, as he became suddenly rather listless, couldn't be bothered to ask me any more of the questions he'd already asked me, and ushered me out of the door with the warning that when the interview was broadcast it would be followed immediately by his review of the play.

In the lobby the bookseller was sitting on a sofa, jangling his keys and muttering. Stephen was standing by the door, rueful at the waste of his time, desperate to be off. He had some trouble getting out of the parking lots, but eventually made it to Lombardi's, where we had a quick lunch. Then into the theatre for a technical run, during which I tried not to concentrate on the set, which nevertheless struck me as ghastly, having in common with the Matrix set for *The Common Pursuit* a high and dominating, i.e. actor-dwarfing, effect, but was unlike the Matrix in that it was so flimsy – almost to the point of transparency – that I felt I could have looked right through it if I peered hard enough at its drably painted walls, which shook when the actors moved. I was pretty sure that the floor shook too.

Stephen and I had a dejected dinner at Lombardi's, discussing the set and what could be done about it, the set designer and what should be done to him, and then back to the New Arts for another technical run that at least, now and then, gave me an opportunity to do some work with the actors. I got back to the hotel at about midnight, slunk into the bar for some malts, then came upstairs, lay on my bed and watched a film Karen Ratcliffe had lent me – a John Wayne/John Ford film that I'd never even heard of, let alone seen – a kind of Victorian melodrama about three desperadoes redeemed by a baby that they have rescued by mistake, and are toting across the desert. Two of them are taken out by a combination of Indians, snakes and thirst, but Big John Wayne, looking both curvaceously masculine and overpoweringly maternal, struggles on to salvation, the babe in his arms. Throughout John Ford had his chorus singing away as usual, only more so. The experience of the film was so bizarre that I couldn't help wondering whether I wasn't making it up. I mean could anyone, even John Ford at his peak, seriously make a film like *The Three Godfathers*? It made me cry a bit, of course, but I cry at almost any film that has choruses singing old Western songs. And John Wayne carrying babies. Though I prefer him carrying guns. After the film I settled into a coma.

## Wednesday, 19 February

Woke up pretty late, and lay on in bed, coasting seraphically, until Beryl phoned. I told her about my life here in Dallas, she told me about hers there in London, we agreed that I'd be home by Tuesday – I'd already told someone at the theatre to book me on to a plane on Monday. I hung up, sinking into a positively voluptuous drowsiness, before getting around to confronting the real facts, the hard facts, about my immediate future, which were: that I had to shave; I had to shower; I had to wash my hair; I had to cut my fingernails, which are beginning to curve around my fingertips like talons; I had to find some way of sawing off my toenails, which are threatening to slice through my soft leather shoes (only pair). I started on my hair in the shower, then had a long, hot bath in the hope of softening my nails down to the clippable. In fact, I was just climbing out of the bath to deal with them, when the phone rang. A woman from the New Arts publicity department to say that she had just sent a journalist over to the hotel to interview me, she would be arriving in fifteen minutes, was that all right? All right? My hair was wet, in fact I was wet all over, and yet in fifteen minutes, without having had any breakfast let alone a glass of champagne, I was going to have to cope with some woman journalist. I said no, sorry, can't, I'm drying myself, I've got to get dressed, I haven't had breakfast, put her off. OK? But of course it was too late to put her off. She was already on her way.

I went down to the bar and downed a glass or two of champagne, my main thought being that it was up to her to find me, and who in the world, apart from anybody who knew me, would think of looking in the bar at that time of the morning? She arrived within minutes, flanked by officious personnel from both the theatre and the hotel, who led her straight to my table, without even having checked out, as far as I could tell, either my room or the various coffee shops. She plonked herself opposite me, and there she stayed. She was a bit older than me, handsome, with a sort of wart on her lip – to the right side of her lip. Spectacles, over which she peered in the manner of a flirtatiously reproving school teacher. A widow. I can't remember what particular questions she asked me, though I do remember that several were highly personal. I also remember that I kept summoning more champagne for both of us while she kept independently summoning more champagne for herself, so that in no time she was drunk. Among the signals she sent out, even though drunk, was that she had no intention of paying for her own champagne, let alone mine. After two hours of champagne and impertinence, she announced that she was hungry, where would we have lunch? I said we couldn't possibly have lunch, I had to get to the theatre, which was a lie, of course. But I was desperate to get away, especially as she'd become libidinous, rapping me on the knee and stroking me on the wrist. No, no, must have lunch, she insisted. Must. I said it was impossible, out of the question, but just to confirm I'd phone the New Arts, check up on my schedule.

I lurched up to my room and hung about, smoking a cigarette, then lurched back down to the bar where she had ordered another glass of champagne, both for me and for herself. I informed her, standing swaying on my feet, that yes, I *did* have to be at the theatre, damn it! The actors were waiting for me. Oh, she said, well in that case she'd drive me. This seemed a prospect more frightening even than lunch, but short of knocking her unconscious I couldn't see how to refuse.* We went to the car exit. While we were getting her keys from the high-booted, tall-hatted bell-hop – I could see the two of us, by the way, reflected in the glittering slabs of pseudo-glass that make up the wall of the hotel, teetering towards each other, swaying away from each other – she informed me that she had to find a toilet. She returned her keys to the flunkey from whom she'd just received them, reeled off into the hotel. Although she wasn't gone long she came back more drunk, as if she'd grabbed another glass on her way to and from her pee. She wavered straight to her car, and tried to get in. I explained that she needed her keys, so back we went to the flunkey, back to the car, into it. We veered and swerved and rolled drunkenly off, watched by the completely impassive flunkey. The journey, which normally takes about four minutes, was an absolute nightmare. She kept going down the wrong streets, her reflexes contradicting my instructions, right for left, straight on for turn. Also she went in for dramatic changes of speed, accelerating whenever she saw a car ahead, whether it was going the same way or coming towards us, but slowing down whenever the street was empty. She braked at traffic lights or passed through them without reference to their colour. We clocked up seven near-accidents on a journey that in real time lasted only fifteen minutes, but in true time lasted a couple of months, to be deducted in due course, no doubt, from my personal account.

When we got to the theatre I tried to behave affectionately – 'If you're ever in London,' I said, kissing her just to the side of the wart, 'Look me up in the phone book. If I'm ever in Dallas, I'll give you a ring' – as not only is she going to be writing up the interview (assuming she made it safely to her home, or her office, or the police cells) she's also, like greybeard of the radio, going to be reviewing the play. Jesus Christ! The last I saw of her she was swerving crazily away from the New Arts, up through the western patch of Dallas, while I, pretending to go into the theatre, was in fact swerving out of it into Lombardi's, where I ordered lunch. It was now nearly two o'clock, and I felt quite ghastly. I was stuffing some food down

* I suppose I could have said, 'No thanks. You're too drunk to drive,' and taken a cab. But I'm a man of extremes. Either blows or acquiescence – anyway, when full of champagne.

myself when Stephen appeared with the cheque for our lectures at the Arcadian college. Its size cheered me a bit, but not enough. We went in for a technical run, hung about for a few hours doing the lighting and sound cues, then went back to Lombardi's for a drink – it was now about six – and then back to the theatre for the first dress rehearsal.

The show was so hideously lit that the actors seemed to be pushed against the walls, featureless, virtually faceless, but possessed of enormous shadows, sometimes double shadows. At times there seemed to be nine or ten people on the stage, six of them silhouettes. The actors struggled gamely, but the great pall of darkness surrounding the sets seeped into their playing. The sets themselves continued to shake and gibber, bits of them seeming to be on the verge of falling down every time an actor moved, while the closing of a door caused the room to sway for about thirty seconds afterwards. The sound effects were equally preposterous. The unseen child, who is meant to be about six, reasonably bright and articulate, made the kind of noises appropriate to the vegetable infant in *A Day in the Death of Joe Egg*. There were a few guests, or volunteers would be the better word, present who laughed politely and applauded politely, but we all knew that they'd had a dreadful evening, though probably not as dreadful as the parties responsible, Stephen and I, had had.

Afterwards, at Lombardi's, I tried to reassure the actors that we would resolve all our little technical problems and, anyway, they were so wonderfully and deeply rooted in their parts . . . I suspect I wasn't very convincing. Anyway they didn't look convinced. Stephen drove me back to the hotel, breaking the news *en route* that I wouldn't after all be flying to London on Monday as there is no plane from Dallas to London on Mondays. So I shall have to leave on Tuesday, arriving back on Wednesday. I had a drink at the bar as usual. When I stood up I found myself tottering, but I tried to keep a certain dignity of demeanour and gesture as I strutted up to my room. Since then – it is now twenty to two, 20 February – I have dictated all this. Tomorrow we have our first preview. There's another preview on Saturday and two on Sunday. Monday, the day I can't go back to London, is the cast's official rest day so I shan't be able to do any work either. But Tuesday, home.*

* *Wednesday* home. But even if I'd got it right, I'd have been wrong, as it turned out.

## Thursday, 20 February

I rolled out of bed at eleven, went downstairs, had my two glasses – he's now actually understood this, the Pakistani, that I have *two* glasses – of champagne while waiting for Stephen to arrive. I don't know if I've said this, but their champagne is actually quite good, though I still haven't got used to the strawberries perching on the glasses' rim. I invariably take the strawberry off and eat it, forget all about it, then when I begin to address myself to the drink I suddenly see the stain, a splash of red, that's left on the rim and start back in alarm, thinking it's either lipstick or blood. When Stephen came, we sat on in the bar discussing aspects of the text, the play, the production, then went and had lunch. Anxious for something light on the stomach, I ordered chicken noodle soup, which arrived in a bowl so large that it made me think of a trough. We went to the theatre, keyed up for the last dress rehearsal before the first preview, to discover that in fact there was to be no dress rehearsal as there were no costumes, somebody in wardrobe having removed them from the actors' dressing-rooms, to have them cleaned. There was however a photographer, who was determined to take pictures whether the actors were in costume or not.

Deciding that the whole enterprise would be a waste of time, I came back to the hotel and watched *Shenandoah*. Then went back in a cab – the temperature has suddenly plummeted, by the way, from the seventies to the thirties, so that for almost the first time during this six weeks or so in the States I find myself appropriately dressed – and at the theatre found Stephen Hoovering the floor of the auditorium, one of the duties of the artistic director of a theatre in Dallas. He asked if I would like to help. I said no,* and went over to Lombardi's, where Stephen – his humble tasks performed (I trust) – eventually joined me. We had the usual pre-first preview kind of conversation, airing our worries about the play, the actors, the set and the lighting. Then back to the theatre, where I briefly inspected the floor and seats for signs of dust, then upstairs to the dressing-room to cuddle the four actors and to tell them that they were looking forward to it as they were desperate for an audience, etc., then down again to the auditorium, and up to Stephen's office,

* Stephen, as he occasionally points out, is younger than me. If it hadn't been for his one or two physical impediments, he might have become a top athlete. I was in no shape to handle a Hoover. Besides, I didn't want to.

where over a glass of white wine so disgusting that I refuse to believe it can have been alcoholic, one of the assistants told me she'd arranged my plane ticket for Tuesday, Super Executive, provided free by British Caledonian – their way, and a splendid way, it seems to me, of helping to subsidize the theatre. Nevertheless, I rejected it, telling the girl to demand a free First Class ticket instead. British Caledonian is throwing a party in my honour on Sunday night which I have no intention of being present at unless I go back to London in proper style and comfort on Tuesday, OK? The girl said OK, she'd pass the message on. Then we went down, took up our seats on different sides of the auditorium, watched the play.

Two vital facts emerged from the experience. One, that from our point of view, the play was fully alive, funny and touching. Two, that from the audience's point of view, it wasn't. They weren't actually hostile. They didn't rustle their programmes, whisper among themselves or jiggle their buttocks about. They sat in stillness, impassively polite, rather like members of the Royal Family sitting through yet another rain dance or fertility ritual.* They made a noise at the end – it sounded like a light rainfall – which I took to be applause. Then they rose, they left, without comment. All quite unnerving. Nevertheless Stephen and I raced up to the dressing-rooms, flung out our arms, drew the actors triumphantly into them, then raced over to Lombardi's and set up the drinks. When the actors joined us we celebrated away as if we'd just picked up a clutch of Tonys.† Michael Rothaar, whom previously I'd only seen sipping at Perrier water, proved that he's not an alcoholic by swigging down vodka after vodka. I set about concussing myself with some malts, but was still conscious when I had Stephen drive me back to the hotel. I managed to put myself to bed, and was just trekking towards sleep when Sam Weisman phoned. There was a dreadful second when I thought he was downstairs in the lobby, wanting to come up, but he was of course in Los Angeles,

* When travelling the far reaches of what used to be the Commonwealth, I mean. We don't do rain dances or fertility rituals in England, although I suppose we might if tourists expressed a demand for them.

† The major New York theatre awards, named after Antoinette Perry – I don't know why, as I don't know who she is, or was. The Tony is in the shape of a statuette conferred each year on the most successful musical, play, actor, etc., on Broadway. Its only value to the straight theatre is that it ensures that at least one play gets to Broadway each year, so that the award can be conferred.

and merely wanted to report that *The Common Pursuit* was going well. Last night the little Matrix had been packed with Hollywood celebrities, he said, *big* stars, really *big* stars. The trouble was the electrical system had cut out just as the play began, so the really big stars had had to sit in complete darkness until Joe passed some candles out. They sat for twenty minutes or so holding the candles aloft, and then departed. One or two of them had said they'd try again, some other evening.

## Friday, 21 February

For the second night running, one couldn't see the actors' faces properly and therefore couldn't follow their emotions, although, on the other hand, who really gives a fuck? The audience probably only vaguely noticed that they couldn't quite see the actors' faces and therefore only vaguely noticed that they weren't following the emotional line of the play, which they probably wouldn't have liked anyway as in one sense it's about a man being unmanned by women, a prospect not truly, I suspect, in the Texan scheme of things. Nevertheless I have never felt such loathing for a lighting man, who is probably very sweet in his personal life. The fact remains that he's buggering up the play. However little that matters to anyone else, it matters to me. After all I have to keep sitting through it.

## Saturday, 22 February

Woke up with the shivers, utterly miserable, but was cheered by a telephone call from James Hammerstein, who read out a review that has appeared in today's *New York Times* of my book, *An Unnatural Pursuit*. A warm, indeed glow-making review, and he read it out in a voice, at once leisurely and dramatic, which made it all the more enjoyable, though he faltered when I asked him to describe the photograph of myself which appears with it. In fact I was sure I heard him laughing slightly, which leads me to believe that once again I come across as a plump and degenerate lesbian.

Morally galvanized but still physically enfeebled, I went down to a late breakfast, for which I foolishly chose catfish in batter (which arrived with a mountain of french fries) and a few glasses of wine, having even more foolishly, I must admit, gone through a few glasses of champagne previously by way of aperitif. Then, my stomach heaving, got a cab to the theatre, where Stephen was attending to the sound and the lighting, and manoeuvring the actors around, perhaps a fraction more rapidly than I cared for – we always come to this directorial problem with my plays. Speeding the actors up won't speed the play up, in fact slows it down, because the audience stops listening even sooner than when the actors move only when there is a reason for doing so. But I left him to it, knowing that in the end the old moves would somehow reinsert themselves.

Went to Lombardi's for a glass of white wine or two, and then sauntered unsteadily back to do my share of the rehearsing, i.e. unblocking and reblocking Stephen's blocking, Stephen viewing me at it with sardonic equanimity. Later, at Lombardi's, he was full of worry about his future, both at Dallas and generally. We discussed his life, moved on to discuss the meaning of life, then the meaninglessness of life, then went back to watch the performance.

It was a pretty full house and a responsive one – in fact the evening went quite well. The lighting was vastly better but the sound effects still dreadful, though in a quite different way – the offstage noises of children playing in the garden at the top of the first scene, which previously had been almost inaudible, now made them sound like a gang of football hooligans on the rampage. Furthermore their voices, instead of just coming up briefly, then going down and then returning even more briefly and then going down, stayed there, shouting and hollering right through the onstage actors' lines, drowning them out. The music we'd chosen to cover the scene changes, 'And did those feet', came in and out in the most eccentric way, so that sometimes we got the thunder of an organ without voices and sometimes the voices but no organ; sometimes we didn't get anything at all because the chap in the sound box had forgotten to put the record on. And so it goes and so it goes . . .

Anyway, after the show, I scurried across to Lombardi's and booked a table, then went backstage with Stephen, collected the cast and took them to dinner. We sat there, drinking, eating, gossiping, joking, reminiscing about old films and plays and rehearsal experiences, etc., – one of those delightful evenings that come so frequently in the theatre.

## Sunday, 23 February

Slept late, finally being pounded out of bed by the lobby piano at about eleven. I sat at the bar sipping champagne and observing – not for the first time – the waiters' obsession with ashtrays. The moment you tap a bit of ash into it, they (actually only one of them) whisk it away and replace it with a fresh one. You thus find yourself getting through about five ashtrays in the course of a single cigarette. I find this exceptionally irritating as it (a) messes up a conversation or a train of thought or even a state of comfortable vacancy, and (b) messes up one's relationship – ideally so uncomplicated that one doesn't notice it – with one's cigarette. At times I feel like demanding the ash back, insisting that it belongs to me personally, they have no right to remove it.

I decided over my third, or possibly fourth glass, that I wouldn't go to the matinée, having had enough of plays of mine at the moment, so I stayed on and had brunch in the hotel – on Sundays they lay out tables and counters of cold crab, cold prawns, cold lobster, lumps of chicken, and quite a lot of food that I couldn't identify. I padded about piling my platter high with a visually stunning assortment of what turned out to be nearly tasteless delicacies, then sat down to read an interview I'd given in one of the local papers. There I was, portly and lesbian, half smirking and half glaring out. The interview was friendly enough but quite pointless because – as the interviewer explained – since I'd refused to discuss the 'meaning' of my plays, or to consider them in any aspect whatsoever, there was nothing much for either of us to say.

At about two thirty I thought I'd better look in on the matinée after all, or at least what would be left of it by the time I walked to the theatre. I passed down the escalator and along an extraordinary underground corridor, the walls of which were lined with photographs of ex-Presidents of the United States. Both Roosevelts were there, I think; Truman, Eisenhower, Johnson, Reagan (no satire intended, I'm sure, in placing him among the dead) but no photograph that I could see of Kennedy, who'd been gunned down not a mile from where I was walking. Anyway, along this peculiar, carpeted corridor, around the corner of Union Station, into the boulevard on which the hotel is situated – the least boulevard-like boulevard in the world, I imagine, being really a sort of freeway, with car-parks and grandiose but mostly empty buildings on either side. Not a bar, not a café, not a shop and scarcely a human being in evidence. Very few sounds, too, and those in the distance, mainly sirens denoting mishap and death. I got to the New Arts just as the audience was coming out at the interval. I sat on a bench opposite, surveying them as they stood chatting, rather angrily it seemed to me, about the play, though it might have been about their parents or their children or the lapses of God.

The second act was poor, full of unnecessary gaps – well, not quite gaps so much as extended pauses that achieved gap-like effects. This didn't depress me too much – after all, a Sunday matinée, the temperature up again, the theatre hot, the actors exhausted from their week – but I made a few notes, especially about Stanley Wilson, who had lost his edge and seemed to be in a dallying mood. After the show I sent a message around to his dressing-room, asking him to meet me in the only restaurant in the vicinity – Chinese, naturally – that was open on a Sunday afternoon. I crossed to the restaurant, and was surprised to find myself half accompanied by a short, tubby man with a red beard,* wearing peculiarly patterned, tartan trousers and a looping leather jacket, the pockets of which looked as if they were bulging with marbles. He stopped on the pavement when I entered the restaurant, and stood swaying, staring after me. I sat down and peered through the window, keeping a look-out for Stanley Wilson but also watching tartan-trousers, who was continuing to watch me, amiably, indecisively, rather in the manner of a well-disposed dog who hasn't yet made up its mind to pick you up. When Stanley appeared, he followed him into the restaurant – large and virtually empty – and when Stanley sat down opposite me, sat down himself, at the next table. We had drinks, he had drinks and a bowl of food, and all the way through our note session he kept his good-natured intoxicated attention on us.

We left him there, Stanley going back to the theatre, I back to the hotel. Dozed for a while, then went down to the bar for a single malt. I was determined to be sober for the evening, as the show was to be preceded by the big-deal, British-Caledonian-sponsored reception. So I sat watching the bugs of elevators sliding up and down the walls, and the men in their stetsons and high-heeled boots

* Sam Weisman has a red beard. So did the man with the knife who followed me in Los Angeles.

and the women in their fur coats throwing coins into the bizarre concoction of a fountain that isn't a fountain but a great inverted bowl with something sliding up and down its side that looks like water but isn't. In fact the whole thing is a *trompe l'oeil* perversion of a wishing well. There's no gap for the thrown coins to fall through so they simply bounce off the top of the bowl and tumble down into the basin, visible but unretrievable.

I stayed on and on, entranced by so much opulent triviality, until I suddenly realized that it was past seven and that Stephen, who was going to collect me and take me to the reception, still hadn't appeared. I dashed out in a panic, got the flunkey to whistle over a cab from the long line that waits, like a kind of dole queue, outside the hotel, and got to the theatre a quarter of an hour late. The lobby was jammed with the usual tuxes and long gowns. I had to push my way through them, quite brutally really, swinging my bag from my shoulder as a kind of flail, to get into the office. There I put on my coat, fished my tie out of my bag* and put it on, then slid back out into the lobby where I bumped directly into Stephen, forcing his way through the packs of Texans towards the door with the intention – or so he claimed – of collecting me from the hotel. He hadn't forgotten me, just forgotten the time, he said, as he took me around and introduced me all over the place. I was smiling and nodding and showing what's left of my teeth in merry grins, when I spotted old tartan-trousers, pulling at his red beard with one hand, his other loosely encompassing a glass of champagne, swaying uncomprehendingly on the other side of the lobby, the only person with quite a lot of space around him. He'd got in, Stephen told me, because anyone who was prepared to spend twenty-five dollars on a ticket to the play could get in. In a fit of something or other – perhaps merely spite – I went over and introduced myself to him, then introduced him to every tux or gown whose name I could remember. He didn't speak a word, just stood there swaying and burping and nodding, possibly on the point of throwing up. The tuxes and gowns dealt with him perfectly politely – perhaps they

* I began the practice of keeping a tie in my bag when I was made a member of the MCC (Marylebone Cricket Club). For reasons that make no sense to any intelligent human being, you have to wear a jacket and tie to get into the pavilion. I always try to wear a dark blue tie against a dark blue shirt in the hope, regularly satisfied, of luring one of the noisy, ill-mannered and officious stewards into the kind of error for which even they have to apologize.

took him for a relation of mine, and certainly, sartorially and possibly in other respects too, we might have seemed to have more in common with each other than with anyone else in the lobby. What I couldn't understand, what I still don't understand, is why he should have wanted to come. Surely he could find something better to do, even on a Sunday afternoon in Dallas, than to attend a performance of *Dog Days*? The last I saw of him he was gaping dangerously at a couple of tuxes and some fur coats, all of whom had the sense to stand well away from him.

We were summoned into the theatre inexplicably early – at about a quarter to eight. I took up my usual seat at the back of the stalls, and prepared to take notes. I was slightly depressed, actually, as I'd become quite fond, through all the work I'd put in, I suppose, of this odd, flawed little play, and felt that I still hadn't done right by it. I don't mean in the production – though I'd made some major mistakes there too, not least in the use of 'And did those feet' as the musical theme, which, in the only version available in Dallas, provided a downward pulsing effect, like an ill-tempered dirge, rather than the rousingly ironic commentary I'd intended* – but in the text. Above all, it was in the text that I hadn't really pulled *Dog Days* off. I was brooding away like this, waiting for the lights to go down, the curtain to go up, when the curtain suddenly went up, without the lights going down. A young civic dignitary, possibly the mayor, wearing a tux of course but with a white silk scarf wrapped carelessly about his throat, stepped forward and gestured towards the wings, out of which stepped a middle-aged chap, the chap who runs British Caledonian in Dallas, as it turned out, who came in for a little peroration of thanks from the youthful mayoral figure for his contribution to the evening – the contribution being, as far as I could make out, to provide ticket-holders with free champagne, and to fly me free First Class back to London – in other words, an extremely important contribution, especially the back to London part. The chap who runs British Caledonian in Dallas then made one of those speeches that sponsors make about his pride and pleasure in being behind the evening that we were about to see – although he'd probably have been better advised to wait until he'd seen the evening before boasting about his responsibility for it.

* We eventually substituted some jolly, but non-committal (in terms of the play) Mozart.

When he'd finished somebody else was called out of the audience to be awarded accolades for something or other, I really wasn't paying much attention, wishing really that we could get on with the show, but when *he* left the stage the mayor launched into a five-minute tribute to yet another chap – myself, as it happened. He finished by gesturing me up to a spot beside him. I felt quite easy about all this, the whole affair seeming quite unreal, dreamlike. So down the aisle I coasted, floated down the aisle, up on to the stage, took up my place beside him with a shy little stumble of feet, and stood through a few more minutes of acclaim which concluded with my being made an Honorary Citizen of Dallas, and being presented with a plaque that apparently entitled me to drive anywhere I like in Dallas without being impeded by the police, and to park anywhere I like without being given a ticket – though presumably not in the grounds or garages of the sort of people sitting there watching me receive it. In fact the plaque wasn't something I'd care to hold out for close inspection, even to the Dallas police, as it looked like an enormous wallet made out of balsa wood and plastic, and covered with varnish, though it's true it had attached to it a sheet of official paper, with some writing and quite a few signatures on it. I accepted it with what I hoped was an overwhelmed smile, made an under-energized joke about my financial condition already announced by my appearance – but how delighted I was to be received into the very bosom of Dallas (its car-parks), what a pleasure it had been to work with Stephen at the New Arts, scooted back off the stage up to my seat, then as soon as the play began, scooted along to the lavatory for a pee, then scooted back, and settled down to the first act.

It was all right. I tried to avoid being irritated by the text by concentrating on being irritated by the sets and particularly the interminable scene changes. The performances were in good nick, especially Karen Ratcliffe's. I really adore her acting, not only her innate delicacy, but what she does physically. I often watch her feet because they act out her emotions almost independently – doing little jumps or turning inwards or pointing towards the character that's talking to her even when her body is turned away – I find her feet very eloquent, very charming.

At the interval I went up and joined Stephen in his office. We congratulated ourselves on the way the act had gone, although worrying a bit that the laughter was coming where it had never come in the previous productions in Oxford and Vienna, nor in the other previews in Dallas. But it was a relief, I suppose, that the befurred and tuxedoed gathering had managed to find amusement, even if it was theirs rather than ours – though I now remember that a couple had left halfway through, the young woman leaning heavily on what I assumed was her husband's arm, either courteously pretending serious illness, or seriously ill.

The second act would have been all right, too, if it hadn't been marred by the interminable set-change back from seedy bedsitter to middle-class Muswell Hill – even longer than the other-way-round change in the first act. I pondered this as I made my way back to the lobby, where I found myself barricaded away from the office by the audience, who wanted to shake hands and drawl out Texan compliments to this newly elected honorary citizen of a city which, frankly, mainly looks as if it's been nuked. What struck me yet again was their dress, or rather the contradiction between their opulent dress and their semi-educated speech, unlike the characters in the play, who are exactly the opposite, dressing shabbily and speaking literately – yes, this is the nub of it, the audience dressed to the nines and speaking down there in the twos, or even the ones, while the play is dressed up verbally to the nines, but is right down in the ones, or even the minuses, in dress.

We – Stephen, the cast and myself – eventually made it across the road to the only restaurant open in the neighbourhood on Sunday nights, to find that they stopped serving food at nine thirty – an excellent policy when directly opposite a theatre that doesn't come down until ten. The mayoral figure was there, at the bar, with an enormous cigar added to the white silk scarf and the tux. He looked, with a lock of dark hair straying over his forehead, like yet another version of the Great Gatsby. He was, in fact, searching for me, having neglected to present me with a plastic key set in a block of plastic wood that completed my honorary citizen's kit. More to the point, as the bar was extremely crowded, he furnished us all with drinks, seeming to have the kind of relationship with the barman that one would like to have with barmen all over the world. In the meantime Stephen had found out about a wine bar some way off, to which we repaired after I had ceremonially thanked the mayoral figure for having presented me with the Freedom of the City. The wine bar was pleasant, the food OK as far as I remember it, and there went another evening.

## Monday, 24 February

A rather strange woman, semi-oriental, possibly Filipino, squat, ill-tempered, speaking almost no English, cleans my room. She completely ignores the 'Do not disturb' sign and glowers indignantly when I explain, with smiles and deferential gestures, that I am actually in my room, intend to remain in it for a while, and would she come back later? She stumps off, and when she comes back after I've gone, evidently turns on the radio, then forgets to turn it off, so that when I return at one or two in the morning, already sufficiently unfocused, I open the door either on voices gravely talking or to an explosion of music. It must be she that's fiddled with this recorder, turning the tape over in the hope of finding something interesting, and leaving it there. The result is that I've recorded over myself – about five minutes wiped, and the five minutes I wiped it with now in the wrong context. Thanks, Filipino lady.

But this has turned out to be an extraordinary day, the break day on which the actors can't be called on to rehearse and no plane flies out of Dallas to London. My plan was to spend it doing things that normal people sometimes do – as for example a film in the evening, in the company of Stanley Wilson, Karen Ratcliffe and anyone else – tartan-trousers for instance – who wanted to tag along. But first I had lunch with Stephen, to discuss various notes I wanted to give the cast before leaving on the plane tomorrow. Halfway through lunch I suddenly found myself saying, 'I wish to Christ, I wish to Christ, that I'd set this play in one room. The set-changes are destroying the production, they're all wrong for the rhythm of the play – I just wish I'd found some way of doing it.' Stephen said, 'I wish you had, I can't stand the set-changes either.' From that moment everything turned on its axis. It suddenly became a positive, a powerful ambition in me to rework the play into one set – I suddenly realized I'd been edging unconsciously towards an attempt to do so ever since I'd seen the first run. I began at once, on the paper table-covering at Lombardi's, where they also thoughtfully provide crayons, for precisely such emergencies, I assume – scribbling out new lines of dialogue, adjusting old ones, changing the end of scenes, the whole operation taking three hours, including a short break for a telephone call home, in which I told Beryl that under the circumstances I'd better come back on Thursday, giving myself a necessary two days to put in the changes with the actors and see how they worked – news that she received with generous equanimity, relieved that at least I'd be in time for the opera on Friday, for which she'd got a couple of very expensive tickets.

When I got back to the table and the crayons, Stephen, who'd been guarding them, went off to rearrange my flight, joining me half an hour later with the news that there was no plane out on Thursday either – no plane on Monday, which had turned out to be a blessing in that it had led to the decision to rework the play; no plane on Thursday, which was a curse – another example of life's quite superfluous swings-and-roundabouts policy, I suppose. And so back to the telephone, and a slightly less fluent conversation with Beryl about how I'd have to miss the opera after all, damn British Caledonian, what was the point of free tickets if the plane didn't actually go when you wanted it to, sort of stuff; and then back to the table, very depressed, because having to stay on and on is very depressing, especially when one adds to that having to give explanations to loved ones about having to stay on and on. The only nice thing was that somebody in the office told me there'd been a nationwide rave for the Matrix *Common Pursuit* on the radio, she'd picked it up over breakfast – ah well, a further, but altogether more laudable, example of swings and roundabouts, especially as there was a double ration of the roundabouts in the form of a phone call from Joe Stern, confirming marvellous feedback, floods of favourable reviews, so forth. But I can hardly recall the days of Joe Stern and Sam Weisman, not even the ugliest days of rehearsal. One good thing about the theatre. It keeps you in the here and now. Which seems to suit my temperament.

The actors, whose break day this is, nevertheless came over to Lombardi's, where I took them through the changes, pointing to this section and that section of the paper table-covering. Then we made plans for tomorrow's rehearsals. I love it about actors that they too seem to live in the here and now. Mine.

## Tuesday, 25 February

Got up about ten, went downstairs to the bar at about twelve, had the usual two glasses, then went to the theatre and rehearsed the alterations with the actors. The physical changes involved very little for the stage management to come to terms with, being almost entirely a matter of elimination – above all, the elimination of the lumbering set-changes. But as always, even minor physical modifications seemed to require endless adjustments of lights, sound, props. After standing impatiently about for an hour or so, I walked back to the hotel, lay down for a while, then went down to the bar, where I kept an eye on this exceedingly tall, let's say about seven foot two, black chap with a relaxed, easy, almost sloppy manner, strolling around the lobby in a tracksuit, being accosted first of all by an elderly Texan in a trim suit, with a white moustache, who seemed to want his autograph – anyway, he held out a little book, which the black chap signed – and then by a little gaggle of women, giggling, who seemed to want to press the flesh, taking his hand, holding it, passing it about amongst themselves. And still he strolled, the only creature I've ever seen in the lobby of the Regency-Hyatt or Hyatt-Regency who has been in proper proportion to it. I got up, and for no reason I could understand, began to follow him about, just plodding along behind him, watching as various other people came up, spoke shyly to him, went away from him waving and shouting good lucks, until we got to the elevator section, where there were two middle-aged women and the elderly Texan with the white moustache who'd already got his autograph. The two women asked for his autograph just as the elevator arrived. They all got in, the elderly Texan now looking angry, angry and puzzled, as the black guy bent over the ladies. I stood watching from the lobby as the bug climbed up the wall, I could see them through the glass, and the thought occurred to me for the first time – I'd been a bit slow because it's a sport that's never interested me – that the black guy was probably a basketball player, a famous basketball player, which was why, of course, they all wanted his autograph. What I couldn't understand, though, was why the white-moustached Texan should be angry with the two women collecting his autograph, having collected one for himself. Unless, of course, the black guy wasn't a famous basketball player, but a famous stud.

I went back to the bar for another drink, Stephen arrived, we went to the theatre, and I was pleased to see that the play, at least as a play, worked better than before, flowing much more smoothly without the set-changes, and was correspondingly better received by the audience, who were, I think, composed mainly of a contingent from Delta Airlines – they, like British Caledonian, have their evening too, but without offering up either free champagne or free plane tickets or the Freedom of the City. But if the play had improved, the performances had deteriorated. Karen Ratcliffe had lost her bite and authority, especially in the last scene, when she boots – according to the script – her husband back out on to the pavement. She kept giving him tender, loving glances against the run of the text and the production, as if playing a scene of a different spirit in a quite different sort of play. And Stanley Wilson, as the booted-out husband, responded in kind, turning lines we'd rehearsed as acid and dignified into pleas for forgiveness in a shared bed. All it needed to be completely disgusting was violin music. So roundabouts and swings again, though again I felt I was up – preferring an improved play to improved or even accurate performances. I whisked the actors off to Lombardi's, manoeuvred the seating to be next to Karen, discussed the scene with her; manoeuvred Stanley Wilson into driving me back to the hotel, discussed the scene with him over a drink at the bar, came upstairs where I am now dictating this.

## Wednesday, 26 February

Woke feeling terrible – tired, hungover and headachy. Took me hours to get up, but I finally managed to get down to the bar, picking up the two Dallas newspapers on the way, to read about the overthrow of President Marcos of the Philippines, then idly turning the pages of one of the newspapers was suddenly confronted by a large Technicolored photograph of myself, under which there's a caption reading 'Playwright Simon Gray has a passion for cinema, especially American movies, but loathes rude movie audiences.' In the article itself he reports on my rumpled appearance, grey hair, pouched eyes and trembling hands, then describes at length my attempts to secure a decent glass of white wine at the restaurant where we met – presenting me, in other words, as both an alcoholic and a snob. By the time I'd finished reading this my hangover had intensified, my head was pounding with a kind of soft, genial dreadfulness. It was pounding softly, pounding genially, killing me. I went up to one of the shops in the lobby and bought a tin of aspirins, which I was unable to open. There was a little message on the lid, that I had to squint at to read, ordering me to press my thumb on the two red spots, but no matter how I squeezed my thumbs down on the two red spots, the lid didn't snap up. In fact, nothing happened at all. It seems to me characteristic of modern life that when you have a hangover and a headache and therefore need to buy an aspirin, you should be provided with aspirins you probably couldn't get at when you are at your most sober and supple-thumbed. I finally gave the tin back to the girl who'd sold it to me, pointing out the problem in strong but controlled terms. She looked puzzled, tried to open it herself, couldn't, passed the tin on to the responsible-looking chap in charge of the shop, who struggled for a while with his thumbs, then with an exclamation whipped off a completely invisible wrapping, and proceeded to thump away until the lid flew up. I got some water from the bar, dropped some aspirins down my throat, and got a taxi to Lombardi's, where I had two plates of carpaccio, a marinated, uncooked beef, served with grated parmesan and a vinaigrette dressing – they offered me a third, on the house, but I wasn't up to it, and anyway had to get across to the theatre, where the cast was waiting.

We rehearsed for three hours, and then Stephen and I went through all the physical changes with the stage management, and then I came back here, feeling distinctly ropy but at least without the headache, and tried to dictate the above. Something had gone seriously wrong with my tape-recorder – as I talked into it, it grew first warm, then hot, until finally, with smoke leaking out of its sides, it began to burn my hand. I went down to the shop where I'd bought the aspirins, bought some new batteries, put them in, started again. The same thing happened, although more quickly this time. It was really rather alarming, having the machine with which and into which I've been so intimate over the last seven weeks, smouldering violently away in the palm of my hand. I suppose its little heart had just given out, worn down by all the worry and anger I've poured into it. Or it was a cheapo to begin with, with a built-in failure system. Either way, there was only one place for it, the wastepaper basket. I phoned up Michael Rothaar, from an instinct that he was a machine-type chap, and got him to agree to lend me one of his tape-recorders, then went in for the evening show, the (for me) penultimate performance, and the last preview.

Everything was going swimmingly along – I wasn't even paying much attention, really – until the reorganized scene between Peter

(Stanley Wilson) and the girl he picks up (Cindy Vance). In the new version, in order to eliminate the protracted set-change, it takes place in Peter's Muswell Hill sitting room, rather than in a borrowed bedsitter. He fails to fuck the girl, denounces her for his failure, shows her out, then picks up the bags he's already packed, glances around the room in which he's spent so much of his young husbandhood and his fatherhood, leaves for pastures new. That's what I wrote down on the paper tablecloth at Lombardi's, and that's what they did last night. Tonight, the lights went down abruptly before he'd shown the girl the door, let alone before he'd had a chance to pick up the bags, bid farewell to the room. Stanley and Cynthia had to blunder off the stage in the dark, leaving the bags on stage. The lights came up almost at once, seeming positively to glow over the two unremoved bags as Peter's wife and Peter's brother discussed the implications of Peter's departure, a dramatic event which the onstage bags emphatically contradicted. Karen Ratcliffe and Michael Rothaar kept darting their eyes towards them, and then imploringly towards the spot in the stalls where they knew Stephen and I always sat. There was of course absolutely nothing either of us could do except what we did do, which was to hurry down into the lobby and have a sullen row, one of the few we've ever had, in which I denounced the stage management of his theatre for their incompetence, and he defended them on the grounds that they were doing their best in exacting circumstances, bound to be mistakes when changes had been made so rapidly, little time to practise them, so forth. We stopped when we'd exhausted ourselves, went to Lombardi's, had a mutually pacifying drink, went back to the theatre, watched what there was left of the play to watch, both of us dejected, and therefore both of us surprised by the warmish response from the audience, anyway a response which suggested that they'd noticed nothing amiss, certainly not an unremoved suitcase, stage left.

After the show Stephen and I hustled back to Lombardi's, waited over drinks for the cast, who joined us for further drinks and a meal, then I came back here, dictated this into a tape-recorder furnished by Michael Rothaar, a sturdy, simply functioning thing (the tape-recorder, not Michael Rothaar) and am now contemplating going down to the bar . . . The temperature today was up in the nineties by the way. The nineties. In February. And tomorrow is the First Night of *Dog Days*. An event I'd intended to miss by some days or so. I really don't want another First Night so soon after the last First Night, especially when that one was in Los Angeles, at the Matrix, and happened twice.

## Friday, 28 February

The morning after the first night before. And yesterday was very conventional, almost like a little model of a First Night day. After spending a couple of hours, woozy hours, watching the glass bugs slide up and down the walls, attempting to overhear various Texan conversations – there was a Manure Marketing Convention in – I tore myself away from the lobby and over to the theatre, rehearsed all the scenes which seemed to me to have been off the previous night, which meant almost all of them actually, had some confidential words with Stanley about the actor's husk he adopts from time to time, had coffee with him and with Stephen at Lombardi's, came back to the hotel, lay down for a while, went back to Lombardi's, where I had a large Scotch, and waited for Stephen. When he arrived we both realized we hadn't got any good luck cards to give the actors, so we set forth in Stephen's car. We drove for about ten minutes in the general direction of a card shop which he believed might still be open, then gave up, came back to Lombardi's, had another drink, then over to the theatre for the opening.

It went OK, I thought – a responsive audience causing the only real confusion, in that they laughed more than previous audiences, louder and longer. The actors didn't quite cope with this, so that some of the better lines were buried under laughs trailing over from a previous line and weren't resurrected by the usual professional means, i.e. repeating them. There was also a dreadful moment when Stanley dried, but then the youngest member of the cast, Cynthia Vance, drama student, came to his rescue by feeding him the information he needed in the form of a question, thus getting him going again. But the curtain came down to decent – no, positively generous – applause. Afterwards the company went on to a bar–restaurant called the Green Leaf, which likes to honour the New Arts after every First Night, and did so with us by issuing us each, as we went through the door, with a ticket that entitled us to one free drink each. The bar was badly lit, full of people who'd obviously never needed a free drink in their lives. I drained off my own as I roamed briefly through the shadows in search of Truth, Beauty or even a recognizable face, then got Stephen to drive me to the hotel, came up here to 328, dictated this.

I packed my bag, got the video into its case – obviously the wrong way around, from its distorted shape – and went down to the bar. There I sat, smoking and sipping champagne, while I watched for the last time the bugs sliding up and down the walls; the men in stetsons and the women in furs tossing coins and dollars into the bogus fountain; the platoons of fat women waddling to their conference rooms and banqueting halls; the children among the rafters, riding on balloons; the cops crouching behind the plastic ferns, guns ablaze; John Wayne stumbling towards the down escalator, his arms full of babies; a chorus of holy ghosts, led by Harold, offering up the yellow rose of Texas; Stephen Hollis, standing above me, suggesting it was time to check out.

At the counter I set one of the bell-hops, a grizzled veteran of some twenty summers, an initiative test by sending him up to 328 for my bags. He passed triumphantly, returning with them in twenty minutes rather than the mere two or three that less experienced mortals would have required – though I admit that his coming down twice, once to check on the number of the room, the second time to collect the key without which, he discovered, he couldn't get in, might have struck a less ardent fan as a form of cheating. Then into Stephen's car, and off – with a majestic salute to the high-booted, tall-hatted flunkey who keeps the doors of the Hyatt-Regency or the Regency-Hyatt – to Lombardi's, for a last lunch with the cast. We sat at a round table by the window, looking out at the only bearable part of Dallas, talking over our memories of rehearsals, hoping we'd all meet again, work together again, possibly do *Dog Days* in New York one day – relaxed and nostalgic, ending the experience in the way in which these experiences should always end. There was one stomach-lurching moment when I thought I saw the small, arm-swinging, red-bearded figure of Sam Weisman crossing purposefully towards us, about to appear at the door as he'd used to appear at the door of Joe Allen's, during the preview nights in Los Angeles. But it wasn't Sam Weisman, of course, and whoever it was went on past the restaurant, down the pavement, in the sunlight.

There was a spot of trouble at the airport, when an exceptionally handsome, broad-smiling chap at the check-in tried to fob me off with a Super Executive. I explained his error in my most civilized manner, and within minutes I had my First Class ticket in my hand, was through the radar-screening, and was just settling down to a last glass of champagne when I was called back to check-in over the public address system, and informed by the magnificent Texan that he'd made a mistake, First Class was full. I said I was one of the people who made it so, had in fact been guaranteed a First Class aisle smoker by British Caledonian's most senior executive at the ceremony at which I'd been made an Honorary Citizen, recommended he phone said Senior Executive before we found ourselves on the way to an international incident, etc. I stood there resolutely, possibly tramp-like in appearance but indisputably aristocratic – Welshly aristocratic – in manner, managing to keep my bags in the way of other riff-raff struggling to check in until his nerve broke. So that was that. I got on to the plane, settled into my aisle smoker, noting sorrowfully as I did so that the magnificent Texan's claim that First Class was full was a lie. It was half full. Or half empty, depending on how you choose to look at it. The seat next to mine was unoccupied, so I had, as these things go, an extremely comfortable flight, reading most of the recent Orson Welles biography, and didn't mind too much that we were in the air for an hour longer than scheduled because Gatwick was frozen over. From Gatwick to Victoria by train, and then across London by taxi, taking in the sights that at various times over the last two months I'd thought I might never see again, all of them covered in snow, which made them for some reason all the more endearing, arriving home just as Beryl was stepping out of the door, on her way to a George Eliot Fellowship meeting. Talked for a while to Hazel, who has become slightly less incontinent, I gather, but sometimes stands for minutes at a time, facing no particular direction, from which I assume that she is now almost blind. Looking at her when she does this makes my heart pinch, but I feel OK, that she'll go on for ever, when she is under my desk (which she is now) stirring every so often.

# 4

# First a Body Count, Then *On With The Show!*

---

[1]

I began writing again almost as soon as I got home, working in succession through three film scripts that I'd left in varying states of suspension.* By the time I got to the third I'd managed to give up smoking, taking up nicotine chewing-gum at last, which made early script conferences with the director something of an ordeal. A thoughtful, imaginative Irishman who chooses his words with fastidious care, he is also an infuriatingly eccentric smoker – treating his cigarettes as finger aids to concentration, sort of worry beads, really. He would take one out of a packet as he searched for a phrase, fondle it, put it back, stare at the packet, revolve it in his hand, take the cigarette out again, put the packet on the table, massage the cigarette, place it between his lips, extract it, revolve it, before lighting up slowly and ceremonially, as if treating himself to an enormous cigar at the end of a banquet. The whole ritual, *sadistic* ritual as I saw it, sometimes took him half an hour to perform. Through it I sat stiffly, concentrating not on what he was saying about the script, but on the effort of not hurling myself across the room to relieve him of the cigarette by force, and smoke it myself. It wasn't until our fourth or fifth meeting that I'd become sufficiently experienced in his ways, and sufficiently habituated to the gum, to enjoy both the work and his company. In fact, it turned out to be a very happy collaboration that demanded tolerance on his side too. He was after all dealing with an impatient, frequently fretful colleague whose jaws only stopped working when one piece of gum was being replaced with another.

* These were *After Pilkington* for the BBC; an adaptation of *Quartermaine's Terms* for the BBC; and a version of J. L. Carr's novel, *A Month in the Country*, for Channel 4 and Euston Films.

In early May Beryl and I went to Lucerne for a holiday. I took with me a throbbing pain, that now and then soared into a piercing pain, in my left ear – the result, I subsequently discovered, of the incessant gum-chewing. All I remember of the holiday now is going about the lake in big boats, muffled against the wind, the sleet, the snow or merely the rain, or whipping through valleys in trains, my head bent over a book in order not to notice the throb in my ear. A perfect companion as always for my wife. When we got back I started a new play, writing demonically through May, June, July, frequently day and night, the Cellophane strips from the gum piling up as the cigarette packets had once piled up, the dead pieces of gum filling my black metal wastepaper basket as the cigarette ends had once filled it. There was a brief spell of about three days when I gave up the gum because I was convinced that it was leaking a stagnant pool of nicotine into my stomach which would poison my whole system. But without either cigarettes or gum I found myself in a state of continuous and unbearable agitation, unable to write, unable to read, and of course unable to sleep. I spent hours sitting jumpily in front of the television set, on one occasion staying up until two in the morning, a bottle of Scotch at my side, just to watch the fight, transmitted from Las Vegas, between Barry McGuigan and some no-hope Mexican called Cruz. Both the Irish champ and the Mexican chump insisted on going the distance, which meant I didn't have to go to bed and try to wrestle myself to sleep until nearly four, by which time we had a Mexican champ and an Irish chump. Cruz, a rather blandly smiling brown boy, slipped coolly about on the shady side of the ring; McGuigan, the tough little towser from County Down, scampered about on the sunny side, looking rather like the infant alien from the film of that name, all claws and knobs, though skewering away at nothing. The whole experience was so unnaturally vivid, almost hallucinatory – the consequence, I suppose, of my nicotine-deprived, over-alcoholed condition – that I've wondered since whether it wasn't my equivalent of a trip on acid.

Either the next day or the day after I went back on to the Nicorettes, and so got back into the play. A few days before I'd actually finished it, but when I knew that it was about to be finished, I went to Lord's* for the afternoon. After an hour or so of

* For the benefit of American readers: Lord's is one of the larger cricket grounds in the London suburb of St John's Wood. As it is a predominantly Jewish neighbourhood Lord's is frequently referred to as the synagogue of cricket.

listless inattention, I went up to the bar, where I sat for a time speculating about the bizarre little man who always sits on a chair in a corner by the window, never turning his head to look out of it and see the game. He's about seventy, with spectacles and a hearing aid, his scalp visible through strands of (dyed, I believe) black hair plastered thinly back, and an odd little thick black moustache (also, I believe, dyed). He wears a heavy suit even on the hottest of afternoons, with his member's tie knotted right up under his chin, and he always has a drink in his hand. That afternoon there was the usual coterie of teasers gathered around him, with whom he was swapping the usual badinage, very loudly as usual. I was trying to imagine him in some other environment – where and with whom did he live? What did he do (had once done) for a living? How did he spend his days during the long months when there was no cricket and the bar was closed? Did he, in fact, exist except in that corner, that chair – when I suddenly found myself hurtling out of the bar, down the steps to the telephones, which, at Lord's, are to be found in antique wooden cupboards that seal you off from the world and its air so completely that by the end of a medium-length conversation you feel on the verge of death by suffocation.

I phoned Michael Codron and told him that I had a new play. He went in for being delighted, urged me to get it to him before I went off to Sestri Levante for the annual family holiday, and fixed an appointment for two days' time, at 4 p.m., in his offices, for the ritual transfer of the script. I spent the next day and a half messing about with the text, mainly cutting, though deciding not to worry about its comparative roughness, both in the writing and the typography. In fact, I rather *liked* its roughness, comparing its effect to that of a violent, but life-enhancing tramp – a tramp of the old school. I arrived at Michael's office, punctual to the minute. In the reception area a girl reading what looked suspiciously like a script by Tom Stoppard or Michael Frayn or Alan Ayckbourn* told me that Michael wasn't ready to see me yet, and invited me to sit on a peripheral sofa, would I like tea or coffee? I sat down, took out of my bag a copy of the *Spectator*, which was nestling beside my play, and with a cup of tea beside me, my mind really full of the impending interview, began to thumb through it. After about ten minutes Michael appeared. Seeing the *Spectator* in my hand, he

* Three English playwrights.

said, 'Oh, you're reading the *Spectator* too, I was just reading it in my office.' So there we'd been, he in his office keeping me waiting while he read the *Spectator*, I in his foyer reading the *Spectator* while he was keeping me waiting. Quite a coincidence when you think about it.

Once in his office, I took the play, which was packed in a cardboard box, out of my bag, and handed it over with a little bow. He put it down on his desk rather hurriedly, then, with his eyes averted from it, went behind the desk, sat down. Though his noble and hawk-like face looked as noble as ever, and slightly more hawk-like, I noticed that his eyes resolutely refused to rest even fleetingly on the encoffined play, nor did his fingers stray absently towards it. We sat there, gossiping vivaciously along, eventually settling on a little incident in which Beryl and I had left at the interval of a play he'd produced at the Aldwych fairly recently. The reason we'd left was not precisely that we'd thought the play bad, but that we couldn't make out whether it was or wasn't, not being able to hear more than the occasional word. We were sitting quite a few rows back in the dress circle (house seats, though I'd paid for them) of a theatre far from full, but the extraordinarily cavernous sets, for what was virtually a conversation piece about sex as far as one could gather, soaked up the actors' voices while diminishing their physical presences. Good actors too, with good voices and presences, there miming dutifully away to thin trickles of meaning. So why stay, once there was an interval to leave surreptitiously in? Unfortunately some people sitting right behind us reported to their friend the director our failure to return, who reported it to the author, who mentioned it to the producer, who was now discussing it with me, in phrases that indicated forgiveness and forgetfulness in counterpoint to my blustering explanations and apologies. We got through all that eventually, on to a bit more gossip briefly, then Michael said, as I was raising my cup to my lips, 'Don't you think that you ought perhaps – I mean, the longer you stay, the less time I have to get to this,' somehow indicating my play without either gesturing or even glancing towards it. And then went straight on to warn me that as a matter of fact he wouldn't be able to read it for a couple of days as he was about to open a new Ayckbourn in Richmond. As he said this he got to his feet, terminating the interview, seemingly unaware that in consecutive sentences he'd established two completely contradictory positions. To wit: that he was desperate to read the play, please therefore would I go; that he couldn't read the play for a couple of days because he was opening a new Ayckbourn in Richmond, nevertheless please would I go. Both positions, however, succeeded in containing the same conclusion – I was to piss off. So back through his reception I went, down the endless stairs, out into the Aldwych, into a taxi, and home.

A week later, on holiday in Sestri Levante, I heard from Judy Daish that Michael had rejected the play, finding it 'too big' and 'too upsetting' – producer's synonyms, perhaps, for too expensive and too uncommercial.* The holiday was further marred by the news from our house-sitter that Hazel, who had fallen down the steps to the back garden, was seriously ill. My brother Piers, who had joined us for a week or so at Sestri, got back to London in time to see her through the vet's visit, into death. I shall always regret that neither Beryl nor I was there at her end, although from Piers's account she was probably past caring. She was over seventeen years old when she died, which is OK for a dog, I suppose, and she was never very bright, and in her prime exceptionally greedy. She was also a coward, a reckless coward, as she would often start fights by yelping belligerently at a passing dog, and then, when the passing dog took offence and yelped back, would try to scale up the nearest human body for safety. She was deeply affectionate, had soulful brown eyes, and stuck by me, under my desk, night after night, when I was at work. Her portrait, done in oils by a friend, hangs above my desk, slightly idealized, as is appropriate for a portrait, and so missing out on her innate gift for the comic gesture or the foolish utterance, but catching something of her lurking spirituality.

[2]

Throughout the spring and summer while I was writing the new play, there was also, of course, *The Common Pursuit* and the question of its future. Some time in mid-March Jack McQuiggan phoned from New York to say that finally, on his fourth attempt, he'd made it to Los Angeles to see the Matrix production, his three previous attempts having been foiled by, respectively, an ailing mother; a back injury actually incurred on the way to the airport; a crisis in the show he was currently producing Off-Broadway. He

* This play – *Melon* was eventually produced by Duncan Weldon at the Theatre Royal, Haymarket, with Christopher Morahan directing and Alan Bates in the lead.

liked the play very much, could see that it worked well on stage, and wanted to produce it in New York. What did I say? I said yes, delighted – which I was. When he'd done *Quartermaine's Terms* I'd thought him the best producer I'd ever worked with. After we'd exchanged a few 'greats' and 'wonderfuls' at the prospect of being in business together again, he went on to say that as far as he could see, there were only two problems: (1) he didn't want to move the Matrix production, being unhappy with some of the casting, and of course the sets, and (2) he wanted me to direct it myself. I was in complete agreement on (1), but not on (2), claiming that I'd dug myself so deeply into the text when rewriting it for the Matrix that I wasn't sure I could keep a cool and detached eye on it yet, but that I'd be happy to co-direct it. OK, Jack said, but who with? What about Ken Frankel, I said, from the Long Wharf production? After all, he had a pleasant personality, so that at least there'd be a relaxed atmosphere in the rehearsal room. I would come over for the last two weeks of rehearsals and all the previews, do everything I'd done with *Quartermaine's Terms* to make sure the show was right, and this time appear as official co-director. Jack finally agreed, though not very enthusiastically – he'd worked with Frankel since *Quartermaine's Terms*, when no other had been present to take charge. We left it that I'd phone Frankel and invite him to co-direct *The Common Pursuit* in New York.

As it turned out, Frankel wanted to resume our previous arrangement, viz. that I'd continue to do a great deal of the work, while he'd continue to take all the director's royalties and the credits. I passed this offer back to Jack, who turned it down with what sounded suspiciously like exhilaration. 'What about Sam Weisman?' I asked. 'But you hated working with him in Los Angeles,' Jack reminded me. Yes, but – but what? Well, he *was* good on the text, and let's hope that he now realizes the importance of a happy rehearsal room. On in this vein until we left it that I'd phone Weisman and put it to him.

But first a call to Frankel, saying he was out, Sam Weisman was in. 'Weisman? In as what?' he asked. 'Well, as director.' How did this make sense, he asked, he only as co-director, Sam Weisman as director? 'Well, you see – ' though actually I hadn't quite worked it out, partly, I suppose, because I hadn't thought about it. What I came up with was that as Sam Weisman had only a month or so previously appeared in Los Angeles as sole director, it would seem a trifle odd if he now turned up in New York as co-director. Whereas he, Ken Frankel, had been involved in *The Common Pursuit* a year and a half ago, a script and a half ago, he'd be dealing in some respects with a new play, so questions wouldn't be asked about his personal demotion, in fact what could be more natural? It all sounded pretty persuasive to me, but didn't persuade Frankel, who cut across to tell me I was being 'stupid' not to do it on our old terms. No good, I said, Jack won't have it. He said again that I was being 'stupid'. I took him, as soothingly as I could, through my arguments again and we ended by exchanging pleasantries, no doubt both of us wishing that there was a reason or a season, like Christmas, to hang them on.

After Frankel, Weisman. Actually not quite. Weisman was directing a production or something or other on the West Coast, couldn't be contacted direct, but as he was in the habit of phoning Joe Stern almost every evening I asked Joe to pass on my message. A few days later Weisman phoned to say he'd love to do the play in New York. I gave him my thoughts on casting – Kristoffer Tabori (Stuart), Judy Geeson (Marigold) and Christopher Neame (Peter) from the Matrix production; Nathan Lane (Nick) from the Long Wharf and Matrix productions; Michael Countryman (Martin) and Peter Friedman (Humphry) from the Long Wharf productions. What did he think? Fine, he said, great – so what was the next move? I said I supposed it would be for him to come to an agreement with Jack, then to meet – or at least talk with – David Jenkins, who'd designed the set for the Long Wharf and would now, I hoped, be designing it for us. Right, he said, he'd get on to Jack and Jenkins straight away. Great. Fine. Thanks. And that was that.

For about a week. Then Jack phoned, to say that he and Weisman had talked, there was one thing he needed to get absolutely clear, Weisman and I would be co-directing, sharing the royalties, the billing, right? Wrong, I said, Weisman was to be to this production exactly what he'd been to the Matrix production (except in manners and behaviour, I hoped). In other words, the sole director. 'Ah,' said Jack doubtfully, 'that's the arrangement, is it?' Well, if I was *sure* that that was what I wanted – was I sure? I said that on balance I *supposed* I was, then moved the conversation to the question of casting, the need for David Jenkins to do the set, the need for a good lighting man, sound man. And that was that.

Some weeks later Jack came over to London, bearing with him

two large trophies won by *Quartermaine's Terms*, one for heading the Off-Broadway baseball league, the other for getting to the finals of the Off-Broadway baseball knock-out competition. He wanted me to have them in my collection rather than his, not because they were endearingly ugly, but because he, along with the director and the cast, had won trophies for their part in the production of the play, whilst the play itself had won nothing. I deserved *some* reward, he said, for being the cause of rewards to others. We had lunch together one day, dinner the next. It was clear that he was already enjoying getting the production under way – he was negotiating with the actors, with David Jenkins, with a top lighting chap (female) and with an excellent sound man. Would I please reconsider my decision not to co-direct? Even better, would I please reconsider my decision not to direct on my own? I said I wouldn't, why? He said he just had a feeling, that's all.

A week or so after Jack had flown back to New York Kristoffer Tabori and Judy Geeson turned up in London. Over lunch at Groucho's,* we had a rather formless discussion about Jack's desire, of which they'd got wind, that I should direct the play on my own. They seemed to have no feelings on the matter, let alone views. Very perplexing, considering the extent to which they were both prepared to relive the horrors of the Matrix, Tabori enacting the several occasions when he'd almost flung himself bodily at Sam Weisman. Perhaps they were just pleased to be doing the play in New York, let who was going to direct direct – Gray, Weisman, Himmler. All my attempts to grill them more closely ended when Judy, either from innocence or guile, deflected me with photographs of myself with massive, shoe-groping dog Digby taken in Los Angeles those months back, myself with their cockatoo those months back – until we ended up in pleasant little rivulets of talk about nothing in particular.

Anyway that was that, and went on being that, until Phyllis Wender (my New York agent) phoned one night in late July, perhaps early August, to tell me that Jack had finally decided against Sam Weisman. As I was deep into the last draft of the new play, I received this information almost absentmindedly, returning to the typewriter the moment Phyllis hung up, and mentally staying there until Sam Weisman phoned me a few nights later, from a television studio in Hollywood, to inform me that his lawyer in

* A club in Soho, London.

New York had just received a letter *by hand* from Jack McQuiggan (or was it from Jack McQuiggan's lawyer?), announcing that he, Sam Weisman, would not be directing *The Common Pursuit* Off-Broadway, other plans entirely were being laid. There was obviously some mistake here, Sam Weisman said, would I find out what was going on? 'Right,' I said, 'and oh, by the way, I'm just finishing a new play and –' 'Great,' he said. 'Fine. So if you'd give Jack a ring. And clear this up. Know what I mean?' I gave Jack a ring. Yes, Jack said, that's right, Sam Weisman was off the show. It was a producer's decision, which was why he'd taken it without reference to me. 'Any particular reason', I asked, 'for taking it?' Well, Jack said, he'd met with Sam Weisman in New York, made a few inquiries about him here and there, thought about him a great deal and come to the conclusion – I could call it a hunch if I wanted – that Sam Weisman hadn't the right sensibility for the New York production, there would be a risk of discord in the rehearsal room, other people involved in the production felt the same, and anyway, right or wrong, there was nothing anyone could say, that Sam Weisman could say, or Sam Weisman's lawyer could say, or I could say, that would change it. Sam Weisman was out, Michael McGuire was in. Michael McGuire was in? Yes, Michael. He liked Michael, he knew I liked Michael. Michael liked the play, and furthermore had trained as a director before becoming an actor, so Michael McGuire* in, Sam Weisman out. *His* decision, as producer.

I sat at my desk, Hazel dotingly under it, and contemplated the history to date of *The Common Pursuit* in America. There was no doubt that its most sensational feature was its high body count. I ticked off the corpses, first from the Matrix in Los Angeles, then from the Long Wharf in New Haven. Twelve in all, if one counted the three discarded directors – Frankel, Tabori, Weisman; and counted Chris Neame† among the discarded actors. I tried doing it the other, more cheerful way around, with a check-list of the

* For information about my previous relationship with Michael McGuire see pp.103-5.

† Chris Neame had phoned to say he couldn't, after all, be considered for the New York production because as a British national he was unable to get a green card, without which he couldn't work in any theatre except a waiver one, like the Matrix. He would have qualified for a card if he'd married the American girl with whom he lived, but we agreed that no one should use the opportunity of appearing in a play, even a play by me, as an excuse for getting married.

survivors. Kris Tabori and Judy Geeson from the Matrix; Michael Countryman and Peter Friedman from the Long Wharf; Nathan Lane from both. And now of course Michael McGuire from nowhere relevant, who so far hadn't had anything to survive. But whichever way round I did my adding up, it remained horribly clear that in New York there would be more ghosts hovering in the wings than players on the stage.

I thought a bit about Sam Weisman, recalled some choice moments from the Matrix rehearsals, wrestled briefly with my conscience,* then 'phoned him and broke the news. He was appalled, angry, disbelieving. I said Jack had said – wanted me to know – that the decision was irreversible. Sam Weisman then asked me to put his case to Jack for him. He would fly to New York at his own expense, if Jack wanted. I agreed, though suspecting that the last thing Jack wanted was Sam Weisman flying to New York, at anybody's expense – especially to see him. I phoned Jack up, and made a coolish and clearish statement of the Weisman entitlement, throwing in one or two rhetorical flourishes. I think I did all right by Weisman, at least I can't think, even now, of a moral stone I left unturned. And there really was some fervour in me, as a consequence of a conversation I'd had a few hours earlier with Joe, whose distress on Sam Weisman's behalf certainly made me anxious to do right by *him*. Jack listened to me, courteously, patiently, restated his own case, which my advocacy hadn't changed a jot, but offered to write a further letter to Sam Weisman's lawyer, giving a fuller account of the reasons behind his decision – his fear that Sam Weisman would jeopardize the atmosphere in rehearsals, that hiring him might cost us David Jenkins, who was crucial to our plans† and had already announced himself out of sympathy with Sam Weisman's approach and manner – and that everybody else connected with the production who'd met Sam Weisman in New York felt as Jack and Jenkins did.

I didn't really believe that the information that *nobody* in New York wanted him to direct *The Common Pursuit* would bring Sam Weisman much comfort, especially when conveyed in a lawyer's letter. All I myself said when I phoned him was that I hadn't been

* When Richard Nixon said the same thing, it was assumed the fight was fixed.

† I'd asked him to repeat his Long Wharf design, with necessary adjustments, given more limited stage space in New York.

able to change Jack's mind, give up, Sam. He said he wouldn't. Joe Stern phoned me again; Kris Tabori, in tandem with Joe Stern, in one of those Los Angeles link-ups, phoned; Sam Weisman phoned; Jack McQuiggan phoned – all this after I'd handed my new play over to Michael Codron and was waiting for his response, and at two, sometimes nearly three in the morning. But really, given the finality of Jack's decision, all the calls were a waste of time and money, and just a day or so before I set off with my family for Italy, they stopped.

In Sestri I received just one phone call relating to *The Common Pursuit*. It was from Jack. He wanted to tell me the schedule (we would rehearse through September, open to previews in early October, have our First Night on 20 October – the night before my fiftieth birthday) and to discuss various actors he'd lined up to audition for Peter, the Christopher Neame part. 'Oh,' he said, when we'd finished, 'and one other thing. You and Michael McGuire to have equal billing as co-directors. All right?' I said no, surely the arrangement was the usual one, that I'd come over for the last two weeks, and all the previews, and see to things in my capacity as author. 'No, not at all,' Jack said. 'You and Michael are co-directing. I never asked Michael to direct. Only to co-direct.' I said that this was the first time I'd been told of this, or anyway understood it. He said, 'Well, I suppose I just took it for granted that you'd understand that that's what I meant. I mean, how else would it make sense?' I hung up, reflecting that Jack, whether consciously or not, had got most of what he'd wanted from the beginning. Which, of course, further increased my respect for him, in that it's always good when producers not only know what they want, but also succeed in getting most of it. On the other hand, I didn't feel so good about being what he'd mostly succeeded in getting, as it meant that I wouldn't be able to turn up at my pleasure and leisure, halfway through rehearsals; nor would I be able to turn up in rehearsals only when I felt inclined (admittedly that was almost all the time). I would have to be there from the very beginning, and turn up at the rehearsals, promptly, at whatever hour Michael McGuire and I called them for. On top of which, taking the credit (which I didn't mind) meant that I also had to take the responsibility (which I might mind) and even the blame (which I would mind). On the *other* other hand, for too many years I had been private director of my plays in the States, going public was perhaps what I secretly wanted, let's do it. It all seemed quite simple, when considered calmly from the terraced restaurant in Sestri, overlooking the harbour at sunset, with a fine Italian meal before me, bottles of wine to hand, nicotine chewing-gum on the go, and my family around me. Although the stomach did lurch a little at the prospect of nearly seven weeks in New York, lived through in a double state of frenzy, given that I was now doubly at risk. A bum play directed by a bum director were the headlines I envisaged. To which I could make the comforting amendment, a bum play directed by *two* bum directors.

During the week between my return from Sestri and my setting out to New York, I received a phone call from the joker in the pack, Michael McGuire. He caught me at a bad time – very late in the evening, when I was full of Scotch, grieving over Hazel's death, waiting anxiously to hear about the fate of my new play,* and in the middle of watching *The Cincinnati Kid*† on television. He was concerned about how we would proceed in rehearsals – how did co-directors actually work together, he wondered. I said, one eye fixed on the screen, one hand wrapped around a glass, 'Well, we'll just say whatever seems appropriate, surely.' Well, no, he said, he'd been giving the matter a lot of thought and he was unutterably opposed to any system that led to our disagreeing openly in front of the cast, they'd lose confidence, not fair on them – 'But don't misunderstand me,' he also kept saying. 'I don't have any ego problem with this play.' A chilling phrase, 'ego problem', as I'd first heard it from Ken Frankel, when he was about to direct the play at the Long Wharf; then from Kristoffer Tabori in London when he was about to direct the play at the Matrix; and then heard it from Sam Weisman in London when he was about to take over from

* It was currently with Sir Peter Hall at the National. Although he seemed keen to do it, he was unable to offer dates in any future that I could foresee. There was also the usual problem, with the National, of communication, i.e. plenty of phone calls and letters from my side through Judy Daish; none at all from theirs. I finally withdrew the play and offered it to Duncan Wheldon who is now producing it. It is called *Melon* and is in rehearsal as I write this.

† A thick-witted rip-off of *The Hustler*, with a climax that depends on the most unlikely event in the history of poker games – and in the history of the cinema – when one of the players (Edward G. Robinson) beats 'the kid' (Steve McQueen) with a straight flush against a full house. *That* isn't skill, that's luck. No. Worse. It isn't even luck, it's merely tawdry plotting, the writer working with a stacked deck, but calling it fate.

Kristoffer Tabori at the Matrix. I couldn't say, though I wanted to, that I *did* have an ego problem with this play as it was by me. Instead, I babbled on incoherently, sometimes drawing on experience so past I could scarcely remember it, sometimes being, or attempting to sound, curtly professional, cutting across his uncertainties with a slurred epigram. But of course Michael was right. One can co-direct one of one's old plays with one of one's old friends, as I'd done in Dallas with Stephen; one can direct while masquerading as the author, which I'd done to some extent at the Matrix, and twice comprehensively at the Long Wharf; but how, when it came down to it, did one co-direct with a co-director who actually wanted to co-direct? I refused to answer the question on the telephone at that time, and as a consequence had to address myself to it again at a crucial phase of rehearsals in New York, when I wasn't drunk, anxious, grieving or watching a bad film on television.

# 5
# But Down There I Wasn't a Duck

## Sunday, 7 September 1986

I flew to New York on Virgin Airlines, in their version of First Class, which they call 'Upper', in contrast to their cheap seats, which they call, with refreshing frankness, 'Lower'.* From the glimpses of 'Lower' I treated myself to, the compartment resembled the hold of a nineteenth-century transport ship, people packed so closely together that they seemed to be sitting on top of each other, weeping or unconscious. 'Upper', on the other hand, is very spacious, and provides reasonable service – somewhere between the Super Club and First Class of the major airlines, though at less than Super Club prices. Virgin also hands out a free 'Lower' ticket to its 'Upper' customers, which you can either use yourself (fat chance!) or pass on to someone in feeble health, in whose life insurance you have an interest.

My old friend, Dena Hammerstein, and her son Simon (named, I modestly admit, after myself) were on the same plane. Simon is actually a bright and charming fellow, but as he's only eight years old, I had reached a pre-flight agreement with his mother that they would sit as far away from me as possible, meeting up by appointment only for a drink at the bar. This was not only mean-spirited but entirely sensible, as it would give me the chance to read a book, watch the film, eat my meal gravely by myself, unmolested. Simon, however, refusing to consider himself a party to this arrangement, quickly took to looming beside me, making all sorts of perfectly normal (i.e. nonsensical) eight-year-old requests; for example, could he have my book to read, could he occupy my seat and listen to the in-flight music through my headphones, as he

* They've since changed 'Lower' to 'Space', presumably on the grounds that what little there is should have attention drawn to it.

was sure that it was better than the music to be heard through his, what about giving him some money? In the end I turned a bit uncley, and consented to show him my favourite, indeed my only, card trick, which in loose outline consists of inviting someone to choose in their head a card from the fifteen spread before them, and then after a lot of flim-flammery, telling them which card they've chosen. It's an absolute whizz of a trick, a jaw-dropper, that has only one flaw – it depends for its success on the complete integrity of the person you're showing it off to. Every time I flourished Simon's card at him, he simply looked away with a bored shake of the head, until I was forced to give up, sending Simon off with a verbal message for the pilot, which he clearly didn't deliver, as he returned unshackled and ungagged well before we reached New York, almost at once in fact. Nevertheless Dena and I managed a few enjoyable gossips before we landed at Newark, the most convenient international airport for New York, as it's sufficiently small for one to be able to pass rapidly through customs and immigration – especially if you make it first to the desk as I did, by means of some pretty ruthless sprinting and hustling, impeded only by my overnight bag. I was in Manhattan a mere thirty minutes after getting off the plane. This might be a record.*

When in New York I stay at the Algonquin, loving its eccentric and animated lobby life, finding safety in the fact that most of the bell-hops' faces are familiar, and feeling at ease in my suite – I usually manage to get the same one, 310, which is comfortable, pleasantly decorated with playbills of famous or poignantly long-forgotten shows, and has three telephones, one of them in the bathroom, beside the lavatory, which conjures up images of myself as Louis XIV, Lyndon Johnson, etc. In other words, for me the Algonquin is home, never more so than now, when I'm not staying in it. For once I've allowed economics to prevail over all the really important instincts, and am in the Pankhurst,† which gives you a special deal if you stay for a month, and pay in advance. As I've paid in advance, I'm stuck here for a month. It comes highly

* From the above I suppose I give the impression of exceptionally ungentlemanly behaviour, even by my own low standards, but in fact Dena and Simon had a limo waiting for them, as had I (Virgin provides a free limo to 'Upper' passengers), so there was no point in jostling through customs and immigration together, only to separate immediately afterwards.

† I have changed the name of the hotel for reasons that will become apparent.

recommended by people in London whose judgement I shall make a point of ignoring in future. I can't remember what it is that they liked about it, although I think somebody connected with the National Theatre said it was 'wonderfully discreet', which should have been enough to put one off, as 'discreet' invariably means a dull lobby in which anything you do will be noticed, and possibly noted. And indeed the lobby is dull, or would be if it weren't actively depression-inducing, its atmosphere that of an ante-chamber to a funeral parlour, the only visible residents extremely old and sitting patiently about as if waiting their turn in the embalming room. I took an instant but for once not entirely irrational dislike to my suite, not least because its décor is an unattractive green, or rather variations on an unattractive green, and there are lots of those bogus classical-style lamps that one comes across in those hotels in the States that go in for being stylish, without any style. Not least I dislike the suite because it's not in the Algonquin, the doors of which my limo actually passed on the way here – I had to check a cry to the driver to stop, hold, this is where I get out. I wish I hadn't. I can't face unpacking. Unpacking will make my being here somehow definitive. By the way, the fridge in the closet-sized kitchen has a morose hum to it, from loneliness, I suppose.

## Tuesday, 9 September, two nights later

Let me do a quick run-down on my dealings with the Pankhurst so far. The gays and other guys at the desk have been infuriatingly well mannered and helpful, easily frustrating my attempts to involve them in the kind of row that might lead them into paying me my money back, and letting me go. So far I've concentrated my attack on the curtains in my suite. They are heavy and brocaded (green within green on green) and hang at all the windows, four pairs in the sitting room, two in the bedroom, and have one redeeming feature – *they don't work!* When you undo the sash and tug and jerk at them, they neither move sideways to meet each other, nor fall down. They just hang there, inertly framing the windows it is their function to cover. I suppose, therefore, that they're ornamental curtains, but the joyous fact is that the blinds behind them are clearly inadequate either for privacy (there is a teeming office block opposite) or as protection against the light, and I therefore require curtains that curtain.

I saw at once that if I handled this properly, I might shortly be on my way out of the Pankhurst with a refund in my pocket, so phoning down to the desk I explained the situation, assuming the restrained manner of a man who means business. Before I could get into the inevitable repercussions – i.e. 'make up my cheque, please'* – I was told that the matter would be dealt with straight away, someone would be right up, sir. And right up came the housekeeper, a burly middle-aged woman of the kind you expect to find in a hotel in Moscow, who spoke English with the kind of accent you also expect to find in Moscow. She tugged futilely at the curtains, then said, 'Have to get man. Have to get man who do this,' and went. I was about to phone down again when man – a male version of the housekeeper, in that he was even burlier, so possibly a brother or husband, arrived with a toolbox and no English whatsoever, and set to work with screwdrivers and such, to no effect. I stood watching him with a drink in my hand, making discouraging exclamations of annoyance, clucking away at his failures. I was slightly drunk. I had, of course, been drinking on the plane but, as always happens with me – I've never quite understood the psychology – the moment I get into my hotel room I decide that it's about time for my first real drink of the day. When man had left scowling and muttering, I phoned down to the desk, and trying to keep the triumph out of my voice, reported on the situation. 'I can't stay here, you see,' I said, meaning the Pankhurst of course, but he took me to mean here in this particular room, and said he would send up a bell-hop to show me another one. I hesitated, thinking it was now or never, then deciding that it was better to clinch my case – there would almost certainly be something to object to in any room at the Pankhurst – I agreed. The bell-hop, a rather maternal middle-aged chap, with a reasonably fluent command of the language (he was Irish), took me down several floors to a suite that was noticeably different from mine in that it was decorated in variations of an unattractive brown, nevertheless sticking to the main house style with classical lamps and non-meeting curtains. Back up I went, and down I phoned, to be told, with inflexible sympathy and courtesy, that the manager had just left, but when he came back in the morning he would surely sort my problem out. I gave it as my opinion, rather grimly, that he wouldn't, but decided

* As opposed to 'Make up my check, please'. The point being that they *they* owed *me* money. Got it?

to leave it at that for the evening, really quite pleased with the progress I'd made.

I stood at one of the sitting-room windows for a while, sipping further malt and watching the lights go out, the office workers departing, in the building opposite, then pulled down the blinds, a protracted and messy business as I can never work out which strings to pull, and invariably end up with one large corner of the blind tilted up and jammed. In fact I was wrestling with just such a corner when I was jolted upright by a sharp, savage ring, not from the telephone, possibly from the doorbell. But probably not from the doorbell either, as when I opened the door there was nobody there, and nobody hurrying down the corridor away from the door, either. This unexplained ring unnerved me. It hadn't sounded accidental, but peremptory, as if there were an urgent purpose behind it. I went out and did some shopping – toothpaste, razor blades, Nescafé, plums, sort of stuff, then had a meal in a nearby and cheerless hamburger joint where I went from brooding over my situation at the Pankhurst to brooding over the fact that so far I'd received no communication from my producer, Jack McQuiggan. When I'd made my way back along the drab and almost empty streets, through the dead man's lobby, up in the space-shuttle lift, into my greenish room, I set about trying to phone him. I had two numbers, home and office, but on both I got his answering service – the same answering service; in fact the same person on the same answering service, his voice cheerful, polite and indifferent, and therefore far more infuriating than a couple of answering machines. Most answering machines at least beg you to leave a message as if afraid of missing out on something. While I was dealing with the voice that I'd only just dealt with, there was another sharp ringing noise. I opened the door. Nobody there. I went to bed, pondering resentfully on the nature of producers,* but finally coasted calmly off on the thought that at least tomorrow, given that the curtain

* No doubt recalling the famous New York producer who was sitting at his desk one morning, when his phone rang. He answered, listened, went white, ran out of the office. His staff was astonished, as he'd never before left his office without letting them know where he was going, and how to get in touch with him. Three hours later he reappeared, sat down, began sorting through receipts. His staff entered *en masse*, convinced he'd been through some terrible experience, and asked him, with passionate concern, whether he was all right: 'Gee, Mr —, we were really worried about you, your rushing off like that, are you sure everything's OK?' Yes, yes, he said irritably, he was fine, fine, somebody had rung up to say there was a bomb in the building, but it had turned out to be a hoax.

problem was quite unsolvable, I would be able to depart for the Algonquin. It even occurred to me that perhaps Jack, and possibly lots of other people as well, had left messages at the Algonquin, out of habit. I was woken at quarter to six by the sun bashing its way through the blinds, unresisted by the unmeeting curtains, just as I'd anticipated. New York blinds can't actually deal with the sun, which finds it perfectly easy to shoulder its way through their slats and get into your eyes.

So there I was at dawn, writing a long, argumentative letter to Harold about a recent anthology of poetry that he had co-edited. I went on for nine pages, questioning most of his inclusions and angrily challenging key omissions, breaking only to make some breakfast (hot-dog sausages, hot mustard and hot tomato sauce, which I'd purchased on my shopping spree the evening before – not perhaps a happy choice of early-morning fodder as it lingered around my intestines all day), until suddenly I realized it was nearly ten o'clock and time to get to the theatre to audition Peters. As I left my suite, I noticed for the first time a little pack of papers squeezed behind a specially fixed loop of metal on the door, which turned out to be telephone messages, most of them from Jack who had phoned before I arrived and then several times while I was out shopping, giving me various numbers at which I could reach him. This explained not only Jack's strange and insulting silence (what a waste of good resentment!) but also, presumably, those extraordinary rings, the bell-hop sticking the message on the door, ringing the bell, immediately departing, leaving me confronting an empty corridor – but how did he manage to do it all so quickly?*

I went down to the lobby and moved into phase two of my escape plan, going to the desk and describing to the guy there what it had been like to be punched out of sleep by a fist of sunlight to the eyes, so to speak. 'Intolerable, quite intolerable,' I said. 'Really, really I can see no alternative but to leave. However much I like your hotel in so many other respects.' Instead of going on the defensive ('No one's ever complained before') or the offensive ('Go or stay, who cares as long as we got your money?') which I would have preferred, he went in for being deeply nice – obviously a show of deep niceness is the long-practised tactic at the Pankhurst desk –

* By hurrying, of course. I subsequently discovered that the lift operator delivered the messages, and as he had to leave the lift door open when doing so, he had to get back to the lift as quickly as possible.

nodding gravely, and exclaiming, 'Oh, that's terrible!' he could *really* sympathize, he appreciated – that was the word he used – 'I appreciate what it's like to be woken so early in the morning with the light,' as if genuinely troubled on my behalf. Not on the hotel's behalf, on mine. Frustrated, I rocked off, still slightly hungover from the night before, more than nauseated by my hot-dog and mustard breakfast, and already exhausted from penning my long letter to Harold.*

When I finally got to the theatre – the Promenade, up on Broadway and 76; the Pankhurst down in the mid-fifties, off Park – I found my co-director, Michael McGuire, and my producer, Jack McQuiggan, already there, waiting for me. We had a brief talk about the cast we'd signed up, the chances of finding a good Peter from the auditions ahead, the problems David Jenkins would have reorganizing his Long Wharf conception in the smaller, proscenium space of the Promenade, and then this and that, until I transferred the conversation to something important – i.e. my video machine. I had sent Jack urgent messages across the Atlantic, as I'd once sent them across the Pacific to Joe Stern, demanding that a video be installed in my room. I think I'd also sent urgent messages to Phyllis, my New York agent, making the same demand, so now I come to think of it, I probably have two videos on order. Jack said he'd put someone on to it straight away. I gave him the precise address of the Pankhurst to pass on to the proper party, forgetting that if luck went my way I'd no longer be staying there when the video arrived. I must at some time, when I have a great deal of leisure, examine this obsession I have with getting a video installed the moment I arrive in the States these days – or rather with trying to get it installed. Perhaps that's the point. That it's not the video itself I need, but the rigmarole of trying to get it installed.

Anyway, on from the furthering of my obsession to another bloody day in the theatre. The auditions for Peter seemed to go on for ever. We saw about twelve actors in the morning alone, of whom only one or two were even remotely appropriate. Of the inappropriate ones quite a few seemed not even to be particularly good actors. So there I sat in the stalls, chewing my nicotine chewing-gum, watching actor after actor after actor after actor

* I never sent it, a cold-eyed reading revealing it to be befuddled in argument while rancorous in tone. There were also, in places, signs of illiteracy.

reading the same lines and failing to communicate any sense of the part, or communicating a perverse sense of the part, or just being desperately at sea. There was one lively moment when an enormous chap, about six foot four, very broad, looking like a college football player in fact, sauntered down the aisle, saying as he came that he was very much looking forward to my lecture in November. I said, 'What?' And he said, 'Yeah, well aren't you going to be there?' I suddenly remembered that I had long ago accepted an invitation to appear at the 92nd Street Y to discuss the process involved in turning a play into a film – the film in question being *Butley*. I said, 'God, yes, you're absolutely right, I'd completely forgotten,' adding, really just to say something while he was clambering on to the stage, 'I wonder if I get paid.' I heard his voice – his back was to me and I was very conscious of his enormous shoulders – drawling, 'Not by *me* you don't.'* This struck me as quite funny and I therefore felt well disposed until he began his reading. It was quite grotesque. There on the stage was this enormous and muscular man with a rather thick and bullish head, giving a pansified account – flouncing and mincing and virtually lisping – of Peter, who is of course relentlessly and unchangeably (I hope) heterosexual. So that was the end of that – a hopeless case. We finally settled for an actor called Dylan Baker, who is clearly very talented and has a lot of charm but is, I suspect, slightly too young for the part, even in such a young company, and possibly also too inexperienced. Not as an actor, I mean, but in life. His face is open and eager, and I'm not convinced it can ever register the exhausted cynicism that should mark Peter out towards the play's end. But it is always best to go for the talent.

We talked a bit, Jack, Michael and I, about rehearsal schedules. Seeing them together again, I was struck again by the contrast between them. Jack is always spruce, fresh-looking, rapid in

* He must have known something. When I returned to New York in November, expecting a select gathering of devoted connoisseurs, I found myself in an enormous cinema – part of the vast 92nd Street Y complex – into which about a thousand people had been packed. After the film was shown I was first of all grilled by a critic from the *New York Times*, and then by quick-witted and erudite members of the audience. I don't remember any of the questions and the only answer I can recall involved my saying, apologetically, 'Well let's face it, two hours is a long time to spend with two guys in a room,' which brought a burst of spontaneous but unwelcome applause from the house.

everything he does, with bright round eyes and a cheerful, determined expression. Michael is lean, sunken-cheeked, somewhat theatrically dressed and haunted-looking, giving the impression that he's back on a short visit from Hades. Nevertheless they have three things in common. They're both Irish, they're both non-drinking alcoholics, they have both cut down from about sixty cigarettes a day to none at all. After we'd finished Michael and I arranged to meet in the evening before going on to have dinner with the cast. I came back to the Pankhurst for a bath while Michael, who's down on 48th and 8th where the sleaze is, went where I want to be – into the sleaze. That's another reason that I want to be at the Algonquin – to be able to step straight out of its sociable lobby into the sleaze. As other people like to step into the snow or the sunshine, I like to step into the sleaze. As far as I've been able to see there is no sleaze around the Pankhurst part of New York, it's just dull. A bit of Third Avenue, a bit of Madison and Park – all perfectly pleasant and respectable with office blocks, etc., and utterly dull.

Michael came over to the Pankhurst at about seven. After he'd expressed surprise and distaste at the complexion of the room, we had a long conversation during the course of which I got drunk, while he sat there sipping water, talking on and on about his lack of an ego problem – with reference of course to our being co-directors – until, drunker and therefore rasher, I said that people who don't have an ego problem don't have to keep saying that they don't have an ego problem, 'because the thing about an ego problem, Michael, is that it never occurs to you you've got one until you've got one and as soon as you've got one you spend your time denying that you've got one'. There was a long pause. He admitted that he did in fact have an ego problem about our co-directing. He was intensely worried about who was going to do what, we mustn't contradict each other in front of the actors, etc. I said,'Listen, I'm co-director, you're co-director, we're after all both grown-up and both sort of human, intelligent, vulnerable. If we make mistakes, why pretend that we don't, and why be embarrassed in front of actors if we have disagreements?' He said, yeah, well he now saw that he did have a bit of a problem to do with his ego on this one and that he didn't really know how it was going to be resolved, he was beginning to find out about himself a little bit through this – the usual American stuff, except that he's an extremely charming and intelligent man, and his writhings were really only with himself – he wasn't trying to wrestle, so to speak, at a distance with me. As we had to go uptown for our dinner with the cast, the matter was left unconcluded.

I'd downed so many malts during the conversation with Michael that I was pretty gone when we arrived at the restaurant, which was up by the Promenade Theatre. Fortunately, or unfortunately, I'm really not sure which, I don't behave very differently when I'm drunk from when I'm sober. I don't fall over, throw up, sing sentimental songs, pick fights (although I admit I'm even quicker than usual to take offence, or start the kind of debate that could lead, but has only once led, to a fight – and then with someone drunker than I was), my speech remains comparatively unslurred, and my thought processes remain fairly uncluttered. To those who know me, I am genial, even affectionate, even *over*-affectionate, but not drunkenly so; to everyone else, and there were a lot of everybody elses this evening whose names and functions I couldn't quite grasp, but were probably mostly backers – one of the perks of being a backer is that you get to meet the company, possibly a greater perk for knowing that the company doesn't want to meet you – to all these I was uncommunicative, irritable, presenting them with a red and sweaty face, slightly unfocused eyes. I really have no memory at all of whom I talked to, or didn't talk to, apart from the actors and Michael and Jack, but I assume that I continued to drink, and I know that at about eleven, when the other guests were beginning to leave, I staggered to my feet with the intention of getting back to the Pankhurst, to discover that Nathan Lane, Kristoffer Tabori and Peter Friedman (our Humphry from the Long Wharf production) were going on to a bar in the neighbourhood, and that I felt an obligation (neither moral nor social) to join them. I had something more – something too much more – to drink. Finally achieving a conventionally and recognizably drunken state, I had myself put into a taxi, the driver of which must have been a man of considerable virtue as he could easily have mugged me at any traffic lights, tumbled me out into the gutter, without anyone, especially myself, being the wiser.

One of the many awful things about being at the Pankhurst is that it is miles from any part of New York you want to, or are likely to have to, be in. The trip back from anywhere you want or have to be is, even when drunk, a foul experience. For instance, from this restaurant near the Promenade we would have bowled rapidly down Broadway, about halfway to the Algonquin, then turned east, where all the streets are choked with traffic because the traffic lights never turn from red to green, or when they do, turn instantly back to red again, and the journey would therefore have taken twice as long as it would have taken to go to the Algonquin. Come to think of it, in terms of actual distance, the Promenade might well be closer to the Pankhurst than to the Algonquin.*

Back and swaying about in my room a salient and terrible fact swam into focus: somebody had been in while I was out and put up a whole new arrangement of curtains – of *working* curtains – thus snatching from me my plan for escape. Depressed, fatalistic and drunk, I clambered into bed, went out like a light.

## Wednesday, 10 September

Woke at eight, made myself a heavy breakfast, went for a walk and then took a taxi to the theatre. First looked at the model of the set, talked to the designer, David Jenkins, and Michael McGuire about the stage furniture and its positioning, then settled down for the read-through, which went OK, the new young actor, Dylan Baker, doing well to keep up with the five actors who had done the part before. Just before the read-through, a girl from Phyllis Wender's office had phoned to say that she'd arranged to have a video delivered whenever I wanted. Knowing that there was nothing but the usual video hassles ahead, I phoned her back after the read-through and said that I would return to the Pankhurst immediately to receive it. Back I went, settling down in my room for a long wait for a video that wasn't going to come, and if it came wouldn't work. Within half an hour there was a phone call from reception to say that the video man had just arrived. Although I'm on the seventeenth floor and it generally takes some time to get up from the lobby, I nevertheless – partly because I can't stand the sound of the bell – went straight to the door and opened it. To my disbelief – it seemed physically impossible – the video chap was coming along the hall towards me, carrying the box loosely and easily under his

* On rainy evenings it took a good twenty minutes longer, *after* I'd got a cab, which often took a bad twenty minutes.

arm, almost as if it were empty. A slightly surreal figure, being a strange racial mix, even by New York standards – a combination of Filipino and West Indian, perhaps, quite young and almost certainly not too good at English. 'Look,' I said slowly, 'the one thing you've got to understand is that I'm immensely stupid and these machines never work for me, did you bring a tape' (I'd asked Phyllis's office to tell them to bring a tape) 'so you can give me a demonstration?' No, he said fluently but in a thick South American accent, he hadn't brought a tape, he'd just have to explain it to me. 'Look,' I said, 'it's no good, I won't understand anything without a tape.' It took him about three minutes to install the video. He then explained to me, with extraordinary rapidity, how to make it work. Actually my attention was fixed on his slightly simian gestures – among other things he was rubbing his thumb up and down under his left armpit. I knew I hadn't grasped anything he'd said and asked him to take me through it again. He said no, he was going. 'Come on,' I said, 'you can take me through it just once more.' 'Aw, is very simple,' he said, and departed, leaving his box on the floor. So the new video débâcle has begun.

I went out. I hadn't had any lunch actually because these hot-dog things I'd eaten at nine o'clock (the same breakfast as the day before) seemed to have swollen my stomach, making me feel rather flatulent. Out into the heat of New York. It's very odd how I've been in the heat in the States all through this year – in Los Angeles in January, Dallas in February, and now here in September in New York, when it should be getting a little cooler. I trudged about looking for a video rental shop without luck, until finally, miles away, right down almost at the Algonquin, I came across one. It had taken me about forty-five minutes to get there. I felt faint. I joined their club and took out *Shane* – just the one video to test on a machine that wasn't after all going to work. I managed to get a taxi back, trembling with fatigue, came up into my room, put the tape into the video, turned on power, then did a kind of peculiar digital computorial thing to do with pressing buttons 3, 0 and 'entry' – how the video man had managed to feed this information into me subliminally, I really have no idea – put the tape in, sat listlessly down, and there, within a matter of seconds, was the title sequence of *Shane*. I watched to the end of the Alan Ladd–Jean Arthur dance scene, and then turned off the set, took out the tape, put it in again and played the scene through in slow motion – all this for practice, before settling down to think about the Gray–McGuire co-directing problem.

I came to the conclusion, out of a desire not to force the issue for the moment – i.e. cowardice – that I'd better stay away from rehearsals for a few days, my argument being that there's not much point my being there at this stage anyway. I've been through the play so often that I'm likely to become impatient, as I did in Los Angeles. The flaw in this argument is that five of the six other actors have also been through the play as well, and that I'm leaving them to be directed by someone who hasn't – so perhaps *they're* likely to become impatient if I'm not there, to help them to start from a fairly advanced stage. Of course there's no harm in Michael's doing some preliminary blocking, a rough sketch, so to speak, from which I can work subsequently. On the other hand, the longer I allow him to do that, the more difficult it will be to get my own grip on proceedings. And so backwards and forwards, facing up to, and not facing up to, the fact that I'm creating, have already created, a dodgy situation that could damage the company's morale before we've properly started. And facing up to a further, practical problem: what do I do instead of going to the theatre, if I don't go to the theatre? How do I find something sufficiently active to do, to keep my mind off rehearsals? Perhaps I should go out and hustle. Hustle what? Hustle myself, on the pavements of Eighth Avenue. But would anyone give five dollars for an hour with me?

## Thursday, 11 September

My hair has felt foul all day. Hardly surprising as I forgot to bring any shampoo and haven't yet got around to buying any. So I went about conscious of this pad of rather unwholesome hair on my scalp. At one point in the day's rehearsals I found myself addressing the problem of Peter's hair with Dylan Baker – Dylan has got a wonderful mop of blond, springy, positively exuberant hair – informing him that one could tell a great deal about the ageing process from people's hair, which changed in some often quite subtle way, not just falling out or turning grey, but visibly losing life and energy. As I talked I could see him eyeing the lustreless pack of dead hair on my own scalp. He's obviously a bright young man who has to be watched very closely, with a view to putting down in him any irony or intelligence that threatens to surface.

After rehearsals I had a pleasant, relaxed and freqently jolly evening with Phyllis in spite of the restaurant, a small bistro-style dump on the East Side, with taped music. Although we arrived slightly late, the table wasn't ready so we had to stand about in the bar before being led to what, from the size of it, might have been a bedside table, one chair at which (mine) blocked the entrance to the wine cellars, thus allowing the waiters to push me backwards and forwards throughout the evening. I knew the food was going to be terrible, too, as all the dishes had chillingly simple names – for instance, crab fishcakes. When the waiter came and took our order – the waiters were ghastly, by the way, poncing about, with suntans and empty grins, as if recently exported from Los Angeles – I decided to have the marinated swordfish, on the grounds that even this lot couldn't mess up something that is served raw, only to be informed that it was off. I said, 'But it's nine fifteen, how can it be off already?' He said jovially, 'Well, it's a very popular dish so it's off.' As the crab fishcakes were even worse than I'd assumed they'd be, there must be a rare talent at work in the kitchen. I tried to get a glimpse of the bill, peering nonchalantly down as Phyllis paid it. The sum that caught my eye was so monstrous that it must have been an optical illusion. I sometimes think that if you can't go to a *good* expensive restaurant, then you should go to a bad expensive one (as long as I'm not paying of course) – it's more fun. Perhaps that's what they've cottoned on to there.

## Friday, 12 September

The theatre was immensely hot, but everything went OK, except for a minor discord between Michael McGuire and myself over the position of a chair, which had been placed right beside Stuart's desk – there's also a chair behind the desk of course. Stuart (Tabori) sat down behind the desk for the beginning of the very long conversation with Martin (Michael Countryman from the Long Wharf production), who immediately sat down beside the desk. So there were the two of them at the desk together, their elbows almost touching, and so it went for the whole fifteen minutes. I couldn't repress the old temper at the tedium, the *pointless* tedium of the experience. Granted that Michael McGuire had no idea what the scene was about and was trying to learn through having the actors sit down and chat their way through the text, I still didn't think it was correct or appropriate for Kris Tabori and Michael Countryman, both of whom have been through this scene endless times before, not to explore it on its feet, so to speak – anything would have been better than their sitting like two elderly club men gossiping about the stock market or X's divorce or Y's divorce or my divorce or your divorce. I said something rather tetchy to Michael McGuire, which led to a minor confrontation. He said he wanted to let the actors get to know each other. I said that they would best get to know each other by working through the scene properly, thus getting the scene on *its* feet. Nevertheless we had a quite pleasant lunch together.

In the afternoon things went on in a dull, achingly hot – it was so hot, one could scarcely breathe – achingly hot way until Marigold (Judy Geeson) came on at the end of Act One to announce her abortion. Whereupon Michael asked her what she felt about the abortion, how the fact of the abortion would show itself in her sense of the scene. I was almost beside myself with irritation. I have been through this conversation not once endlessly (in London), not twice endlessly (at the Long Wharf), not three times endlessly (in Los Angeles), but now for the fourth time, endlessly. I got up – this was an hour before rehearsals were due to finish – swung my bag over my shoulder, made some very blurred apologies to Michael, and left the theatre. I knew that I couldn't sit solemnly on in an un-air-conditioned auditorium on a boilingly hot and airless day in New York, taking part in yet another discussion about what sort of state Marigold would be in when coming from her abortion.*

Came back to the Pankhurst, had a bath and then had dinner with Caroline Lagerfelt, who is extremely pregnant, as the consequence of an affair she'd had with an actor. She was buoyant, eyes sparkling, cheeks rosy, stomach bulging. I found myself feeling very emotional on her account.

* What exasperation prevented me from making clear here is that in Los Angeles the actress concerned was also Judy Geeson. If we'd had a new actress in New York, I would of course have been prepared to go through the conversation again. At least I hope I would. Michael had no option but to go through the scene with Judy, as it was his first time round and he had still to learn how it worked.

## Sunday, 14 September

Various members of the company have had to go off to do commercials, so Lois, the cheerful and rather portly stage manageress has been reading variously the part of Nick, the part of Peter – every part in the play in fact except Stuart, Kris Tabori not having to go off to make a commercial, which I suppose is bad luck on him. But it's all going along as well as can be expected, given the fact that everyone, except Dylan, is far ahead of Michael McGuire, who so far is doing all the blocking and most of the talking. He shows his worry every time I intervene, so I suppose the old ego problem hasn't been disposed of after all. Actually I don't know quite how long we can go on like this, or at what point I shall have to do something about it. Thank God we have lots of time. Otherwise we get on very well, Michael and I.

I should mention that yesterday I damaged my back getting out of a chair in my hotel room. I knew even as I moved that I'd done something wrong. It's one of those chairs where your back can't meet the whole of the chair's back, which curves away from the base of your spine, leaving a gap that you have to be very careful about readjusting your body to, when you move – which I wasn't. I spent most of the day in agony. Sitting down, getting up, bending, anything like that – getting into bed, getting into a bath – all painful. The prospect of picking up the *New York Sunday Times* from outside my door this morning was so depressing that I put it off until I'd lumbered about the room a bit. The sheer weight of the *New York Sunday Times*! I've heard that a small dog was actually crushed to death when a copy landed on it, thrown by what must have been a very muscular newspaper boy. The dog was found pasted to the underside of the front page, and shortly became news itself.

During a (physically) uncomfortable drink I had with Michael in the evening at a Parisian-like sidewalk café he told me he'd heard that Sam Weisman is going to sue Jack McQuiggan for breach of contract.* It seems to me astonishing that Weisman should want the world to know that the producer didn't have confidence in him as a director. He should surely have bowed gracefully out, using the usual 'artistic differences' as an explanation, which in this case

* To the tune of $3,000,000 I learnt later.

would have been accurate, as there genuinely *was* an artistic difference – the difference being that Sam wanted to direct the play and Jack didn't want him to. We were in the middle of discussing this when a Russian lady, an actress that Michael knew, came past. He rose, embraced her, and insisted that she join us. She is one of those ladies that laughs an awful lot because – or so I like to think – she has absolutely no sense of humour, e.g. when Michael, suddenly remembering a Mickey Mouse joke I'd told him, and asked me to repeat it. The Mickey Mouse story derives from a cartoon in the *New Yorker* I'd seen years ago. Mickey Mouse, with a five-day stubble on his face, is sitting on a stool in a bar, hunched over a drink, smoking. Two respectably dressed middle-aged men are watching him, one saying to the other, 'I don't know exactly. But they say he used to be big in Hollywood.' I told this joke – or rather described the cartoon – with considerable *élan*, I felt, to the Russian lady, who actually stopped laughing before I'd finished it. I mean she had laughed all the time before I began to tell the joke, and then partway through the joke, but went silent before the end of it, stayed silent, looking puzzled, then asked, 'That's the joke?' I got a cab to the Pankhurst and went to bed, my back made worse by the journey. When I phoned home this morning, I got Ben, who told me that Beryl had pulled a muscle in her leg at approximately the same time, I worked it out, as I'd ricked my back.

## Tuesday, 16 September

Yesterday was a day off. I spent most of it with my brother, Piers, who arrived on Sunday. We walked around New York. The only time I feel comfortable is when I'm up and walking.

## Wednesday, 17 September

I'm waiting for Michael McGuire to turn up for what we call a showdown conversation. Yesterday at ten o'clock there was meant to be a run-through, which I'd decided not to attend because it seemed more important to find a chiropractor, my plan being to miss the run-through, which I didn't believe could be of much value at this stage, have my back fixed, and get to the theatre in time for rehearsals – the real day's work, as far as I was concerned. Also I had a particular reason for wanting to be at rehearsals as Michael

McGuire had phoned me on Monday evening, to question me about the function and intention of Act One, Scene Two, which struck me as odd – surely it would be much simpler for me to address the actors directly, rather than going through him. Until it further struck me that perhaps he didn't want me to address the actors, the old ego problem again, in other words. Anyway, some time in the late morning I phoned the theatre to say that I hadn't been able to get hold of the chiropractor, at least the one that had been recommended to me, my back was extremely painful, how far along were they in the run-through, what time roughly would rehearsals begin, only to be told that they had been rehearsing all morning as the run-through had been cancelled – Judy Geeson not being well. They had been concentrating on Act One, Scene Two.

I phoned Jack McQuiggan and said we'd better talk, to thrash out once and for all the co-director question. We met in the hamburger joint around the corner from the Pankhurst, an appropriately seedy place where, in films, the cop gets his rake-off, the stoolie his bullet between the eyes. He told me what I already knew – that the actors were getting bewildered and fed up, why wasn't I running the show, why didn't I assume my proper role? I said I could see now that the co-directing idea had been a bad one, how did one apportion the work, we should have sorted it out before, to which he replied that he thought he had sorted it out – his understanding being that I'd do what he'd seen me do with the New York production of *Quartermaine's Terms*, concentrate on discovering all the details of the text with the actors, and help them to realize it, while Michael could deal with any problems on the technical side. He'd hoped that my being officially co-director would make my control of the production easier to achieve, not harder. How had I managed with Stephen Hollis in Dallas? I gave him a brief description, but said I didn't think anything could be learnt from it – Stephen had always assumed I'd take over completely after the second week, had indeed wanted me to, but I was pretty certain that the longer Michael went on doing what he was now doing, the harder it would be to take over from him. I wouldn't be able to insinuate myself into command as I'd done at the Long Wharf, because any move I made would be seen as a director's, a rival director's, move. In fact I had the worst of both worlds, unable to function either as playwright or as director. The situation had to be turned around, we both agreed, and as quickly as possible. But with proper respect for Michael, who was working hard and doing his best in an utterly false situation.

We cabbed down to the theatre, to find Michael running Dylan Baker in his big scene at the end of Act One. It was quite clear that they were both at a loss. At the end of it Michael proposed running the scene again. Dylan objected, asking to be allowed to stop whenever he was uncertain about the way a line should be played. Michael said no, don't stop, I don't think we should stop, let's run it. I stopped the scene almost at once, took Dylan back, discussed a line with him, started him again, stopped him again, every sentence or so. In fact I took over the direction in a manner that was not only high-handed, it was brutal, cutting across Michael whenever he showed signs of speaking, until he sat back impotent, no doubt humiliated. At the end Michael came over, unable to hide his distress, and said, 'Now we have a real problem. Who's going to direct? Who's going to talk to the actors?' We arranged to meet tomorrow at ten (now, in fact) before rehearsals, to answer this question after we'd both had a chance to think it through, but as far as I'm concerned the question is answered. It would not only be a nonsense, but an irresponsible nonsense, to let things go on as they've been going on. What makes it difficult, though, is that I know it's my fault: if I had acted decisively at the beginning, instead of passively waiting for my temper to erupt, as I sort of knew it would in the end, all this could have been avoided.

*Late that night*

Michael came and we talked. A long and painful conversation, though its tone was civilized. He quite agreed that his attempting to direct a play that he knows far less well than I is preposterous. On the other hand, he certainly hadn't understood that Jack had always intended him to be in a subsidiary role, and if he had so understood, wasn't sure that he would have accepted the job. I said that I felt it would be subsidiary only during the next stretch of rehearsals, that once we were in the run-through and preview period, his eye, his ear and his judgement would be invaluable. He said his main problem would be how to deal with the actors. They would be aware of what had happened – Kristoffer Tabori had already given him a look, and he didn't think he could stand that sort of thing, especially as years ago he had been a sort of uncle figure to Kristoffer. I said that I didn't think he'd get that sort of thing from any of the other actors, and proposed that today he should go in as usual and do anything he wanted in the first two hours but before he began, he should say that I was going to come in later and do some very close work on the text, of the sort that I had done yesterday with Dylan Baker. Michael said that if I was going to take over he would prefer me to do it immediately, which left me with the prospect of five hours' rehearsal without a break – too much, really, given my back and the nature of the work. But we both agreed that from now on I would be running the rehearsals, which brought the conversation to an end. As it turned out I had enough stamina for only three hours, but they were three hours of intensely detailed work – the only sort of work I can do as a director. But then I don't think myself there is any other sort of work worth doing, as everything from the specific physical moves to the general shape of a scene grows out of it. I was absolutely exhausted by the end. As I didn't get much sleep last night, God knows how I'm going to cope with tomorrow's rehearsals.

## Saturday, 20 September

The composer is young, bulky, bearded and on crutches, having snapped his ankle in a skiing accident, I suppose – it was never quite clear how he'd snapped his ankle, now I come to think of it. He lay, semi-recumbent on a sofa, outside the rehearsal hall, with his crutches beside him, telling me that, though my play was very 'neat', he planned to juice it up by slipping some music in under the dialogue. Music and dialogue to be going on at the same time, as in a movie. I tried to be polite, ordering him up a glass of champagne from the bottles I keep stored in the rehearsal-room fridge, and then decided to be dictatorial immediately about what I expected from him, in order not to have to be even more dictatorial later on. Music only where specified in the text – Bach, Wagner, etc. – and no music, by God, anywhere else, but particularly not under the dialogue. He lay there, his crutches beside him, a glass of champagne in his hand, shaking his head in bewildered disappointment. He has a habit of referring to himself by his surname, which I can't remember, but supposing it to be Plumbell (it was something like that), he would say, 'You mean it's going to be just Wagner and Bach and no Plumbell? Plumbell doesn't get a chance to use his own music. Is that what you mean?' I have an idea that this isn't going to be a happy collaboration, although I'm assured he's very talented. The trouble is we don't want a very talented Plumbell, we just want a good, solid, professional chap, who is modest about his own music and is anxious to serve the play with well-chosen passages from Bach and Wagner, etc.

Post Plumbell Michael and I went and had a drink, as is becoming our habit. As least I have a true drink, an alcoholic drink, and he has club soda with a twist of lemon, or a Perrier with a twist of lemon. At the end of rehearsals I'm usually so tired that the first drink tips me over – when I say first, I'm not counting the champagne I sip very moderately while working. Anyway, the moment I get into my first Glenfiddich, I go plummeting into pleasant semi-oblivion. But Michael wanted to talk again about his position in the production. I said I needed him both as companion and friend, and as a highly intelligent and experienced man of the theatre to whom I could turn for some kind of judgement – on this move or that move, on this line or that. I also said that I needed his opinions on how the actors were progressing, and that he would certainly come into his own when we got to the preview stage. Besides, I said, it seemed to me extremely important that he should be present at every phase of the process so that he would be in full possession of it for any future productions, which he would be directing on his own. He said, yes, he understood all that but it was driving him crazy just sitting there not speaking. Furthermore, I'd got into a habit of doing something that he found particularly disturbing: talking to the actors without in any way referring to him, in fact going off with them, standing with my back to him, so that he couldn't even hear what I was saying. I apologized, explaining that I hadn't been aware even that I was doing it – that it was really just a matter of strolling with an actor as we talked and ending up where we happened to end up. He said that as far as he could see he had three options: either he could stay on as a co-director if he had an equal contribution to make to the production, but he didn't think he had; or he could withdraw entirely; or he could stay on as a consultant, in which case he would want his title changed, because he wasn't going to pass himself off as a co-director of a play he hadn't co-directed. I said I didn't give a damn what he was called as long as he was there for me to refer to on the terms that I've described. It was again an extremely civilized conversation. When we parted he said he'd go home and think about it. Fortunately, his young lady has arrived from Los Angeles so he will have somebody to discuss it with.

## Sunday, 21 September

They're putting the set into the Promenade, so we've moved rehearsals down to the Village, on the third floor of a tall building – tall, anyway, for the neighbourhood. It's a very spacious room, and would be a joy to work in if it weren't for one of the walls, which consists of two sliding doors. When they're closed, the room is almost unbearably hot. When they're opened, they lead you directly out on to the street. By way of a 60-foot plunge. A death plunge. As I suffer from both a fear of heights and a fear of death I ordered the doors to be shut, and worked throughout the afternoon in suffocating heat. If the actors ever decide they want to exclude me from rehearsals, all they have to do is to demand that the doors are kept open. There is bound to be an Equity ruling that gives them the right to do so.

After rehearsals Michael McGuire and I had a drink at a nearby pub, the White Horse. It's a commodious and casual sort of place, with tables on the pavement outside, and inside lots of dark rooms, some small, some large. While I was downing my Glenfiddich I suddenly remembered that this was the bar in which – or rather, outside of which – Dylan Thomas pegged out after knocking off a dozen or so double shots of whatever it was he was drinking. Whisky, vodka. Perhaps both. He set them up in a line on the counter, threw them one after the other down his throat, lurched out of the main bar past the pavement tables, and collapsed into the gutter, from which he was removed to the hospital and death. At least so I've always understood. So I'll have to watch it at the White Horse – order my drinks one at a time, allow as long an interval as possible between each, confine myself to three doubles at the most. I don't want to end up in the White Horse gutter. Especially as I'm not that keen on Dylan Thomas's poetry. Not keen enough to be taken for a disciple, anyway.

Michael and I steered clear of the co-directing question. We mainly talked about New York, swapping stories about street encounters, most particularly about cab drivers. He told me what is apparently a famous story (i.e. probably untrue) about a yellow cab and a chequered cab, always in intense competition with each other. On one occasion, so this story goes, a chequered cab drew up beside a yellow cab at the traffic lights. The yellow cab driver looked across at the chequered cab, and seeing an extraordinarily fat woman sitting in the back, yelled out to the driver, 'Hey, that's some fat lady you got there! What a fat lady you got there!' The chequered cab driver shouted back: 'Listen, this lady is my passenger! She's a fine lady! Special! What do ya mean talking about this fine, fine lady like that? That's dreadful, you cunt, you shithead, you puke-maker *and* you fuck-all, you're talking here about an important passenger of mine!' The traffic lights changed. Driving off, he turned and said, 'How's that for telling 'em, fat lady?' Now I'd probably have forgotten this story, if it hadn't been for the driver of the cab that took me from the White Horse to the Pankhurst. He was a Greek, and informed me, within minutes and very quietly, that in his view New York was a zoo, yes, a zoo, he said, and everyone in it was an animal. 'They call it Manhattan, but for me it is a zoo.' Suddenly the cab in front did something with which he disagreed, whereupon and still in thoughtful flow, he pulled down the window, leaned out to scream, 'Hey, you fucking cunt, you shithead, you big, big swine, what you doing there?' The other taxi driver did whatever he was going to do anyway, and my driver, calmly winding up the window, resumed his discourse on Manhattan as a zoo. The thing is that Michael's story is a well-known fiction, and mine is simply a report of something that happened a mere few hours ago, immediately after I'd heard Michael retelling the fiction. And yet they tell almost exactly the same story. Perhaps it repeats itself, in slightly different form, every few minutes in New York.

Back at the Pankhurst I had a bath, then dinner with Piers in what I have taken to be the hotel restaurant. Afterwards we came up to my suite, and had a very nice time rocking about with glasses of Glenfiddich in our hands until the Glenfiddich ran out. I phoned down to the desk, and asked them to tell the bar or restaurant to send up more. Neither could do it, I was told, as neither was attached legally to the hotel. And the hotel couldn't do it, as it didn't have a licence. Thus I discovered that the Pankhurst isn't even a hotel, it's a kind of condominium. Which certainly explains why I've never felt at home here. If we wanted a drink, I was told, we'd have to come down to the bar. Where we wouldn't get one, as the bar was already closed. How then had it come to pass, as I was assured by someone or other that it had, that a famous actor had drunk himself to death in the bar. With only a few hours at his disposal, he must have been an even more impatient suicide than Dylan Thomas, who could take his time at the White Horse, open day and night.

## Tuesday, 23 September

I'd just got back to the Pankhurst from rehearsals when Ronald Harwood, in from London, phoned. We arranged to have dinner in the restaurant downstairs. It was a very jolly evening, with lots of laughter, decent wine, OK food, and an unbeatable, almost unpayable, bill. Ronnie was only staying the night, at a very splendid hotel, having been Concorded in (he was also being Concorded out) by a film company for a few conversations which, he said, could easily have taken place on the telephone. We wondered how it is that I never get involved in deals like his, Virgin 'Upper' being pretty well the limit to what people are prepared to offer me – and then I have to stay weeks and weeks to justify it. We agreed that Ronnie gets Concorde and big film deals because he is (a) handsomer, (b) more successful, (c) older, (d) shorter. After dinner I walked him down the street towards the Waldorf, then turned back to the hotel. I was, I must admit, rocking, swaying, in fact scarcely able to keep my balance, but I'd almost made it to the Pankhurst when this Jewish guy, with a rabbinical sort of hat on, swarmed up to me, gripped me by the shoulders and said he wanted twenty dollars. Otherwise he'd have to kill me. I said, no, there was no possibility of my giving him twenty dollars. He said, well, what about ten? I said no, not ten either. He said, well what I'm going to do, I'm going to kill ya – 'I gotta kill ya,' he said. 'I gotta kill ya or I don't get home, what am I going to do?' So I said, 'Well listen, take this.' I poured all the change from my pockets – about 75 cents – into his hands, and left him there. He was about six foot three, about twenty-five years old, and very Jewish with his Jewish skull cap on (I forget what they're called).* He stood there, where I'd left him, counting up the change.

* Yarmulkas.

## Wednesday, 24 September

Arranged to meet Michael and Jack at the White Horse before rehearsals to discuss yet again the question of Michael's status in the production. Horrible ride, with the taxi driver masquerading as a sociologist – or, an even worse thought, a sociologist masquerading as a taxi driver – doing an in-depth analysis on the subject of the major change in New York life, viz. that some years back New York was a place where intelligent people gathered together to talk (he made the whole city sound rather like Les Deux Magots), but now it was just a place where people wanted to buy condominiums.* That was it. That was his whole analysis, though he spun it out by repeating it endlessly.

Michael was already at the White Horse, at a pavement table. I think he's the only person I know who is more punctual than Harold – if, that is, punctual also includes being early. Jack was late of course. He is, I think, the *least* punctual man I know, always deflected on his way to meetings by meetings that give rise to further meetings. As I've said before, he is a very dapper dresser, with a well-knit figure and a neat-featured, wholesome, round face, and there he stood on the pavement of the White Horse, late, in his smart suit with highly polished shoes, his usual collar and tie, his hair slicked back, while around his chops was a five o'clock shadow at least three days old. Thick, grey-black stubble is what it was. I said, 'Jack, what's going on here?' He said, 'Well I just – I've decided not to shave until we've opened. You know, like baseball players or football players who don't shave until they've got through the championship. A superstition.' He was quite hard to take actually, because he looked simultaneously immaculate and sordid.† The conversation that then took place – on whether Michael should have a change of title or quit the production – followed the same course as the one Michael and I had already had, Jack's contribution being merely to support me in my determination to keep Michael with us, although he was strongly against a change of title on the grounds that it would cause unnecessary fuss in the press. It was once again friendly in tone, and once again ended with the matter unresolved. At least as far as I know. Jack

* Perhaps he meant 'condoms', which would have made more sense.

† I'm glad to say that it was a short-lived combination, as the stubble came off next day. I like to think that it was the look on my face that did the trick.

and Michael stayed on, talking, while I rocked up to the West Beth Theatre Complex, or whatever it's called, to conduct rehearsals.

Afterwards, Nathan Lane, Michael Countryman and I went back to the White Horse, and over drinks talked about the real nature of rehearsing and directing, the relationship between the director, the playwright and the actors, etc., all in very general terms. Bonhomous, philosophical, rambling, unproductive, except in the pleasure it gave us while it was going on. Then Michael Countryman got on his motorbike (though I've been begging him not to ride it until after we've opened – or even better, after we've closed). Nathan and I went on talking and getting increasingly drunk, until first Dena and James turned up – we'd arranged to meet for dinner – and then Stephen Hollis, who was in town from Dallas to cast *A Streetcar Named Desire*. Nathan went rolling off into the night, his feet sort of skipping drunkenly across the pavement, while the remaining four of us crossed the road to a Chinese restaurant where the food was merely bad, while the drinks were positively appalling – Stephen receiving a glass of white wine which actually tasted like pear juice, though claiming to be a Chablis. Nevertheless we had quite a nice evening, just sort of relaxed and chatty. Stephen and I lingered on to talk about the triumphs and the horrors of the Dallas production of *Dog Days*. There were very few horrors, as we agreed, but then there were very few triumphs, we had also to agree. He went on to say that he was actually rather depressed about the situation at the New Arts, as since *Dog Days* every single member of the company apart from himself had been fired. We discussed the implications of this for his career* until, waving about from drink, I came back to the Pankhurst where I am now, reporting into the tape recorder. It's one in the morning, and though I've had quite a rough day and a far too sociable evening, I feel all right. A lot of good things are going on in rehearsal, the play seems to be becoming more vivid, breathing in a more relaxed way, and yet growing firmer and firmer. I am deeply tired, carrying on with this monologue because I'm convinced there's somebody out there somewhere that I need to communicate with – rather like E.T. trying to phone home, I suppose.

* About three months later the New Arts went bankrupt and the theatre was closed down. It was then that I discovered that I hadn't received any royalties, either as playwright or as co-director, and therefore ended up heavily out of pocket.

## Tuesday, 30 September

Back on stage in the Promenade, with a major problem in the form of Kristoffer Tabori. During the last few run-throughs I'd noticed that he'd begun to regress, offering first a stale imitation of his best Los Angeles performances, rather as if he were doing it from memory or that it was something he'd brought with him like a suit, that he could just slip into when needed; and then through that to his worst Los Angeles performances, his Lee J. Cobb period, though with some extra mannerisms stuck on. It was a heavy piece of impersonation, in fact, though I was never sure who he was impersonating. Sometimes he reminded me of a befuddled elderly academic; other times – this was a matter of the voice – of Winston Churchill summoning the nation to war: in his first speech of the play, which needs to be crisply thoughtful, we get, 'I just don't *kno–o–ow* – I just don't *kno–o–ow* – there's a letter here from *Le–e–e–avis*, full of *words* like *emba–a–attled* and *bele–e–eaguered*.' For the most part, though, he was using voice to comment on Stuart's language, elaborately stressing certain words and phrases to indicate that here he was being ironic, there forceful. It became impossible to judge what was going on in any scene in which he appeared – he appears in almost every scene – because it was cluttered by his actorish gesticulations and his bizarre vocalizations. No notes I gave him out in the open seemed to have any effect. He didn't actually resist them, but – again – seemed to be impersonating an actor listening to a director.

The final straw came towards the end of today's rehearsal, during the long dualogue with Michael Countryman, a very difficult passage, which works only if we can persuade the audience to listen intently to every word, which in its turn can be achieved only by having the actors listening intently to each other. During one of Michael Countryman's speeches Tabori took off his spectacles, blew on them, wiped them, put them back on, fingered his ears, stroked his chin, and stared down at his feet – he'd never done any of this before but now he did all of it and all of it within Michael Countryman's fairly short speech, which therefore went for nothing. I decided the time had come to confront him directly, but in such a way that I wouldn't seem to be making a big deal of it. So, of course, in trying not to make a big deal of it, I succeeded in making a big deal of it.

First, I chose a patch in the play, the beginning of the Epilogue, in which every actor except Tabori appears, then telling Michael what I planned, asked him to run it a few times, as often as necessary in fact, while I took Tabori out for a drink. We went to the bar next door, where I ordered myself a large whisky, plugged a glass of whatever he'd asked for into his hand, and began to tell him what he was doing. I employed my tentative smile and shy, uncertain voice technique, explaining the effect all his gesticulating and his mannerisms were having on his performance. He said but that was *him*, that was real life, he couldn't help it, that's what people did in life if they were naturally gesticulative people. I said yes, perhaps, but the trouble is that the character he's playing is intensely still and watchful, he was *written* that way. He made a vague gesture towards understanding this, and I recalled with a spasm of hope that we'd gone through almost exactly the same conversation in Los Angeles, to very good effect. I moved on with more confidence to discuss the question of his growing tendency to explain and comment on the text with his voice. I'd hardly got into it, in fact was in mid-sentence, when he said, 'Thank you very much for the drink, I don't want to hear any more, goodbye.' And, turning on his heel, walked out. I stood in the bar for about thirty seconds, thinking, ah yes, of course the Matrix strikes back* – the Matrix being the only theatre I've ever worked in where actors taking umbrage and flouncing off were likely punctuations in the day's work. I knocked off the rest of my drink and hurried after him, catching him as he was just about to turn into the theatre. Swallowing pride, bile, I said something oily along the lines that we really must continue this conversation, if offence had been given, none had been intended, etc. It was either that or *force majeure* (like a blow to his groin). But with the first public performance two days away, I realized it was wiser not to engage in a pavement brawl with my leading man. We went back to the bar for further drinks. After a preliminary and debasing conversation about his feelings and my feelings, our relationship in Los Angeles, when I was the playwright and he was first the director and then an actor, and now in New York where I was the director and he was again an actor, I manoeuvred the conversation around to the primary subject – his performance. I got most of the things said that I

* I thought a number of other things too which are recorded on tape but don't sit prettily on the page.

wanted to say – several times in fact – and he appeared to be taking it in, when we were interrupted by a member of the stage management who said that Michael McGuire had finished running the scene. We went back to the theatre where Michael told me he had finished running the scene about eight times and didn't have the nerve to run it yet again.

## Wednesday, 1 October

Rehearsals proceeded smoothly until there was another confrontation with Tabori. It came, as before, towards the end, when everybody was exhausted. He had obviously done his best to cut out as much of the distracting fussiness as he could but there were still lots of places where he was getting in the way of the play. I pointed them out to him as we came to them, with remorseless politeness and implacable good nature, though I could sense his smouldering resentment. When we returned to the top of Act One, Scene Two, I took him through his long conversation on the telephone, which he was concluding with a swivel in his swivel chair, as he simultaneously seized the datebook* and began to scan its pages with the telephone clamped under his ear, speaking into it as he made to jot something down. I knew that he was particularly fond of this piece of business as it had become more and more complicated but having started on my road I was determined to keep going down it. 'Kris,' I said, with the air of a man about to move on to more important things, 'don't swivel in the chair and don't use the datebook.' Whereupon he asked to have a private word with me.

We went out into the foyer, where he launched into a feverish account of what he thought he was as an actor and what he thought acting was about. I found it very hard to listen to him because what I most of all noticed was that he was doing all the things he'd been doing on the stage, gesticulating, taking off his glasses, stepping forwards, stepping sideways, as if really bent on showing me that everything in his performance came directly from his personal observation of his own behaviour. Finally he allowed me to explain why he couldn't use the swivel and the datebook while speaking into the phone – that I wanted the audience to take in the significance of what he was saying, rather than admire his agility

* In England, known as a diary.

with props, although I put it more tactfully. He said I was stripping him down, stripping him down of everything he did as an actor, until there would be nothing left at all. He said that he really felt that if I went on doing this to him he would have no choice but to leave. He would open in the play of course, and then give his two weeks' notice immediately.* He didn't see he had any alternative, I was destroying him. I don't know whether I believed him or not and I don't know whether, at that moment, I cared or not, and I can't remember how we finished the conversation. But shortly afterwards we ended up back on the stage and went through the telephone conversation again, without swivel or datebook. He did it very well and it worked very well.

I then broke for the day, but before I could get off with Michael for a drink, Tabori somehow trapped me and began a curious debate about the principles of acting, he lying full length on stage, I standing in the aisle below him, my throat parched and full of yearning. Actually it wasn't a proper debate – I hadn't touched on the principles of acting, not knowing what they are. Nevertheless he claimed that he agreed with everything I'd said, he simply had a different approach. He was perfectly friendly and I suppose that, as the producer and the other actors were still hanging about the theatre listening, all he was really doing was showing that he and I were still talking to each other. Later, over my drink, I spoke to Michael in recuperating terms of my feelings – every other actor is doing so well, the rehearsals are in every other respect so harmonious and enjoyable . . . This drink, by the way, was taken at a bar–restaurant along 56th Street called Melon's, after the owner. The décor is all melons – drawings, watercolours, oil paintings, lithographs, photographs, everywhere you look there is a representation of this visually entertaining but otherwise rather dull fruit. As my new play is called *Melon*, after the central character, I find it slightly eerie. Certainly portentous. But of what?

* One of the serious disadvantages – perhaps the only serious disadvantage – of having a play done Off-Broadway rather than On-Broadway is that Equity allows actors the right to give two weeks' notice, thus jeopardizing the stability and continuity of the production. The Equity argument is that actors are paid comparatively little Off-Broadway and should therefore be in a position to accept on the spot any work for which they might get paid more. In an Off-Broadway production of one of my plays some years back the leading lady did in fact give two weeks' notice just before we went into previews, which meant that she left the day after we'd opened.

## Thursday, 2 October

Our first public performance, though not an official preview. In fact Jack had told us he'd merely invited a small group of friends. The auditorium, however, was packed and it turned out that almost everyone had paid for their tickets. This isn't a complaint, rather a little memorandum of admiration to Jack. I'd much rather play before a full house, whatever the circumstances, and so would the actors once they get going. And of course I'd always rather people paid for their tickets, especially when I get a percentage – two percentages in this case.

The show went OK for a first go. The nature of the work still to be done was pretty evident, mainly a matter of translating the rehearsal tempo into a theatrical tempo, eliminating irrelevant pauses, coming in far quicker on cue, re-examining a number of moves that now suddenly seemed redundant – the usual kind of stuff. And Kristoffer Tabori. He had in a sense proved his point. Now that he'd had everything stripped away he was nothing, or anyway gave us nothing, except a voice humanly hollow but nevertheless commenting and intoning. He allowed interminable pauses before speaking and made a point of not looking at the actors when they spoke to him, or indeed when he spoke to them. Instead he looked at the ground pointlessly, his shoulders slightly hunched. A particularly unfortunate posture in this lighting – the lighting clearly also requires a lot of work – as he invariably lowered his face into shadow, thus making himself look to the audience like a loser, a jerk and a loser. No, that's intemperate and not quite true. He has considerable physical charm on stage, so what he really looked like was a hounded schoolboy.

## Friday, 3 October

I spent the morning rehearsing Tabori, trying to get some animation into his performance without allowing him to become a windmill. The worst aspect of this situation is that I've begun to neglect the other actors, all of whom need (or anyway *think* they need) attention. In the afternoon we had our first official preview. I would have been delighted by it, as would McQuiggan and McGuire, if it hadn't been for Tabori's performance. After the show the three of us proceeded to our table at Melon's, and over our respective drinks – two club sodas for them and a very large Glenfiddich for me – considered ways, some of them very sinister indeed, of dealing with our problem. Nothing in the end seemed feasible except the obvious one of my continuing to try to get from him what we all wanted – a live, quick-witted, uncommenting, ungesturing, fully expressed Stuart on the stage.

I went back to the Pankhurst, feeling dejected and defeated, had a bath, returned for the second preview. It went very much as the first had done. Michael McGuire and I went up to the dressing-rooms to see the actors. The dressing-rooms are actually one room divided into two sections. In the first section are Kristoffer Tabori and Judy Geeson, in the other section everybody else. But in order to get into the second dressing-room you have to go through the first – a kind of rite of passage. The first person I saw was Tabori – he was taking off his make-up. Our eyes met in the mirror. I smiled at him with sickeningly cheerful intensity, gave his shoulder a half-squeeze which I tried not to make punitive, then turned to Judy and gave her a cuddle of real enthusiasm. I have come to admire her performance enormously – fresh, warm, uncomplicated and honest, which, given the fact that she spends almost all her time on stage telling lies, is a remarkable achievement. Then, liberated, through into the next dressing-room, with heartfelt embraces and compliments for Michael Countryman, Nathan Lane, Peter Friedman and Dylan Baker. Dylan, having struggled far behind the others with the text in rehearsal and often quite clearly full of doubt, blossomed remarkably from the moment – it came very early – when he got his first laugh, and spent the rest of the evening joyfully garnering many more.*

Over a drink at Melon's Jack and I again debated the Tabori problem for a while, considering further alternatives. There *are* no alternatives, of course, but animated dismissals of impossible solutions somehow give one hope – or at least give one the illusion of doing *something*. We had to break off to go to a party, which was being held in the penthouse of the theatre. We were rather late – Michael McGuire and the cast had already gone up – and we made ourselves even later by not being able to find any route from the lobby to the penthouse, until we stumbled on a heavily

* Subsequently, in fact, he became so successful at laugh-garnering that he began to threaten the structure of the scenes and had to be held somewhat in check.

disguised lift that took us, not only up to the penthouse, but right into the vast sitting room in which the party was underway. It was a very lavish, beautifully appointed apartment, or at least so I was told by several young men clustered about the place, whose role I couldn't determine, but it was so dimly lit that I couldn't make out much more than the essentials – i.e. where the sofas and chairs, drinks and food were located. It did however command a magnificent view of the river, though I sometimes think that almost every apartment I've been into in New York commands a magnificent view of the river – or, if not the river, of the park. I wasn't sure who the apartment belonged to, but I suppose – logic suggests – that it would be owned by the guy who owns the theatre, but as I didn't know what he looked like (still don't) I made a point of treating every rich-looking, unidentifiable male as the host, issuing compliments on the food, the view, etc. Among the people I talked to early on was Kristoffer Tabori's mother, the actress Vivica Lindfors, and Holland Taylor, the actress who'd played Anne Butley opposite Alan Bates on Broadway all those years ago.

I gave neither of them full attention because all the time my eyes were fixed on Michael McGuire and Kristoffer Tabori, who were engaged in what looked like rather passionate conversation on the other side of the room. Suddenly Tabori broke away, looking angry, distressed, something, and I remembered that at Melon's, after the afternoon preview, Michael had offered to talk to Kristoffer as his old friend and mentor. So let's say that Tabori looked exactly like a chap who's just been talked to by an old friend and mentor. I slipped up to Michael, and asked him what had happened. He said he'd offered his services – anything he could do to help improve Tabori's performance, talk, go through the scenes, whatever. Tabori first went – or pretended to go – into a state of shock, then asked why we were all ganging up on him, what was the matter with his performance, he thought it was fine, everything had come together for him, he knew exactly what he was doing, perfectly happy, why couldn't we leave him alone? This deepened my depression. If Tabori really believes that he is ace in the part, *and* is convinced that all criticism and offers to help are merely part of a plan conceived by bullies to give him a bad time . . . I sought out Tabori, trying to look genial and yet impassive, but before I could start, he wanted to know what was going on, why we were all ganging up on him, etc., he thought he was doing just fine – after which I delivered a little pack of clichés, with an anchovy of a compliment on each, about the differences between the actor's view and the audience's, our need to develop, even change slightly, our perspective, and what harm could it do to talk to Michael, they were both intelligent men, after all Tabori could aways discard anything that didn't seem to him useful, *such* a difficult part, as we all knew . . . In the end he agreed to talk to McGuire, although only on condition that he didn't have to listen to him. Reminiscent of the kind of arrangement I used to come to with Ben, my son, when he was having a dodgy time with the teachers at Highgate Primary School.

## Sunday, 5 October

Yesterday afternoon I went into a bout of what I already recognize as uncontrolled paranoia (I like to think I live most of my life in a state of *controlled* paranoia). I sat through the matinée which, I think, went very well, and I know I took lots of notes, because I've still got them, on such technical things as pauses, looks that go astray, etc., but my only memory is of my eyes, mind, heart, soul being fixed in a kind of cold passion on Tabori, as he walked about the stage with the measured pace that no human being really walks with, *except* on stage, and certainly no *young* man should ever walk with, even on stage – walking in a stately way about the stage, and delivering his lines in a stately but strangled voice, then dropping his eyes to his feet, thus dropping whatever actor he was playing with (usually Michael Countryman) into the shit, as no other actor, however good he is, can play effectively on stage with someone who isn't there. But it was above all the lines, the way he delivered my lines. *My* lines. That was the point. So suddenly the playwright shouldered aside the director, crying out – how can this be allowed to happen? How could you let this guy maul my language? Real paranoia, or possibly schizophrenia in that there were suddenly two of me, one of whom was giving the other absolute hell.

I went to Melon's, spent most of the evening preview there, looking in on the theatre to glare at Tabori, before ducking back to Melon's. And did much the same during today's two performances, unable to stay longer than twenty minutes at a stretch during the matinée, making an occasional note, managing to go back and see the actors afterwards, grinning out compliments at Tabori in a tone as unnatural, I imagine, as his on stage. But really I was in a different world, a world of drink and anger. I spent almost all the evening performance at Melon's, either by myself or with Jack and/or Michael – they kept darting back to see bits of the show, coming back to report on the lack of change in Tabori's performance. It must have been about halfway through the second act – anyway Jack was there and Michael wasn't – that I rose from the table and without even knowing I was going to do it, got some change at the counter, went to the cigarette machine and bought a packet of cigarettes. I smoked my way through them, one after the other and sometimes probably two simultaneously, and felt – I suppose this is the worst part – such joy, such release to have the murderous old friend swirling about in the lungs again. (Swirling about *now*, drifting through my nostrils, filling the room *now*, as I dictate this.) I won't say the paranoia leaked away on the spot, but I was able to discuss rationally with Jack, and then with Michael, how I intend to proceed with Tabori. I'll simply go on giving him notes, *all* the notes I make, closing him down in details, eliminating every pause, every look at his feet, force him to deal eyeball to eyeball with the other actors – in fact, assume that if we can't get him into the play as Stuart, we can get him out of its way as an imposter. Drill him into submissive service. That, it seems to me, is the director's duty to the playwright. Though I can't say I'm looking forward to performing it. It's now two in the morning. I have an overflowing ashtray and an almost empty cigarette packet beside me. If I smoke myself out, will I be able to start tomorrow afresh? *Afresh!* Hah!

## Thursday, 9 October

Tomorrow I'll have done my time at the Pankhurst, and can move out. I've booked myself into the Algonquin, Suite 310, which they've assured me will be ready by lunchtime. I can't quite believe it, expecting at any moment to be summoned by a warder and taken down to see the Governor, a severe but compassionate man, who will break the news that there's been a hitch, the Parole Board have reviewed my case and come to the conclusion that I'm still not ready to be returned to society. If so, I'll make a run for it.

On my desk, by the way, there's a cable from Joe Stern. It arrived this morning, to the accompaniment of the usual savage ring at the door. Catching his name before I took in the contents, I assumed it was a premature First Night good-luck message. In fact, it's a short, angry statement to the effect that I'd given him my word that the name of the Matrix Theatre would appear on the title page of the Promenade programme. Obsessed as I've been with previews, I hadn't even looked at the programme. I did so immediately of course, and couldn't at first see any acknowledgement of the Matrix anywhere. Eventually I located it, in superfine print on a back page, squeezed into a paragraph of many other acknowledgements, one of them to a meat-packing company. (But what has a meat-packing company contributed to the production? Nobody eats meat in the course of the play. At least to my knowledge.) I spoke to Jack who's promised to move the Matrix to the title page, in large letters. What strikes me as a bit of a mystery, though, is how Joe got hold of the information about the Promenade programme? Somebody must either have sent him a copy or phoned him about it. But who? And why the coldly recriminatory cable, when he could easily have phoned? He can't really have believed that I, personally, put him down there with the meat-packers, can he? Or does he see me, since the *affaire* Weisman, as Perfidious Albion?

Anyway, at this moment – 11.30 p.m. – Perfidious Albion is lying on the green sofa of the all-green sitting room for what he hopes is the last time, a cigarette between his lips, a glass of malt in one hand, the tape recorder in the other, trying to get his mind back to tonight's preview. I haven't yet looked at my notes, but I have the general impression that it went OK, given that we're still nowhere very much with our leading man, though at least he's beginning to speed up, move the scenes along, and keep his eyes at eye-level. There was a great deal of applause at the end, which I chose to take as heartfelt, and even some 'bravos' – but then New Yorkers famously love to explode into 'bravos'. It's part of their idea of an evening out. It's part of my idea of their evening out, too, as a matter of fact.

In a few minutes I shall clamber to my feet, and make my way slowly and carefully a few hundred yards up the road to the Drake Hotel. I shall sit in the bar there and hope that the limp-wristed pianist who a few nights ago infuriated a large couple from Houston with a pansified version of 'The Yellow Rose of Texas' is on again tonight. If so I shall encourage him to have a go at pansifying 'Rule Britannia'.

## Friday, 10 October

Came straight back from the matinée, packed my bags, and departed from the Pankhurst, shiftily announcing to everybody in earshot – which included the usual clutch of imminent ghosts – that I'd been very happy there *indeed*, would they please forward any mail to the Algonquin, to which I was having to move for convenience's sake, under-tipped the doorman from nerves (I usually do the reverse) and cabbed jauntily down here to the Algonquin, savouring the atmosphere of the familiar, much-missed lobby as I made my way to the desk, where I was informed that Suite 310 was not, after all, free, as its present occupant, some thoughtless swine of a senator, has postponed his departure until tomorrow morning. So I'm presently installed in 506, a pleasant enough suite which I took a violent dislike to moments before I saw it. As I'm only here overnight I haven't bothered to unpack my bag or the various carrier bags which I've used for transporting all the stuff – mainly unread paperbacks – that I've accumulated over the last four weeks. I've brought the video with me, too, of course, which I've insisted on having plugged in on the grounds, I suppose, that it will have to be unplugged and replugged in 310 tomorrow morning, and on the further grounds that I'll be too tired to watch anything on it tonight, when I get back from the theatre. Perhaps the need to be in possession of a functioning video has now passed beyond a neurosis into a kind of monomania. All I know is that now I've tested it with a few minutes of *Shane*, I feel much more comfortable, ready to descend to the lobby for a Glenfiddich and a couple of cigarettes before going on to the Promenade, for the evening preview. I probably won't even bother to pause at the desk, to make a further scene about being kept out of 310.

*Later*

Tonight's was our eighth preview. It was also the night on which Tabori made his breakthrough. Everything about him was simple, direct and focused. As a consequence he had authority, a real power, so that for the first time one understood why his friends look to him as a kind of standard-bearer. I don't know how he's managed it – though I noticed that he'd stopped straining for a characterizing English accent, which must have helped him relax considerably.* I know I haven't given him any real help. From the moment he walked out on me in the bar I've found it impossible to talk to him except in very specific terms – 'Don't pause there,' 'Don't look down or away there,' 'Don't stress this word – and this – and this –' – all the steady drip, drip, drip of notes could do was limit his room for manoeuvre, not actually give him the kind of life he had tonight. Anyway, I was exhilarated, positively bounding up the stairs to the dressing-room to salute him. He could tell – at least I hope he could – that for once I was paying him tributes from the heart, not simply flinging compliments around like confetti as a way of getting into the real business of dishing out notes. I gave Judy an extra dose of cuddles – I could see she knew something special had happened, and was thrilled by it – then went on into the second dressing-room, where I found an extremely distressed Michael Countryman. Hardly surprising. He's got so into the habit of playing Martin as if he's alone on stage that suddenly finding himself confronted by a real human being who looked him in the eye and asked him questions threw him completely. He'd gone from floundering to sinking and now sat in the dressing-room shaking slightly, scarcely able to speak.

I slipped along to Melon's, had a drink by myself, to toast the arrival in the play of a real Stuart at last, and then remembered that I was expected at a bar on Columbus Avenue, where Dylan was celebrating his twenty-eighth birthday. I rambled along to it, revelling in my first anxiety-free half-hour since I'd arrived in New York. The bar, small, noisy and Irish, was called the Emerald Isle. Judy Geeson and Kristoffer Tabori had already left but Peter Friedman, Nathan Lane, Michael Countryman and his girlfriend, Dylan Baker and his girlfriend were there, all packed into one small booth. I squeezed on to the end of the banquette, which had room for only my right buttock, and talked a bit to Michael about what had happened tonight. And then, looking around at all these young faces, I suddenly decided to leave. I felt – I don't know quite what I felt exactly, perhaps just that I'd reached an age when both my

* I've always felt it far more important for American actors to worry about the intention of the text than to worry about how, precisely, to pronounce it. In my view dialect coaches are the bane of English plays in the American theatre, creating stress and self-consciousness over irrelevancies, and therefore undermining an actor's confidence in who and what he is. I don't mean one shouldn't try to get the accent right. Only that one shouldn't make an issue of it.

buttocks require support, at least when sitting down. I came back to the Algonquin, lingered in the lobby, and over a drink or two and more than a cigarette or two, I thought about my smoking. At the Pankhurst, just before I started smoking again, I had a succession of nightmares. In the most vivid and disgusting of them I was staggering along, carrying in my arms an enormous block – a convict's load, in fact – of nicotine gum, out of which thick, black hairs were growing. So here I am, back on the weed, with all the old effects back too. The filth accumulating in my nose and lungs, the uncontrollable whistling wheeze, my voice enfeebled as I talk into this machine, up in 506. I shall leave a light on through the night, by the way. When the lights are out the blackness is impenetrable, but full of small noises. I've also got it into my head that somebody I know of died in 506. Was it Peter Lorre? I'm pretty sure he died in the Algonquin.

## Saturday, 11 October

As soon as I awoke I phoned down to reception to arrange my move into 310. I was told that the bloat senator was going to stay on for another night. I got myself together very slowly, bathed, shaved, made a few phone calls, including one extremely long one home, then went down to the lobby for a glass of champagne, before plodding the hundred yards or so down 42nd to Un Deux Trois, the English papers under my arm. They get the English papers regularly at the Algonquin, only missing out on the days that really count – the report of the last day of a Test Match, for instance, after you've been allowed to follow avidly the reports of the first four days. I ordered a business-like cheese omelette and a glass of red wine, consumed all of the latter and about an eighth of the former. Not the fault of the omelette. I'm having a great deal of trouble eating at the moment. Glanced through the papers, fretting away about whether Tabori would keep what he'd found, or was it an accident? Or had I deceived myself? etc., then dragged myself out on to the pavement into a cab up to the Promenade for the matinée. When I went up to the dressing-rooms to give some notes I kept my eye fixed casually on Tabori, looking for any significant change in his response. He took his own notes readily enough but without much show of interest. This depressed me. Neither the matinée nor the evening preview were quite up to last night. Tabori, while at least, and thank God, remaining real, had slowed down a fraction, especially in the second show. Hair-line stuff, *just* a fraction, but a fraction on almost every line. Dangerous, as so many fractions spread the play out, imperceptibly, towards boredom. I talked it over with Michael and Jack at Melon's afterwards. Jack, who hadn't seen last night's performance, and therefore saw only the leap that Tabori had made, was elated. Michael, who saw the leap diminished, rather less so. I began to outline my plans for the next day's rehearsal, then gave up and got a taxi back to the Algonquin.

It was an extraordinary ride. The driver had his radio going, was jouncing his knee and singing as he ate either a hot-dog or a hamburger, I couldn't see clearly which, while sucking on a can of Coke, while smoking a cigarette. He was quite clearly in charge of everything except the cab itself which swerved and dodged crazily in and out of the traffic, narrowly failing to smash up the cabs in front. But he had about him a kind of gaiety which communicated itself to me so that I actually enjoyed the ride almost as much as he did. It suddenly struck me that *The Common Pursuit* is precisely about this kind of gaiety, the gaiety of life, that every moment, however dreadful the surrounding circumstances, has its own inherent gaiety.*

I had a drink in the tumultuous, post-theatre Algonquin lobby, straining hard but unsuccessfully to overhear the conversation at the next table between a gaunt but healthy-looking young man of about twenty-five with close-cropped yellow hair (dyed, I think) and a diminutive girl in slacks, dark, hollow-eyed, with ragged fingernails, which she kept gnawing at. It was a very intense conversation, the man seeming to be confessing something, the girl seeming to be confessing something back to him, but there was an impatience between them, as if they found it difficult to hear each other out. I couldn't pick up more than the occasional word, though I think I caught 'butter' and 'soufflé', so they might merely have been swapping recipes. But then I also caught, or thought I caught, 'groin'† from the girl. When I finally came up here I had a premonition that the unspeakably selfish or (politically more dangerous) indecisive senator in 310 was going to stay on and on,

* This is nonsense. There have been many moments in my life that have been entirely without gaiety – even the inherent kind. Whatever that is.

† This might have been 'loin', as in 'loin of lamb'.

and decided to unpack my bag. I hung my few trousers in the closet, sorted out my dirty laundry, then settled at an angle to the video and allowed a fear to surface that I'd managed to suppress at the end of the preview: that the set, which I was sure I had seen falter during the second performance, might actually stick one night during the spectacular last change. Though it was a possibility too ghastly to contemplate, I contemplated it, until deciding that the stage-hands knew best and would certainly have alerted me,* and so slid my mind away to other aspects of the evening, discovering note after note, all of which I wrote down while trying not to smoke and smoking, keeping my eyes averted from the boxes of nicotine gum packed on top of the video. Ever since the nightmare about the hirsute block of gum, I've been unable to look at them without gagging. In fact, the mere memory of chewing the stuff makes me gag. Why do I keep it around then? Perhaps as a penance. Without it, I wouldn't even notice I'm smoking.

## Monday, 13 October

Woke fairly late, phoned down to discover that the senator was about to depart from Suite 310, packed all my stuff and put it on the sofa to be moved down by the bell-hop, then went off to Melon's for brunch, which consisted of a glass or two of champagne, a mouthful of eggs Benedict, and some cigarettes. When Michael joined me we shuffled through our notes and then went into the matinée, for the best account of the play I've ever seen. Ever. Everything moving along at the right kind of pace, the first act fast, the second act not weighted down, as it has been from time to time, by being the *second act*. I burst out of the theatre, hurtled upstairs, flung open the door of the Geeson–Tabori dressing-room, to find not Geeson and Tabori, but the four chaps sitting with their backs to me, staring out at me from their various mirrors. They had changed dressing-rooms before the performance because, apparently, the Taboris like it warm, and the chaps like it cold – although it could also be that the Taboris have more chance of getting away from my cigarette smoke in the second dressing-room. I dished out a few notes, hurried back to Melon's, had a drink or two and a

* My inaction here has helped me to understand why ships and planes go down, trains crash, etc. The moral is not only to imagine the unimaginable, but to act accordingly. I hope, but don't assume, that I've learnt it.

snack, then back to the evening show. It really is as quick as that – the matinée begins at three thirty on Sunday, the evening show at eight. By the time everyone is out of the theatre after the matinée it's nearly six o'clock, which leaves exactly an hour before the 'half'.* At seven I went back, gave them a few more notes, things I'd recalled over my drinks, went down and saw a fairly solid account of the play, though there wasn't the same intensity as in the afternoon. Far more disturbing was my sudden realization – why has it taken me so long? – that there is something wrong with the first scene. Instead of being sprightly but serious, it is cutely charmless, and Tabori, who was fine everywhere else, looks like a bad actor badly directed. The fault is in the writing. Talked the scene over with Michael, had a few drinks and then further drinks, came back to the Algonquin, to find to my amazement that I was still in 506 because the utterly sordid senator in 310 had decided to stay on yet another night. So there I was with all my bags packed on the sofa, and nowhere to go, obliged to stay in 506, no alternative – well, what alternative did I have, actually?

Went to bed depressed and couldn't sleep, my mind busily melding together the injustices of Suite 506 with the inadequacies of Scene One as I nursed whiskies, smoked cigarettes – right back to the old habits, which of course depressed me further. At one point I got up and lay on the sofa beside my bags, brooding drunkenly, the room full of smoke, my lungs full of smoke, on such large questions as 'Whither I?' and 'When?' Pretty soon, I guessed, if I went on like this. I must have made it across the room back to the bed, as I woke in it very late. I shambled fraily down to the desk, to register my matitudinal complaint about being in 506 instead of 310, while preparing myself for the news that the senator had decided to live out the rest of his life in 310. In fact he'd already gone. No doubt leaving behind him a trail of bad debts and broken promises.

I accompanied the bell-hop with my bags, a triumphal little procession, my heart soaring as I stepped into the familiar room, with the familiar playbills (some of them representing work by my rivals, none work by me) on the walls, then phoned down to reserve a bedroom off the suite, to make it a two-bedroom suite for Beryl's arrival, our policy being always to have an extra bedroom available, for one of us to retreat to when I snore, which I do fairly

* Actors have to be in the theatre half an hour before the performance starts.

frequently, for reasons both obvious and shameful, and was told by the chap at the desk that there wasn't a bedroom off any longer. 'Nonsense,' I said, confident that my knowledge of the intricacies of 310 far surpassed his, 'there are two. I can see the doors. I'm looking at them now.' 'Doors, yes,' he said, 'but one door opens on to a bedroom that's been permanently booked, the other opens on to nothing, that room no longer exists, it's been removed.' I was so appalled by this news that I didn't get around to asking him *how* a room could be removed. The upshot of our exchange was that I could have Suite 510, which is identical to Suite 310, *and* has a bedroom off. He said he'd looked up the records and discovered that I've actually stayed in it quite a few times before. I began to protest that I've *always* stayed in 310, and then began to think that perhaps I haven't, that 310 and 510 have somehow become as one in my memory, so that whenever I've stayed in 510 I've just assumed, afterwards, that I'd stayed in 310. Anyway, up we went, the bell-hop and I, to 510. My immediate response, as I surveyed the playbills (also for the plays of rivals), was one of affection and nostalgia. So I settled in comfortably, unpacked my bags definitively, and arranged to have my video installed. Actually the only advantage of 310 over 510 is that it's closer to the lobby, to and from which one can walk to one's rooms. One can walk down from 510, but not really, given one's habits, up. A nuisance, as the Algonquin elevator sometimes vanishes into a kind of Bermuda triangle somewhere between the seventh and tenth floors.* The advantage of 510, on the other hand, is that it has a fridge, in which I can store my champagne. And I've also worked out that Beryl and I must have occupied it for the successful New York opening of *Quartermaine's Terms*, so to complete my sense of comfort I've also decided that Fate has brought me, in its usual fussy and roundabout way, to the right place. 510 had been available all the time I was waiting in 506 for 310. Waiting patiently for me to be delivered into it. So I like to imagine.

I had a pleasant lunch with Phyllis at Un Deux Trois, then walked about, thinking of the first scene in the play, until somewhere up by the bookshop on 6th and 48th I had what I took to be a revelation – that I hadn't connected the Prologue properly to the Epilogue. In the Prologue Stuart is too lightweight and playful,

* Charles Laughton once said he'd spent twenty years of his life at the Algonquin, most of them waiting for the elevator.

opening the play on a jolly up-beat, whereas he ends it in a quite different spirit, an intensely serious young man. And yet the Epilogue is virtually a continuation of the Prologue. In previous productions we'd often rehearsed the two together, flowing from the Prologue into the Epilogue, leaving out all the text in between. What, I wondered, if we rehearsed it the other way around, running straight from the Epilogue into the Prologue, thus helping Tabori to continue the serious Stuart into the Prologue, and so (I hoped) eliminating all its present coyness? Highly excited by what I took to be a flash of directorial inspiration, I hurried back to 510 and phoned Tabori. I apologized for interrupting his rest day, did he mind? – 'Well' (pause) 'no–o. Well' (pause) 'go ahead.' I explained what I had in mind. He reacted as if I'd merely found a new and labyrinthine way of criticizing him personally, embarking on a long defence of his acting, using truly ghastly words that I'd hoped never to hear again once I'd given up teaching – 'epiphany' was one of them. In the end, though, he agreed to give my little scheme a whirl. Actually he has no choice, given that I am the director and he the actor, but I suppose he doesn't want to be thought to be obeying me, merely to be agreeing with me. I believe C. S. Lewis had a dog like that.

## Tuesday, 14 October

This day week I shall be fifty. Christ! But at least Beryl will be here to nurse me through it. And through the First Night, the day before. Therefore we shall be reading the reviews together on my birthday. What better form of celebration?

Last night, drunk and chain-smoking, I furiously wrote down a synopsis of the characters in the play as I've come to understand them through this production. One of the things I'm wondering is whether, with the critics coming in throughout the rest of the week, I dare risk reading it out to the actors. On the whole I think I will, because it will give me a chance to slip in some important points about Stuart to Tabori, in the open, where all the other actors will hear them. The synopsis, by the way, includes an account of what I've come to believe is the right tone and dramatic direction of each scene, so that I won't simply be talking about the characters, but about the responsibilities of each actor in each scene.*

* I read out an abbreviated form of the synopsis, then hurried on into notes.

## Wednesday, 15 October

It's just gone one thirty in the morning. A good preview – worryingly good, for the night before the critics come. The law that controls these things probably guarantees that tomorrow, when among others we have Clive Barnes of the *Post* coming in, it won't go as well. May not go at all. What I must remember to tell the actors is *not* to try to duplicate tonight's performance, but to come on stage as if it hadn't happened, to find their world afresh, *listening* to each other, *talking* to each other. Also I must fix a couple of blank moments in the first act. For instance, Tabori went right back to his Dullard's view of Hamlet, standing gazing down at his toes in order to avoid looking at the other actors, and on one occasion, after taking up an over-relaxed position by the banister, suddenly slumping across it, and staying there, as if he'd fallen asleep. This doze, or whatever it was, seemed to refresh him as he then became hyperactive, laughing at Humphry's jokes when only smiles were in order (had in fact been ordered) and with such abandon that he swivelled violently in his chair, slopping his drink out of both his glass and his mouth, thus going a long way towards undermining the dramatically necessary idea that here was a chap in a state of considerable tension, an idea he expressed very well elsewhere in the act. It's true that he's honoured every note I've given him recently. Now I'll have to make sure that he doesn't start implementing a few of his own, on the side, or even worse, start improvising mid-performance. I'd thought that the improvising tradition was dead in New York. I'd *hoped* it was dead. But something closely resembling it twitched sporadically into unwanted life on the stage of the Promenade tonight. On the other hand – *on the other hand, don't forget* – he's cut out all the bogus gesturing, and is full of *wanted* life throughout most of the play. So on the whole we had a very good evening.

At the end of it, when I was scooting through the door that leads backstage, I was astonished to find an old colleague of mine from the English Department of Queen Mary College waiting to speak to me. He is an American, from New York, a specialist in eighteenth-century literature, who now occupies my old office – took it over in fact with rather unseemly haste, moving his books and self in slightly before I'd moved mine and self out. Anyway, there he stood, looking appreciative. Face red, but tone appreciative. I paused to appreciate the appreciative tone and even the face red – red from shyness, I flatter myself, as I know him to be of very abstemious habits. Or was, before he moved into my office. I have no idea what he's been getting up to since. He introduced me to his mother, who was also appreciative, with face pale. Buoyed by compliments I sped on up to the actors, to give out cuddles and congratulations all round, and some immediate notes all round too (i.e. Tabori's laughter), then on to the round table at Melon's, where I was joined by Dylan Baker and lovely old Nathan Lane, followed by Michael McGuire. We had a boisterous evening, making appalling jokes in abysmal taste on such subjects as ——.* After they'd gone I stayed on by myself, slumped pleasantly over the table in a posture reminiscent of Mickey Mouse in the cartoon, and then came back to old 510, went through the notes I'd made, added some more. Drinking, smoking, thinking, writing. Now here we are, at one twenty-seven in the morning, on Wednesday the 15th, with the critics-in phase of the production beginning tomorrow (today, come to think of it).†

## Thursday, 16 October

Had lunch by myself at Un Deux Trois, where by sheer persistence I've become a welcome, or at any rate familiar, figure. I was hustled past a gratifyingly long queue to a quiet and comfortable corner. I love these long, solitary, meditative lunches, or breakfasts, I suppose they are, really, letting my mind drift around last night's performance, jotting down additional notes while my eyes drift around the waiters, the waitresses, the clientele. After lunch I went to Melon's, where I met Michael McGuire, went through our notes with him, then went into the theatre to give them.

During these sessions I sit at the edge of the stage, the actors sit in the auditorium, near the front. On previous occasions the chaps and Judy Geeson have sat on one side of the aisle, Tabori has sat by

* Shame prevents me from specifying the subjects.

† Checking back to the first sentence of this extract, I see that I appear to have begun it three minutes after I'd ended it. So either I'd misread my watch, or my watch had started going backwards, or it took me minus three minutes to make the report. Whichever, I've decided to leave the error in. I distrust the *apparent* continuity of time even more than I distrust my ability to record its obvious deceits. Besides there are Bergsonian, even Kantian, implications that will appeal to many readers, I know.

himself on the other, creating yet another peculiar separation. Once, about a week ago, on one of the hottest afternoons, he sat not only apart, but in an overcoat, his collar turned up, looking haunted and poetical, with a touch, he said, of flu. Every time I wanted to speak to him I had to swing my head around, keeping my voice soothing and respectful, fearful of sending his temperature soaring. But now, this afternoon, for the first time, Tabori was sitting among the cast. Consequently the atmosphere was congenial, the note-giving what it should always be, relaxed and even funny, but concentrated. It occurred to me that Tabori might here have made a breakthrough as important, almost, as the one he's made on the stage, that will also help him on the stage.

Seizing the moment, I dismissed everyone except Tabori and Michael Countryman, and rehearsed the dreaded and treacherous Act One, Scene Two – the scene that I suspect I still haven't got quite right in the writing, and which the actors therefore have to get more than right in the acting. It was here that Tabori had threatened to send the audience into a doze by miming gloomy speculations before seeming actually to fall into a doze himself, over the banister. In fact I didn't rehearse the scene, I ran it, standing so close to it that I was very nearly in it, my eyes fixed pointedly on Tabori as he hunched his shoulders, dropped his eyes and lowered himself into the slough of despond. I stopped it about a quarter of the way through and said in a tone that I hoped was both affable and intense – it's the old question, Kris, I said, of not connecting. 'Your worry about the future has to be expressed as an active, inner tension, an *active* one. When people speak to you you've got to reply to them directly, not withdraw from them.' I pounded softly away at him, softly, softly, on and on, until neither of us could stand it a second longer.

I went back to Melon's, met McGuire, had a morale-enhancing Glenfiddich or two, and then into the theatre to sit amongst the first batch of critics and watch the show. I trained my eyes away from six or seven Clive Barnes look-alikes, at least one of whom must actually have been Clive Barnes, and kept my mind fixed on Tabori as if practising long-distance hypnosis. He was even better than on the night of his breakthrough. He is naturally so personable on stage that all he really has to do, in this part anyway, is to trust himself, concentrate, and never ever do anything that looks like *acting*. In fact if the evening hadn't been rather calamitous, I would now be prepared to consider myself a deeply satisfied chap, with nothing to fear from any conscientious and decent-minded critic except the usual slovenliness and ill-will.

Calamity Number One: the set of course, which, having behaved normally since the evening when I'd thought I'd seen it nearly choke, now choked. The present began to glide off towards the wings, then stopped. The past began to glide forward from backstage, and also stopped. So there they were – Nathan, Dylan, Peter and Michael in one set, neither upstage nor down but in a kind of limbo, listening to Wagner; and there in the other set was Kristoffer Tabori, halfway to the wings, immobile on the stairs, looking like the captain of a ship that has perversely decided not to go down after all. I suppose this ghastly tableau lingered a mere fifteen seconds or so before the sets began to move again – I didn't time it precisely as I'd almost immediately run from my usual folding chair under the circle and out on to the stairs, shaking a fist and mouthing obscenities. What's called a diversionary tactic. It certainly diverted several people in the circle, among them the manager of the theatre, who was standing just inside the exit, but I doubt if anyone else, apart from Michael McGuire of course, would have realized that what had happened on stage was entirely God's fault and not simply another example of the director's bad timing.

Calamity Number Two: the audience. They were determined to laugh, even where laughter was positively (by me anyway) unwanted. Furthermore it was peculiar laughter, hysterical and undifferentiated, that inevitably bewildered and upset the actors, who equally inevitably began to lose their concentration. When I went backstage, pondering on the one hand on how to put it to God that I preferred him not to concern himself in my affairs, and pondering on the other the possibility of applying some kind of aptitude test to members of the audience before they were allowed into the theatre, I found an extremely emotional Jack McQuiggan, who told me that at the interval Peter Friedman had accused him of planting friends, or possibly even hirelings, among the audience – under orders, presumably, to laugh continuously and so persuade the critics that a terrific time was being had by all. Jack's eyes, usually round and clear from abstinence and ambition, were now moist, almost protuberant, from disbelief and fury – I've never seen him like this before. Not only would he never *want* to do a thing like that, he said, but he'd never be allowed to get away with it. People would find out in no time, he'd be finished as a producer in New York. I left him in the backstage lobby, went up to the dressing-rooms, gathered the actors around, and said that there wasn't the slightest question of Jack's having rigged the audience, though yes, indeed, it had been an odd, undisciplined house and probably not the only one we'd get during the run. I suggested that as the play has already developed a reputation for smartness, some people would want to seize any opportunity, even the wrong one, to establish that they were pretty smart too. But they, the actors, I plonked, must never again allow themselves to be thrown by inappropriate responses. If every line they uttered were to be met by boos and jeers they were still to play their characters, play the play, etc. – the obvious kind of stuff in fact. Peter Friedman then issued a statement to the effect that he was mortified by his previous loss of control, now realized that Jack was innocent on all charges, and said he would apologize personally.

Someone – I think it was Nathan – then asked which critics had been in, had we had the 'biggie'? Yes, someone else – Michael Countryman, I believe – asked, had we had 'the crucial one, the big, big one'? What they really wanted to know, of course, was whether Frank Rich, of the *New York Times*, whose review would settle our fate, had been in. As a matter of fact he hadn't – he's coming in tomorrow night – but as they hadn't named him directly, I made a lightning decision to answer their questions literally. Yes, that's right, I said, tonight was the big one, the biggie, crucial. And so it was. Every night's a biggie as far as the playwright's concerned. There was a silence, almost of reverence, while they pondered the fact that the die was cast, there was no going back, we were already marked down as a success or a failure – though we wouldn't know which until the review was published after our official opening.* Someone, probably all of them, said what actors always say in these circumstances, viz. why did he have to come tonight, we were much better last night – and the audience – and the set! And so forth,

* Theatrically, New York is a one-newspaper town. Thumbs-down in the *Times* usually closes a straight play within days. Thumbs-up usually guarantees a run. With my first play in New York, *Wise Child*, almost every review was favourable except the one in the *Times*. We closed after three performances. The reason for this peculiar, indeed dreadful, state of affairs is that New York theatre-goers take the *Times*, and aren't going to risk quite a few dollars on the possibility that the reviewer has got it wrong.

until I stopped them with what I imagine directors always say in these circumstances, viz. that, well actually, it was a very good evening, anyway no point in worrying about it, from now on you can relax, concentrate on your work, play the play. Let's have a drink.

On a note of rising conviviality, tension-free at last, we gambolled down to Melon's, where Judy (Daish) was waiting, having flown in this afternoon. She had seen the show, and was very jolly. Everybody was very jolly. Riotously jolly. By about half-past midnight everyone but Nathan and myself had gone home. We stayed on, getting more riotously jolly by ourselves, until it was clear from my behaviour that the time had come to put me into a cab. I was in the middle of proclaiming the virtues of (a) the play and (b) this particular production, when I suddenly found myself out of control, my feet carrying me eagerly towards two men just emerging from a restaurant. Nathan grabbed my arm, swung me around, pulled me across the street – rather dangerously given the traffic – and ordered me to shut up. The two figures staring after us were, apparently, John Simon, theatre critic of *New York Magazine,* and Mel Gussow, theatre critic of the *New York Sunday Times*, who had been in to see the show. Nathan shovelled me into a cab and dispatched me to 510 via the lobby (a pause for refreshment) where I set about my late-night task of drinking and smoking myself into a stupor.

## Friday, 17 October

Woke dully, clambered lethargically about my suite like a drugged ape, trying to keep my mind closed to the thought that in the evening we really would have the crucial one, the biggie, while keeping it open to the thought that in the evening Beryl would be arriving, possibly in time to share the anxiety. Or double it, depending on her view of the performance. I was on the point of falling down the stairs into the lobby for a glass of breakfast when Ian Hamilton rang. He's in town for a couple of days to deal with lawyers over his Salinger biography. Apparently Salinger is attempting to block publication on the grounds that he doesn't like being written about. We had lunch at Un Deux Trois at a series of tables, moving in little zigzags about the room, until we finally settled at one where I could both sit comfortably and hear almost everything he said. That's the only problem with Un Deux Trois – a lot of other people like it too, and furthermore insist on talking loudly over their meals. We discussed the Salinger problem, then the Frank Rich/*New York Times* problem. He offered to sit in on the show tonight, in return I offered to sit in on his legal hearings – possibly posing as a surprise witness – and then, just before we left, he told me a rather touching story about a woman whose husband, a brigadier, had died recently. Wanting to make contact with him, she went to a medium for a seance. Eventually she succeeded in getting through. 'Well, what's it like up there?' she asked. 'Oh, it's wonderful,' he said. 'I sort of have a bit of sex and then I swim and then I have a meal and then I have a swim and then a bit of sex and then a meal and so it goes on. It's absolutely glorious.' And she said, 'Is that all you do?' He said, 'Yes, that's all I do really, swim, bit of sex, meal, swim, bit of sex, perfect.' She said, 'But you weren't very interested in sex as I remember when you were down here, in fact I remember very well that you weren't interested in sex. And you hated swimming.' 'Ah yes,' he said, 'but down there I wasn't a duck.' I have no idea why this lightened my spirits so much – perhaps simply the prospect of living through eternity on such straightforward terms. Especially as I'm extremely fond of swimming.

From Un Deux Trois straight to Melon's, where Michael told me that he had checked out the set, which seemed to be – he verbally crossed his fingers – OK. We picked over our notes from last night's performance, then went in and did a spot of rehearsing. I tried to make my manner cavalier, not wanting the cast to wonder why, if they'd got over the crucial one and were now to relax and enjoy the play, we were still rehearsing the production. 'Might as well get it *absolutely* right while we're at it,' I said jovially. 'Tighten it up. That sort of thing.' Then back to Melon's, of course, for an hour's jittery talk with Michael and Jack, then backstage for some bogusly carefree salutes and fraudulently casual injunctions to go out and *really* enjoy yourselves tonight, eh, and down to the auditorium. I sat on my folding chair, trying to spot Frank Rich. I'd got the idea from someone or other that he's a stripling of a mere three decades or so, who doesn't even look his age, and is a natty dresser, but all the youthful males I rested my eye on were hirsute, ill-dressed and looked old for their years – old and self-righteous. Possibly a pack of critics up from the *Village Voice*. Again there were several Clive

Barnes look-alikes, not one of which was likely to be Clive Barnes this time around, unless he'd come back for seconds. The music rose, the lights went down, and we were off on our biggie.

I don't believe I've ever watched a show so intently in my life. Afterwards, on balance, weighing this against that and taking everything into account, I decided that it was perfect. Well, almost perfect. Furthermore, the set worked. If Rich didn't like it, then at least he didn't like what I wanted to be on offer. I went upstairs to the dressing-rooms feeling – above all feeling a vast relief. The first person I saw was Kristoffer Tabori. I blurted out a heartfelt compliment, accompanying it with several emotional cuffs and strokes on his arm. He gave me an odd, shy look and muttered 'thank you' out of the side of his mouth. A real 'thank you' it seemed to me, in return for something done. I like to think that this was an acknowledgement of the whole stretch of misery, suppressed ill-temper and frustration we've experienced with each other, and also an acknowledgement that nevertheless we'd got it right in the end. But of course he might just have been thanking me for something very specific, like – I don't know – picking up one of his shoes. Although I can't remember actually picking up one of his shoes. When I went back into the other dressing-room someone – I think it was Peter Friedman but it might have been Michael Countryman – asked if I knew who'd been in. 'Well,' I said, smirking slightly, 'one or two. You know. Critics. Frank Rich, of course.' It took them a moment or two to rally from shock to outrage. They accused me of having lied, claimed that they were too relaxed to have given of their best, would have been more concentrated (i.e. tried harder – exactly what I wanted them to avoid) if they'd known. Nonsense, I said, nonsense. For one thing I hadn't lied, merely not told them the truth,* my decision had been totally justified by the performance they'd given, a much better one than last night's, so why all the fuss, shut up, time for a drink. If Rich doesn't come through with the goods, they'll no doubt blame

* This position has since been somewhat discredited by the head of the British Civil Service, Sir Robert Armstrong, when giving evidence on behalf of the British government in Queensland, Australia. But our situations were entirely different, as I hope Sir Robert would be the first to admit. He was not telling the whole truth merely to save the government embarrassment. I was not telling the whole truth to a positive end – to keep the actors' morale high, and to unwind them for the crucial performance.

me. And I'll blame Michael McGuire. Or Jack. Or the audience. And of course Frank Rich.

Later, at Melon's everyone was much calmer, if also much louder. Now they really can relax and enjoy playing the play. At least for as long as the reviews allow us to. I felt pretty good, very good really, and particularly enjoyed introducing Ian, who'd seen the show and was waiting for me in Melon's, to Tabori – the part of Stuart is based on Ian, or at least on his experiences when he was running a literary magazine in London, years ago. As I'd also introduced him to Nicholas Le Prevost, who'd played Stuart in London, on the critics-in First Night at the Lyric, Hammersmith, I felt that Fate had pulled off a notable double here. I was just settling into a Glenfiddich or two and working on soliciting some compliments in the form of comments from Ian when Judy appeared, to announce that Beryl had arrived at the Algonquin, was safely ensconced in 510, was a mite exhausted from the flight (which had been preceded by a morning's teaching), wasn't quite up to coming down to Melon's, see me when she saw me. I scooted out of Melon's, into a taxi, but got here too late. Beryl was already deeply asleep. Is now deeply asleep. So here I am rollicking about on my own in the living room of Suite 510, in a state of high excitement at the realization that at the very least I've done what I set out to do all those months ago in Los Angeles. The play is on the boards in New York, the die is cast, and there is my wife, for the first time it seems in years, asleep in a nearby room. Could a chap want more? Yes. He could want a clutch of good reviews, topped by a rave from F. Rich in the *New York Times*, to guarantee a decent run. That's what he could want. Along with another drink.

## Sunday, 19 October

I went down to the lobby, had a glass of champagne, read the London papers until Beryl returned from her walk. There are very few things she likes better than roaming the streets of New York, unaccompanied, which I refuse to accept as evidence of a death-wish. When she got back she took me straight out for my constitutional, i.e. the 100-yard slog along 44th to Un Deux Trois. We had a long leisurely lunch, during which she slipped morsels of food into my mouth whenever she could take me by surprise. These attempts to save me from death by malnutrition nearly ended once or twice in death from choking. We talked mainly about the production, which she'd seen last night. She said she was keen on the new version of the play, liked all the actors but did find herself wondering whether here and there I hadn't allowed them to become physically trapped. I pointed out that the task, darling, had been to keep Tabori still and focused, and in doing that, my love, I'd perhaps inadvertently curtailed the freedom of the other actors, so yes, perhaps sweetie, now that the Tabori problem was solved I might find myself giving them some physical independence, though not too much, angel, given my almost pathological hatred of unmotivated stage movement. Thank you for the note, always my best critic. Thank you.*

We moved on to a discussion of how we would spend the afternoon – a walk, a film? Which would be best for keeping the prospect of the First Night, and more consequentially, the prospect of the reviews out of our minds? – until I suddenly remembered that I hadn't got the cast and company any First Night presents, and as the performance started at half-past six, we'd better get on with it. We zipped up to Scribner's, across and up a few blocks, my plan being to get seventeen copies of T. S. Eliot's *Collected Poems*. This isn't quite as pretentious as it sounds. Over the weeks I'd developed a peculiar habit of paraphrasing the Stetson lines from *The Waste Land* every time I chanced unexpectedly on an actor during rehearsals, clapping my hand to my forehead, reeling backwards, and crying out, 'What Nathan/Michael/Peter/Dylan/Judy *you* here!' I don't claim that this is a great joke. Come to think of it, I can't claim it's a joke at all. But repetition made it funny, and more importantly, made it comforting – one of those details of the rehearsal experience that years from now we'd probably all remember. Would *certainly* remember, if I underscored the relevant lines in the text. As it turned out Scribner's had only one copy. I'll repeat that. Scribner's had only *one* copy of *The Collected Poems of T. S. Eliot* in the shop. A large shop too. Pausing only to make a brief scene – time was getting too short for the comprehensive one that the situation deserved – we sped about plucking from the display stands all available copies of John Houseman's latest volume of autobiography, all available copies of Oliver Sachs's *The Man Who*

* Beryl was quite right, of course. I did loosen the blocking before I left New York. On the other hand, I also cut out some moves.

*Mistook His Wife for a Hat*, all available copies of a collection of *New Yorker* cartoons – a bizarre assortment, the collecting principle of which was merely panic. It was now four thirty. We would have to leave the Algonquin, showered and changed, by five forty-five at the latest. So we stood at the counter, Beryl passing the books to me and I scribbling into them love, gratitude, etc., before carrying them over to a highly intelligent young man who not only agreed to wrap them for us, but to mark on each wrapped copy the initials of the person to whom the book was going.

We dashed back to the hotel, showered and changed, got a cab, stopped off at the bookshop, picked up the books, proceeded to the theatre, arriving ten minutes before the show was due to start. The taxi driver, a West Indian hopelessly befuddled by the excitements of the last half an hour, not only couldn't break my twenty-dollar bill, but seemed unable to think of any scheme for doing so, and just sat shaking his head, fumbling with coins and bills, mumbling forlornly. Beryl took the twenty dollars, dashed to a news-stand, where an elderly and dignified gentleman gave her change, extracting for himself, as we subsequently discovered, a one-dollar commission. I escorted Beryl to the front of the theatre, got her her ticket, deposited her with James and Dena, then carried the books to Melon's, where, over a drink or two, I translated the initials into proper names. I dumped the books at the stage door, went round into the auditorium for the closing moments of the first act, returned to Melon's where I was joined by Michael McGuire and his girlfriend, back to my folding chair for the second act, upstairs to do my round of cuddles, back to Melon's to settle my long-running tab, then on to the party which was being given at Le Petit Bistro or was it Le Bistro Pathétique? Word had already got out that the *Times* review would appear at about ten thirty, leaving us with over an hour to get through.

One of the features of the party was that, although there were at least 350 souls – if souls is the appropriate word – there was no food, apart from a rarely sighted tray of canapés, while any real drink as opposed to cheap red and white wine, one had to pay for. It was hot, glum and crowded, in other words, its sole purpose being to give the investors a chance to tangle with the company. I was passed about from person to person, like a large, possibly contaminated parcel, waiting to be unwrapped by Frank Rich. The only encounter I can now remember was with Robert Vaughn, the

Man from U.N.C.L.E. We were presented to each other with great ceremony, and then stood facing each other in silence – each waiting for compliments or comments, I suppose. He was very eloquently dressed in dinner-jacket, silk scarf, etc., but was otherwise mute. I was totally mute, sartorially as well as vocally. At least I hope I was mute sartorially, having come out of my tramp persona into humdrum and unnoticeable respectability for the occasion. Except for my shoes, of course. But nobody can see anyone's shoes at a crowded party. The silence lasted until we turned away from each other, he to a cluster of (I hope) admirers, I by a series of social ricochets to a table where James, Dena, Eduardo (Dena's co-playwright) and Judy (Daish) were sitting. We started a small, cheerful party of our own, fuelled by drinkable drinks that Judy and James had somehow conjured out of a bar they'd managed to locate, but remained invisible to me all evening. Beryl was on the far side of the room, by the way, having an excited, even dramatic-looking conversation with Caroline Lagerfelt, who was now very pregnant indeed. Suddenly there was a small tumult at the door.

The Frank Rich review had arrived, earlier than expected. One of the girls from Jack's office was carrying it urgently towards Jack, who stood in the centre of the room with some of his investors. There was a strange buzzing, or even droning noise from the guests, which sounded like the prelude to a tribal chant, as Jack received the review, began to read. Two members of his production team took up a position at each elbow and lowered their heads to read with him. Everyone within their immediate vicinity – top-ranking investors presumably – stood back, watching them warily. Eventually Jack lifted his head, and gazed around, as if confused. Ominous. He passed the review to someone else who read it rapidly, shook his head in confusion and handed it to someone else. More ominous. Beryl, blithely unaware of what was happening, hurried over in great excitement to tell me something about Caroline, then seeing what my eyes were fixed on, fell silent. We stood watching as people skimmed through the review, handed it on. There were neither cries of joy nor moans of despair, just these small, imperceptible signs – head-shakings, shoulder-shruggings, muttered questions – of confusion. I was so transfixed – I've never seen a review have quite this effect before – that it would probably have passed through every hand in the party except mine if Beryl hadn't walked briskly over to the trio currently in possession and asked whether the playwright might be allowed a peek, please. We tucked into it together, James, Dena, Eduardo and Judy peering over our shoulders and around our arms.

One thing was immediately evident. The review was very long and carried a large photograph of Tabori and Judy Geeson. What was not immediately evident, as it took some deciphering, was that the review was not so much equivocal as actively equivocating, leading off with a string of vivid descriptive sentences that could have been compliments, followed by a small paragraph of reservations, followed by further and clear compliments punctuated, but not completely punctured by, further reservations. It didn't so much give with one hand and take with the other, as give with both hands simultaneously both praise and blame, sometimes within the same sentence. I also had a sense, in spite of the personal interest that I brought it, that it amounted to a rather dull read – nothing like as dull as Dan O'Sullivan's,* of course, but dull by normal standards of readability, and far duller than anything I'd previously read by Frank Rich, whose style I usually found both perky and elegant. It was as if he weren't quite himself, assuming a tone he hoped might find favour with the characters in the play, rather than presenting his actual experience of the play to the readers. Could it be that a part of Frank Rich *wants* to live among the failed English literati, I wondered, be out there on the stage, so to speak, hobnobbing with the likes of Nick, Peter, Stuart? It hardly seems possible, given that in his present position in New York he has the power to ruin a celebration completely with one of his reviews, keep a celebration going for two days with another of his reviews, or bring a celebration to a baffled standstill, as he'd just done, with yet another of his reviews. A wizard's power, in fact. A few paragraphs on Monday conferring fame and fortune, a few paragraphs on Tuesday delivering failure and despair. Not just a wizard, when you come to think of it, but for many people (in New York anyway) the living embodiment of the Massy Wheel of Fortune.

Actually I doubt if these thoughts went clearly through my mind at the time. Instead I was listening with dunce-like intensity to Beryl, who was taking me through bits of the review, pointing out all the quotable quotes, and then listening with dunce-like intensity

* Of the Matrix production, in the *Los Angeles Times*.

to Jack when he read some of them aloud, every now and then stating emphatically that it was OK, this was a review he could build on, that he *would* build on, we were going to run, he'd see to it.*

Nathan came over, glanced quickly through the review, then embarked on a long, angry and very funny monologue on the nature of reviewers, their personal habits, sex lives, innate life-hatred, etc., a magnificent solo, full of riffs and variations, until he'd subdued himself through sheer vocal and emotional exhaustion. I passed about amongst the other actors, looking grimmer, Beryl told me subsequently, than was good for morale or than the review warranted, and then we – James, Dena, Eduardo, Beryl, Judy and I† – went down to the nearest restaurant for dinner. Either we ate outside (surely unlikely, at that hour) or we were surrounded by glass. At any rate we were obviously on public display, because Peter Friedman and his girlfriend dropped by for a few minutes, followed by Ben Sprecher, the theatre manager, who strolled insouciantly in, dropped the early-morning editions of the two other papers, the *Post* and the *News*, on our table, and strolled insouciantly out. The two reviews were raves, and if we preferred the Clive Barnes, it was only because it was the longer. A good note to end on, and for once I decided to end on it. On the way back here in the taxi Beryl told me what it was she'd come over to announce just as the Frank Rich review had arrived – that Caroline had left the party for the hospital, having gone into the preliminary phase of labour. Which brings something together very neatly, although I'm not sure what. It occurs to me now that as soon as the baby shows its face we should send Frank Rich over to review it. You can't start coming to terms with the Massy Wheel too early. As he's known to be a family man he should be favourably disposed. Or unfavourably, depending on the kind of family he's got.

## Monday, 20 October

Woke late, and lay in bed attempting to come to terms with the fact

* I believed him – with good reason, as he's the only New York producer I know of who's kept a production (*The Foreigner*) going for two years after it had been panned, not only by the *Times*, but by almost every other New York newspaper and magazine.

† Michael McGuire and his girlfriend, were also at the party; but we never met up. He told me later that they were trapped in a corner table from which there was no exit.

that it's at last all over. No more rehearsals, no more previews, no more notes, and today at least, as it's the rest day, no need even to go to the theatre. I told my heart, therefore, to be still. And it *was* still. Still enough for me to refuse to get up and join Beryl in a shopping expedition for Caroline's baby. I clung on and on in bed, not awake, not asleep, not dozing – mere, I suppose, inactivity, until just after midday, when I finally managed to dress and shave, then make it down to the bar where I quaffed back two mimosas* with great rapidity, sedately ordering a third and pretending it was my first when I saw Beryl arriving with packages of rattles, Babygros, etc. We went off to lunch at Un Deux Trois, I leaning on her like a valetudinarian, trying to ignore the pint of mimosa swishing around in my stomach. Over lunch Beryl and I read, very cold eyed, through Frank Rich's review and decided that it really was OK, the first paragraph especially so, and that most potential theatre-goers wouldn't worry too much about the subsequent equivocations, indeed probably wouldn't even get to them. I phoned Jack from the restaurant to discuss what quotes to use for the ad. He said that in fact Frank Rich had been on the radio this morning in a follow-up review, in which he'd been more openly complimentary, so we'd be able to synthesize both the radio and newspaper reviews to what would amount to a rave, almost.

When we got back to the hotel, Jack phoned and said quite simply, 'It's a hit.' The box office had been immensely busy, we'd taken an enormous amount of money and might even be on our way to breaking a record or two. I phoned up each member of the cast to let them know that all was very well indeed, the only ones I failed to contact being, somehow inevitably, the Taboris. Then I phoned Caroline Lagerfelt's hospital and was told that she'd been successfully delivered of a baby, although they seemed unable to give details, i.e. sex, weight, etc. We were going out to dinner with James and Dena to celebrate Dena's birthday, and I reflected, as I lay down on the bed to read the latest volume of John Houseman's memoirs (Beryl having dashed up to Saks in search of a sweater), on the life-enhancing coincidence that within twenty-four hours we'd had the First Night, the birth of Caroline's baby, now Dena's birthday, with my own birthday turning up tomorrow. It was at

* Known in England as a Bucks' Fizz – a combination of champagne (or if you're unlucky, sparkling wine) and fresh (or if you're unlucky, packaged) orange juice.

about this point – anyway before I'd got properly into the Houseman – that Kristoffer Tabori phoned to say that he just wanted to apologize for having left the party early (actually I hadn't noticed). He'd found the heat, the lack of food and drink and the imminence of the Frank Rich review too much to take. I said I quite understood. There was an awkward pause and then he said, 'It's a wonderful production.' To which I didn't say, modestly, as I should have done, 'Oh, really, do you think so, I'm glad you think so,' whatever. I said, 'I'm very proud of what's on the stage.' There was a pause, and he said, 'Yes, right. OK. Well, before you go perhaps we could have a drink?' So perhaps there is some one further stage to go with Kristoffer Tabori.*

## Tuesday, 21 October

One day into my fifty-first year. I failed to get out of bed in order to join Beryl on an expedition to the Frick, even though it's my favourite museum and contains my favourite painting, a Rembrandt self-portrait. Before she left Beryl phoned the hospital several times, and unsuccessfully, for news of Caroline and her baby, and after she'd gone I tried several times myself until finally discovering that the baby, far from having been born, was being delivered that very moment. There's no point in wondering how the hospital could have made such a mistake. In my experience hospitals tend to get such matters as births and deaths hopelessly wrong.† Anyway if the baby gets a move on it should make it on my birthday which, as it's also Trafalgar Day, is an excellent day to be born on, carrying with it historic associations of triumph in glorious battle.

I met Beryl at Un Deux Trois for a long, lingering and chatty lunch, after which we strolled down to Grand Central Station, picking up *en route*, after trying about five news-stands, a copy of

* We never got around to the drink. The truth is, I didn't really want to, and I suspect he didn't either. For my part, I felt that the wounds hadn't yet become the kind of scars that we could reminisce over. His association with the production ended only a few months after we'd opened. While Judy Geeson was taking a break from the show, to organize their newly bought house in Los Angeles, Tabori had a disagreement with Jack, and left the show. Judy never came back.

† My father had just died, his three sons were grouped, weeping around his bed in a classical tableau of grief, when a nurse entered, put his lunch down on the table beside him, with a cheerful admonition 'to eat up', and departed smiling.

*Woman's Wear Daily* which Jack had told me was both very influential and contained a highly favourable review. It was indeed favourable, and furthermore stood out on the centre page in astonishing black type. But what I don't understand is, if *Woman's Wear Daily* is so influential, how come you can only pick it up from one news-stand in six? Beryl decided not to come to the theatre, preferring, quite rightly, to lounge around 510 and watch television – she finds American television highly addictive, for about two or three days, and then ODs on it – but would join us all after the show for a birthday dinner with the cast at Melon's.

I went straight to Melon's where Michael McGuire and I were interviewed by a rather nice man from the *Post*. I can't remember any of the questions, so suppose they must have been the usual questions, though he employed a charming, if practised, timidity when asking them. Michael left before me and I was a little late – about ten minutes late in fact – getting to the theatre. I was therefore somewhat surprised to discover Ken Frankel, the director of the Long Wharf production, negotiating for a ticket at the box office. He was wearing a very red sweater with words on it and a peculiar jacket.* He turned, saw me and behind his beard his face assumed an expression – actually I don't quite know how to describe it. Aghast. That was it. He looked aghast. Like an aghast sheep. He managed a strangled greeting, then asked me whether we could speak at the interval. I said no, I wouldn't be around at the interval because I always made a point of avoiding the audience, didn't he remember? OK, he said, then perhaps afterwards. We went in together, then separated, he up one set of stairs to the right-hand side of the theatre, I up the other set of stairs to the left-hand side of the theatre, to my folding chair. From there I watched him emerge into the auditorium, bustle down the aisle and push his way along a row, causing a lot of commotion in the audience and nearly as much on stage. Two of the actors from the Long Wharf production, Peter Friedman and Michael Countryman, became briefly paralysed, their eyes initially caught by the boisterous redness of the sweater, then by the thick beard which presumably reminded them of someone, then by the face behind it which they identified. They played the rest of the scene with two much

* I can no longer remember in what respect the jacket was peculiar. I clearly have a blank spot about jackets. I can't remember the words on his sweater, either.

consciousness. Who could blame them? Late entrances are bad enough without the late entrant also being the one-time director and then the rejected director of the play you are currently performing in. I suppose Ken Frankel's intention had been to slip surreptitiously in for peek at the show, though it's hard to imagine how, short of yodelling too, he could have made a worse job of it.

I kept an eye trained on him – he sat impassively, arms folded – for the rest of the first act and the opening of the second act, until I became fairly absorbed, then at last completely absorbed in the play. A few seconds before the end I had one of those strange jolts, a prickling of the scalp, the sense of a familiar presence close by. I glanced to the right and there, sure enough, was Beryl standing at the exit. I got up and slipped out with her just as the lights went down and the applause started. We made it to the top of the stairs and then stopped dead. Frankel was bounding tumultuously down the stairs opposite, his face set in a peculiar kind of rage. He trampled across the lobby, through the backstage door, out of sight. I hurried after him, upstairs to the dressing-rooms, where I found him already surrounding the three actors from the Long Wharf production, embracing them angrily with his arms, while he exclaimed in a voice throbbing with fury, 'It works beautifully, it works beautifully like this!' When he saw me he froze – had he wanted to be in *and* out before I arrived? – stepped dramatically close, and began a conversation that was only marginally longer than the one we'd had in the lobby. He said he was in a rush, I said OK, give me a ring, let's have a drink, talk, I've written a new play, would like to give him a copy, he said he'd be interested to read it, maybe a drink, difficult, he was in the middle of a production himself, well, OK, gotta be off, goodbye. He made an ambiguous gesture with his arm, added another guttural farewell, and off he went, down the stairs, presumably into the night.*

* When I was back in London I received a letter signed by Frankel and four of his colleagues at the Long Wharf, Edgar Rosenblum, John Tillinger, Arvin Brown and Anne Keefe, congratulating me on my success at the Promenade, and undertaking, in return for a credit and some money, not to expose me as a fraud who had stolen Ken Frankel's Long Wharf production. My reply, in which among other things I offered to discuss publicly the exact nature of Frankel's contribution to the Long Wharf productions of both *Quartermaine's Terms* and *The Common Pursuit*, and fuelled as it was by anger, contempt and downright disgust, is too long to publish here, and was probably not worth the writing. At least in as much as it is still unanswered, eight months after it was posted.

Afterwards at Melon's, with Beryl, Michael McGuire and the cast, my birthday dinner. Lots of drink. Lots of laughter. A wonderful party. A real birthday party in fact. Marred only by the absence of Jack. He's made such a thing of my birthday, and then failed to turn up at the party. Not only at the party, he failed to turn up at the show, almost for the first time ever. Odd. Anyway Beryl and I are now back at the Algonquin. Beryl's asleep – she leaves tomorrow evening for a teaching commitment – and here I am, at ten to two in the morning, in the living room of old 510, pondering the implications, trying *not* to ponder the implications, of being fifty and a day.

## Wednesday, 22 October

I hung about in bed while Beryl phoned the hospital and at last managed to speak to Caroline whose unfortunate infant had failed by a mere hour or two to make it for my birthday. In all other respects, however, his prospects look pretty good. He weighs seven and a half pounds and is unbearably beautiful, luminously intelligent, with some hair. Beryl imparted this information while I was climbing out of bed and she was dashing out of the door on the way to see mother and son. I dressed very slowly, like a man palsied, and presented myself in the foyer for an interview with somebody or other – I don't know who he was, or even what publication he represented, but I do recall that he was short and plump, and was sitting contentedly in an armchair, a drink in his hand, with one eye gleaming and one eye dead. So whatever journalist in New York has a botched-up right eye, with an alert left eye, is probably the chap who interviewed me today at twelve noon. I sat down in an opposite armchair, but before we could get into any kind of stride we were interrupted by the production's press officer, an exceptionally devoted, hard-working and considerate chap, who clearly suspected that I was coming to the end of my tether and needed moral support. Or perhaps he just wanted company. Anyway he spread himself on the sofa that stretched between our two chairs, indeed lay so comfortably along it that I thought of summoning the bell-hop and ordering him up some blankets and a pillow, and began to engage interviewer and interviewee in lively conversation. Even when prone he exhibited an unnatural gift for converting my weedy, almost monosyllabic answers into an opportunity for a monologue – on the state of the theatre, on New York architecture, whatever – rendering me virtually redundant. I sat back, my eyes half closed as if in admiring attention, until it was time to make my way to Un Deux Trois, where I had arranged to meet Dena and Beryl for lunch.

I was almost out of the lobby when I was called back to the telephone. Jack to say would I please be in the Algonquin in two hours' time for an extremely important interview. *Extremely* important. I said, oh come on, Jack, Beryl leaves this evening. He said, 'No, no, you must really. This is really the BIG time.' So I thought OK, I mean I'm all for the big time really when it comes to it, and said I'd talk to Beryl and find out how she felt about me and the big time. Then to Un Deux Trois where Dena was waiting. Beryl arrived a few minutes after me to report emotionally that Caroline's baby lives up to its reputation for intelligence, beauty and hair, and furthermore has a pointed head and is charmingly chubby. We toasted his achievements several times, then I went back to the Algonquin and presented myself to the interviewer, who given his bulk, might have been described as Falstaffian except that his eyes didn't twinkle; his eyes were actually quite dead. Both of them. Which put him one ahead or one behind the pre-lunch interviewer, depending on which way you look at it. After an hour of intense intellectual jousting, which left me feeling completely drained, he explained that he wasn't really doing an interview at all, merely hoping to pick up a useful quote or two for his review. I detached myself from him on the spot and went upstairs to 510 to collect Beryl.

We sauntered along to Grand Central Station, studied the walls and the roofs, watched the trains arriving and departing, had a drink in the Oyster Bar, and were just on our way out through the 42nd Street exit when we were stopped on the pavement by a bizarre drama. An elderly woman with a demented, wrinkled face but with lustrous, obviously much-shampooed red hair tumbling down her shoulders, was holding two dogs – Pomeranians, I think they were – on a lead. She was screaming abuse at a respectable-looking young man who was evidently some kind of Evangelist. They stood facing each other, he talking in a low implacable, impersonal voice about the Church and its truth, she screaming back at him that *she* was the Church. 'I am the Church! I am the Church!' And while this was going on, he rigid talking, she screaming that she was the Church, the two Pomeranians were fucking at her feet. In a most peculiar way too, like humans. One of the Pomeranians lay on its back with its legs spread, the other Pomeranian lay on top of it, burrowed into it, and fornicated away, in a ghastly imitation of human sex. We watched them for a good ten minutes, then went back to the Algonquin. Beryl changed and packed. We went down to the lobby, out on to the street where her limo was waiting.

After she'd gone I sat in the lobby depressed, sipping Scotch, smoking, almost unable to move. Although in fact I did. Up here to 510 where, shaved and changed, I am dictating this. I have to be at the theatre by the end of the show as Jack is giving me a birthday party. He'd got the dates wrong which explains his absence last night. There is to be champagne and a cake on stage.

*Later*

No second fiftieth birthday party after all. Jack had forgotten that the cast had agreed to have a discussion with the audience after the show. He was keen to wait until it was over, but feeling too depressed to go through the ritual of a party, especially of a party celebrating a birthday that was already over, and a fiftieth one at that, I suggested he pack the cake back into a box, put the champagne back into the fridge, and bring both out again on Friday, my last evening in New York.*

Michael McGuire and I went to Melon's, sat at the usual round table. He said that he was very tired, I said I was very tired, I said I was very depressed, he said he was very depressed, and so it went. We came back around midnight in a taxi. And here I am, back in my suite, still trying to understand how it's come about that on the occasion of my biggest success in New York, I have no energy, and certainly no joy, no pleasure in what's taken place. I feel in a peculiar way completely defeated by the circumstances of life. Though what these circumstances are I don't know. No doubt I've demoralized myself by the intensity with which I've returned to smoking – back to between sixty and eighty a day. I sit slumped in bars, in corners of sofas or in armchairs, or at the corner of tables in restaurants, drinking, smoking, my stomach swelling, my head

* I never saw the cake or the champagne again. A relief actually, as I've never been particularly keen on cake and think of champagne as strictly a lunchtime beverage.

pounding slightly, not eating. I'm going to bed now. I hope tomorrow I shall feel much springier. I don't understand it.

## Friday, 24 October, my last full day in New York

Lunch at the Players' Club. Over it, Michael McGuire, Ben Sprecher, the manager of the Promenade, and I agreed that we would resist any attempts – there's been considerable interest apparently – to move *The Common Pursuit* to Broadway. Came back to the Algonquin, 510. Thought of dictating into the machine, couldn't face it, tried to read, couldn't face that, lay on the bed and tried to sleep, couldn't manage that, then walked around and around the living room, still depressed, but also restless and irritable – a sign of reviving life, I hoped. At about five the phone rang. Nathan, down in the lobby, come around for a farewell drink. We sat in the lobby and chatted our way through our experiences from New Haven to New York by way of Los Angeles, then, in seemingly good time, hustled over to 8th Avenue where we somehow missed cab after cab, or cab after cab somehow decided to miss us, until – Nathan now desperate at the prospect of being late for the half – we got one to take us to the Promenade. Nathan hurtled up to the dressing-room, I went on to Melon's, where Michael McGuire was waiting for me. We were both coming out of our depressions, beginning to laugh again. We whipped up to the dressing-rooms, dished out a few notes to the actors, then down into the auditorium to a full house. I sat in my folding chair by the gangway, Michael took up his seat at the other end of the row. It went well.

Afterwards to Melon's where I'd reserved five adjoining tables for a farewell dinner. There was a young couple ensconced at the middle table, apparently embarking on what promised to be a long and complicated courtship. So there we were, one group of us crammed in on one side of this couple, the other group crammed in on the other side, and there *they* were, cutting us off as they reached across their table to touch fingers, whisper, sit bolt upright in excitement, crouch forward conspiratorially. Alone, in love, buggering up our evening. In spite of angry grimaces from me, constant polite attempts from the management to dispatch them by delivering their bill, taking it away, redelivering it, they would not *go* and they would *not* go. They did in the end, of course, allowing our two groups to join together at last. But it was too late. The impulse to celebrate, embrace and say goodbye had drained away. What remained of the evening passed in exhausted, humdrum affability. We split up early, and yet not early enough to do anything else with the night. Michael McGuire and I shared a last taxi together. I dropped him off at his rented apartment somewhere around 46th and 8th, and came on a few more blocks to the Algonquin. I packed my bags, arranged a morning call, ducked down for a Glenfiddich in the lobby, came back up and recorded this. Tomorrow midday I shall be boarding Concorde, heading for home.

## Monday morning, 27 October, London

I got back late Saturday night, London time. Concorde was very cramped. Their idea, really, is to treat you as if you are a Strasburg goose, strapping you into your leather seat so that your knees rise fairly close to your chest while they stuff food down you. Alcohol too, I'm glad to say. Hated it, really.

I had a ragged night, starting out of my sleep fairly regularly to work out where I was, and why, then sinking back into a hotel room, but not my Algonquin suite, 510.

Yesterday I spent meandering woozily around the house, re-affirming contact with my family, the three cats and the garden, half looking for Hazel, whom I half expected to appear at any moment, blindly sniffing her way towards a loving presence. In the afternoon Beryl and I walked up to Highgate Cemetery and examined the grave of George Eliot, which Beryl is trying to get properly restored.

Tomorrow or the next day, some time soon anyway, I shall try to give up smoking.